Advanced PHP
for Web Professionals

ISBN 0-13-008539-1

The Prentice Hall PTR Advanced Web Development Series

- **Advanced JavaScript: Insights and Innovative Techniques**, Livingston

- **Advanced Macromedia Flash MX: ActionScript in Action**, Second Edition, Livingston and Justiniano

- **Advanced PHP for Web Professionals**, Cosentino

- **Advanced SOAP for Web Development**, Livingston

- **Developing SVG-Based Web Applications**, Pearlman and House

Advanced PHP
for Web
Professionals

Christopher Cosentino

Prentice Hall PTR
Upper Saddle River, NJ 07458
www.phptr.com

A CIP catalog record for this book can be obtained from the Library of Congress.

Editorial/Production Supervision: *Kathleen M. Caren*
Senior Managing Editor: *John Neidhart*
Cover Design Director: *Jerry Votta*
Cover Design: *Talar A. Boorujy*
Manufacturing Manager: *Alexis R. Heydt-Long*
Marketing Manager: *Bryan Gambrel*
Editorial Assistant: *Brandt Kenna*
Series Design*: Gail Cocker-Bogusz*

© 2003 Prentice Hall PTR
Prentice-Hall, Inc.
Upper Saddle River, NJ 07458

Prentice Hall books are widely used by corporations and government agencies for training, marketing, and resale.

The publisher offers discounts on this book when ordered in bulk quantities.
For more information, contact: Corporate Sales Department, Phone: 800-382-3419;
Fax: 201-236-7141; E-mail: corpsales@prenhall.com; or write: Prentice Hall PTR,
Corp. Sales Dept., One Lake Street, Upper Saddle River, NJ 07458.

Printed in the United States of America

10 9 8 7 6 5 4 3 2 1

ISBN 0-13-008539-1

Pearson Education LTD.
Pearson Education Australia PTY, Limited
Pearson Education Singapore, Pte. Ltd.
Pearson Education North Asia Ltd.
Pearson Education Canada, Ltd.
Pearson Educación de Mexico, S.A. de C.V.
Pearson Education — Japan
Pearson Education Malaysia, Pte. Ltd.

Contents

CHAPTER   2

Session Management   *15*

CHAPTER   3

Multiple Database Interaction   *37*

CHAPTER 4

Better Form Processing

CHAPTER 5

Using What You Have Learned—A Simple Shopping Cart

CHAPTER   6

Working with Files

CHAPTER   7

PHP Authentication Schemes

Index

About Prentice Hall Professional Technical Reference

With origins reaching back to the industry's first computer science publishing program in the 1960s, Prentice Hall Professional Technical Reference (PH PTR) has developed into the leading provider of technical books in the world today. Formally launched as its own imprint in 1986, our editors now publish over 200 books annually, authored by leaders in the fields of computing, engineering, and business.

Our roots are firmly planted in the soil that gave rise to the technological revolution. Our bookshelf contains many of the industry's computing and engineering classics: Kernighan and Ritchie's *C Programming Language,* Nemeth's *UNIX System Administration Handbook,* Horstmann's *Core Java,* and Johnson's *High-Speed Digital Design.*

PH PTR acknowledges its auspicious beginnings while it looks to the future for inspiration. We continue to evolve and break new ground in publishing by providing today's professionals with tomorrow's solutions.

PRENTICE
HALL
PTR

Preface

- Goal of This Book
- Who This Book Is For
- Getting the Code
- Acknowlegments
- The Fine Print

Goal of This Book

The goal of this book is to help you get a better grasp of PHP, to learn some of the less commonly used features, and to help you build some applications that are useful in your work or hobbies. I hope it gives you some ideas on how to make your own applications easier to code and easier to use.

Who This Book Is For

This book is for those who have done some basic PHP programming and wish to learn about some of the more advanced techniques to make applications easier to use and easier to program.

I received many emails from across the globe from readers of my first book, *Essential PHP for Web Profes-*

sionals (also published by Prentice Hall), who liked the concise style and ample examples I had provided. I received literally dozens of emails from people who said they had read other PHP programming books, but they didn't really grasp how PHP worked until they read my book. I can't tell you how happy that makes me feel. I hope to do the same with this book.

This book is for those of you who are ready to take the next step and learn a little more about PHP. This book isn't a reference book, nor does it cover every advanced aspect of PHP. It does, however, stretch beyond the basics and introduce some more concepts that can help you with your PHP programming.

Getting the Code

All of the code for this book is available on the Advance Web Series Web page at *www.phptr.com/advancedweb/php*.

You can download all of the examples for each chapter on the page.

The Web page will also have any updates or errata, as well as answers to frequently asked questions.

If you get really stuck with something *in this book,* feel free to email me at *cosentino@digital-salvage.net*. I say *in this book* because I get a lot of email asking for help with PHP. If it's a simple problem, I can usually answer any question, but I've been getting a little overwhelmed with email lately (who hasn't?), and I may not be able to respond to questions unrelated to my books. Please note that I can't always answer your questions right away. I try to answer as fast as I can, but sometimes the turnaround may be a few days.

Acknowledgments

I wish to give a heartfelt thanks to the editors for this project, Karen McLean and John Neidhart, for their support and patience. I'd also like to give a great big thanks to Jan Schwartz for her production work on my first book.

Thanks also to Micah Brown for his work on this book and on the Essential and Advanced Series of Web design books from Prentice Hall.

I'd also like to thank Leon Atkinson for his thoughtful comments on the drafts of this book, as well for writing the first PHP book I ever purchased, *Core PHP Programming*. It helped to get me started with PHP programming.

Sincere thanks and gratitude also go out to Allan Brumer for his helpful comments and testing of the code on BSD. Thanks for your help, Allan! I'd work on another project with you in a heartbeat.

A special thanks goes out to Professor John R. Nelson, Jr., *"il miglior fabbro,"* from the University of Massachusetts for his help, guidance, and wisdom, and for helping me to get my start. Thanks, Uncle John!

And of course a very sincere thanks and much love to my darling Sarah for her patience and support while I spent, yet again, hours upon hours in front of the computer while working on a book.

Finally, thanks to the readers out there who sent email just to let me know that my first book has helped them. Thank you! I hope this book helps you as well.

The Fine Print

What follows is from the GNU Web site at *http://www.gnu.org/*

The programs detailed in this book are free software; you can redistribute and/or modify them under the terms of the GNU General Public License as published by the Free Software Foundation—either version 2 of the License or (at your option) any later version.

Here's the fine print:

GNU GENERAL PUBLIC LICENSE TERMS AND CONDITIONS FOR COPYING, DISTRIBUTION AND MODIFICATION

0. This License applies to any program or other work which contains a notice placed by the copyright holder saying it may be distributed under the terms of this General Public License. The "Program", below, refers to any such program or work, and a "work based on the Program" means either the Program or any derivative work under copyright law: that is to say, a work containing the Program or a portion of it, either verbatim or with modifications and/or translated into another language. (Hereinafter, translation is included without limitation in the term "modification".) Each licensee is addressed as "you".

Activities other than copying, distribution and modification are not covered by this License; they are outside its scope. The act of running the Program is not restricted, and the output from the Program is covered only if its contents constitute a work based on the Program (independent of having been made by running the Program). Whether that is true depends on what the Program does.

1. You may copy and distribute verbatim copies of the Program's source code as you receive it, in any medium, provided that you conspicuously and appropriately publish on each copy an appropriate copyright notice and disclaimer of warranty; keep intact all the notices that refer to this License and to the absence of any warranty; and give any other recipients of the Program a copy of this License along with the Program.

You may charge a fee for the physical act of transferring a copy, and you may at your option offer warranty protection in exchange for a fee.

2. You may modify your copy or copies of the Program or any portion of it, thus forming a work based on the Program, and copy and distribute such modifications or work under the terms of Section 1 above, provided that you also meet all of these conditions:

   a) You must cause the modified files to carry prominent notices stating that you changed the files and the date of any change.

   b) You must cause any work that you distribute or publish, that in whole or in part contains or is derived from the Program or any part thereof, to be licensed as a whole at no charge to all third parties under the terms of this License.

   c) If the modified program normally reads commands interactively when run, you must cause it, when started running for such interactive use in the most ordinary way, to print or display an announcement including an appropriate copyright notice and a notice that there is no warranty (or else, saying that you provide a warranty) and that users may redistribute the program under these conditions, and telling the user how to view a copy of this License. (Exception: if the Program itself is interactive but does not normally print such an announcement, your work based on the Program is not required to print an announcement.)

These requirements apply to the modified work as a whole. If identifiable sections of that work are not derived from the Program, and can be reasonably considered independent and separate works in themselves, then this License, and its terms, do not apply to those sections when you distribute them as separate works. But when you distribute the same sections as part of a whole which is a work based on the Program, the distribution of the whole must be on the terms of this License, whose permissions for other licensees extend to the entire whole, and thus to each and every part regardless of who wrote it.

Thus, it is not the intent of this section to claim rights or contest your rights to work written entirely by you; rather, the intent is to exercise the right to control the distribution of derivative or collective works based on the Program.

In addition, mere aggregation of another work not based on the Program with the Program (or with a work based on the Program) on a volume of a storage or distribution medium does not bring the other work under the scope of this License.

3. You may copy and distribute the Program (or a work based on it, under Section 2) in object code or executable form under the terms of Sections 1 and 2 above provided that you also do one of the following:

a) Accompany it with the complete corresponding machine-readable source code, which must be distributed under the terms of Sections 1 and 2 above on a medium customarily used for software interchange; or,

b) Accompany it with a written offer, valid for at least three years, to give any third party, for a charge no more than your cost of physically performing source distribution, a complete machine-readable copy of the corresponding source code, to be distributed under the terms of Sections 1 and 2 above on a medium customarily used for software interchange; or,

c) Accompany it with the information you received as to the offer to distribute corresponding source code. (This alternative is allowed only for noncommercial distribution and only if you received the program in object code or executable form with such an offer, in accord with Subsection b above.)

The source code for a work means the preferred form of the work for making modifications to it. For an executable work, complete source code means all the source code for all modules it contains, plus any associated interface definition files, plus the scripts used to control compilation and installation of the executable. However, as a special exception, the source code distributed need not include anything that is normally distributed (in either source or binary form) with the major components (compiler, kernel, and so on) of the operating system on which the executable runs, unless that component itself accompanies the executable.

If distribution of executable or object code is made by offering access to copy from a designated place, then offering equivalent access to copy the source code from the same place counts as distribution of the source code, even though third parties are not compelled to copy the source along with the object code.

4. You may not copy, modify, sublicense, or distribute the Program except as expressly provided under this License. Any attempt otherwise to copy, modify, sublicense or distribute the Program is void, and will automatically terminate your rights under this License. However, parties who have received copies, or rights, from you under this License will not have their licenses terminated so long as such parties remain in full compliance.

5. You are not required to accept this License, since you have not signed it. However, nothing else grants you permission to modify or distribute the Program or its derivative works. These actions are prohibited by law if you do not accept this License. Therefore, by modifying or distributing the Program (or any work based on the Program), you indicate your acceptance of this License to do so, and all its terms and conditions for copying, distributing or modifying the Program or works based on it.

6. Each time you redistribute the Program (or any work based on the Program), the recipient automatically receives a license from the original licensor to copy, distribute or modify the Program subject to these terms and conditions. You may not impose any further restrictions on the recipients' exercise of the rights granted herein. You are not responsible for enforcing compliance by third parties to this License.

7. If, as a consequence of a court judgment or allegation of patent infringement or for any other reason (not limited to patent issues), conditions are imposed on you (whether by court order, agreement or otherwise) that contradict the conditions of this License, they do not excuse you from the conditions of this License. If you cannot distribute so as to satisfy simultaneously your obligations under this License and any other pertinent obligations, then as a consequence you may not distribute the Program at all. For example, if a patent license would not permit royalty-free redistribution of the Program by all those who receive copies directly or indirectly through you, then the only way you could satisfy both it and this License would be to refrain entirely from distribution of the Program.

If any portion of this section is held invalid or unenforceable under any particular circumstance, the balance of the section is intended to apply and the section as a whole is intended to apply in other circumstances.

It is not the purpose of this section to induce you to infringe any patents or other property right claims or to contest validity of any such claims; this section has the sole purpose of protecting the integrity of the free software distribution system, which is implemented by public license practices. Many people have made generous contributions to the wide range of software distributed through that system in reliance on consistent application of that system; it is up to the author/donor to decide if he or she is willing to distribute software through any other system and a licensee cannot impose that choice.

This section is intended to make thoroughly clear what is believed to be a consequence of the rest of this License.

8. If the distribution and/or use of the Program is restricted in certain countries either by patents or by copyrighted interfaces, the original copyright holder who places the Program under this License may add an explicit geographical distribution limitation excluding those countries, so that distribution is permitted only in or among countries not thus excluded. In such case, this License incorporates the limitation as if written in the body of this License.

9. The Free Software Foundation may publish revised and/or new versions of the General Public License from time to time. Such new versions will be similar in spirit to the present version, but may differ in detail to address new problems or concerns.

Each version is given a distinguishing version number. If the Program specifies a version number of this License which applies to it and "any later version", you have the option of following the terms and conditions either of that version or of any later version published by the Free Software Foundation. If the Program does not specify a version number of this License, you may choose any version ever published by the Free Software Foundation.

10. If you wish to incorporate parts of the Program into other free programs whose distribution conditions are different, write to the author to ask for permission. For software which is copyrighted by the Free Software Foundation, write to the Free Software Foundation; we sometimes make exceptions for this. Our decision will be guided by the two goals of preserving the free status of all derivatives of our free software and of promoting the sharing and reuse of software generally.

NO WARRANTY

11. BECAUSE THE PROGRAM IS LICENSED FREE OF CHARGE, THERE IS NO WARRANTY FOR THE PROGRAM, TO THE EXTENT PERMITTED BY APPLICABLE LAW. EXCEPT WHEN OTHERWISE STATED IN WRITING THE COPYRIGHT HOLDERS AND/OR OTHER PARTIES PROVIDE THE PROGRAM "AS IS" WITHOUT WARRANTY OF ANY KIND, EITHER EXPRESSED OR IMPLIED, INCLUDING, BUT NOT LIMITED TO, THE IMPLIED WARRANTIES OF MERCHANTABILITY AND FITNESS FOR A PARTICULAR PURPOSE. THE ENTIRE RISK AS TO THE QUALITY AND PERFORMANCE OF THE PROGRAM IS WITH YOU. SHOULD THE PROGRAM PROVE DEFECTIVE, YOU ASSUME THE COST OF ALL NECESSARY SERVICING, REPAIR OR CORRECTION.

12. IN NO EVENT UNLESS REQUIRED BY APPLICABLE LAW OR AGREED TO IN WRITING WILL ANY COPYRIGHT HOLDER, OR ANY OTHER PARTY WHO MAY MODIFY AND/OR REDISTRIBUTE THE PROGRAM AS PERMITTED ABOVE, BE LIABLE TO YOU FOR DAMAGES, INCLUDING ANY GENERAL, SPECIAL, INCIDENTAL OR CONSEQUENTIAL DAMAGES ARISING OUT OF THE USE OR INABILITY TO USE THE PROGRAM (INCLUDING BUT NOT LIMITED TO LOSS OF DATA OR DATA BEING RENDERED INACCURATE OR LOSSES SUSTAINED BY YOU OR THIRD PARTIES OR A FAILURE OF THE PROGRAM TO OPERATE WITH ANY OTHER PROGRAMS), EVEN IF SUCH HOLDER OR OTHER PARTY HAS BEEN ADVISED OF THE POSSIBILITY OF SUCH DAMAGES. END OF TERMS AND CONDITIONS.

1

PHP Review

Overview

 his book assumes that you have some experience with PHP. This book is not meant to be an introductory text on PHP programming but is instead a book on some of the more advanced uses for PHP that you won't find in many of the introductory books or tutorials on the Web.

Having said that, I am still providing here a brief introduction to PHP for those who may need a quick refresher or are already familiar with a similar language, such as PERL.

PHP Syntax

PHP is a language that was designed to be easily embedded into HTML pages (although you don't have to do it that way). Most PHP pages have PHP code and HTML intermixed. When a Web server reads a PHP page, it is looking for two things to let it know it should start reading the page as PHP rather than HTML, the start and end PHP tags: <?php and ?>, respectively.

If you have configured your *php.ini* file to accept "short tags" (which are enabled by default), then you can use the syntax <? and ?> instead. Additionally, you can configure your *php.ini* file so that it accepts ASP style tags, <% and %>. This feature is turned off by default, and its only real purpose seems to be to allow certain HTML editors to recognize the in-between code as something other than HTML, in which case the editor won't mangle the code by imposing its own set of HTML syntax rules upon the code.

A brief example of PHP embedded in HTML:

```
<h1>Welcome To The Web Site Of <? echo $company; ?>!</h1>
```

The code above, when viewed via a Web server, simply prints out the name of the company in place of the PHP code.

In general, individual lines of PHP code should end with a semicolon, although it is not necessary to use semicolons if a beginning or an ending bracket is used (this will make sense when you look at if/then statements).

For example:

```
<?
echo "<p>a line of code";
echo "<p>another line of code;
?>
```

Variables

You can also easily intertwine small segments of PHP into HTML, such as when printing out the value of a variable:

```
<h1>Today's Date is <?= $date ?>.</h1>
```

The "<?=" syntax in the php, when followed by a variable, is used as shorthand for the echo() function.

You can include comments in your PHP scripts. Comments are ignored by the Web server, and any comments contained within the PHP code are not sent to a browser. There are three forms of comments:

- #—Used just like it is used in PERL; comments out the remainder of the line after the # symbol.
- //—Used just like it is in JavaScript; comments out the remainder of the line after the // symbols.
- /* and */—Comments out anything in between the two sets of symbols. This is the same syntax used in C to comment code.

Examples of comments in PHP code:

```
<?
echo "Hello"; #prints out "Hello"
echo "Hello"; //prints out "Hello"
/* The following
prints out "Hello" */
echo "Hello";
?>
```

You will most often see comments denoted using the // characters or the /* and */ characters. The # character is rarely seen, although it is still valid.

Variables in PHP are denoted by the "$". To assign the value "Hello World" to the variable $a, you simply call it in your code:

```
$a = "Hello World";
```

Strings must be enclosed by quotes, but they can contain variables themselves:

```
$a = 4;
```

```
$string = "The value of a is $a";
// $string = "The Value of a is 4";
```

PHP variables do not have to be declared ahead of time, nor do they require a type definition. Note that you may get a warning about using undeclared variables if you try to use them before giving them a value (depending on how you set up error reporting in *php.ini*, see Chapter 8). For example:

```
$a = 4;
$c = $a + $b;
// $c = 4, but a warning appears "Warning: Undefined
variable..".
```

Warnings do not stop a script from continuing. If you forgot to add a semicolon at the end of one of the lines, then you would get a Parser error, which prohibits the script from running.

Since PHP variables are not typed, you don't have to worry about performing mathematical equations on the wrong type, as you might in C. For example:

```
$a = 4;
$b = "5";
$c = $a + $b;
// $c = 9;
```

PHP also supports boolean variables, which can be assigned either a one or a zero, or the words true or false:

```
$a = true;
$b = 1;
//$a = $b
$c = false;
$d = 0;
//$c = $d
```

Operators

PHP support for operators includes the following:

Arithmetic Operators

PHP supports the standard mathematical operators:

```
$a = 4;
$b = 2;
//Addition: $a + b = 6
//Subtraction: $a - $b = 2
//Multiplication: $a * $b = 8
//Division :$a / $b = 2
//Modulus (remainder of $a / $b): $a % $b = 0
//Increment: $a++ (would equal 5 since $a = 4)
```

Assignment Operators

The two main assignment operators in php are "=" and ".". The equals sign should be obvious; it assigns a value to a variable:

```
$a = 4;
$b = $a;
// $b = 4
```

Comparison Operators

PHP supports the standard comparison operators, as shown in Table 1–1:

TABLE 1–1 Comparison Operators in PHP

OPERATOR	DESCRIPTION
$a == $b	test if two values are equal
$a != $b	test if two values are not equal
$a < $b	test if the first value is less than the second
$a > $b	test if the first value is greater than the second
$a <= $b	test if the first value is less than or equal to the second
$a >= $b	test if the first value is greater than or equal to the second

PHP also supports the standard increment and decrement operators:

```
$a = 5;
$a++;
// $a = 6
$b = 5;
$b--;
//$b = 4
```

Concatenating Strings

The "." operator concatenates two values:

```
$sentence_a = "The quick brown ";
$sentence_b = "fox jumped...";
$sentence_c = $a . $b;
//$sentence_c = "The quick brown fox jumped...";
```

Arrays

PHP supports both numerical arrays (array items are indexed by their numerical order) as well as associative arrays (array items are indexed by named keys).

```
$a = array(1, 2, 3, 4);
//$a[0] = 1
//$a[1] = 2
//$a[2] = 3
//$a[3] = 4
$b = array("name"=>"Fred", "age" => 30);
//$b['name'] = "Fred"
//$b['age'] = 30
```

If/Then Statements

One of the most common PHP language constructs that you will encounter is the if/then statement. The if/then statement allows you to evaluate an expression and then, depending if it is true or not, take a course of action. For example:

```
$a = 1;
if($a) {
        echo "True!";
}
```

Since $a = 1, then PHP interprets it in the context of the if statement to be a boolean type. Since 1 = true, the if statements prints out the message. Literally you can read it as "If True, then print out "True!".

Another example, but this time with an "else" clause:

```
$a = 5;
$b = "10";
if($a > $b) {
    echo "$a is greater than $b";
} else {
    echo "$a is not greater than $b";
}
```

PHP doesn't care that $a is an integer and $b is a string. It recognizes that $b also makes a pretty good integer as well. It then evaluates the expression, "If $a is greater than $b then print out that $a is greater than $b; if not (else) then print out $a is not greater than $b." It's also important to note that you don't say, "$a is less than $b," since it is possible that $a could be equal to $b. If that is the case, then the second part of the expression, the else statement, is the part that runs.

Note the use of brackets to enclose the actions. Also note the lack of semicolons where the brackets are used.

One final example is the if/elseif/else statement:

```
if($a == $b){
    // do something
} elseif ($a > $b) {
    // do something else
} elseif($a < $b) {
    // do yet something else
} else   {
    // if nothing else we do this...
}
```

Switch Statements

In the C programming language, switch statement support arose out of the need for a little something extra when doing if/then types of computation. With the if/then statement, you are locked into a single condition. Switch statements allow for additional evaluations of the data, even though one of the cases may have been met. Switch statements can also save you from typing many if/elseif/elseif/... statements. PHP follows C's use of switch statements.

```php
$a = "100";
switch($a) {
    case(10):
      echo "The value is 10";
      break;
    case (100):
      echo "The value is 100<br>";
    case (1000):
      echo "The value is 1000";
      break;
    default:
      echo "<p>Are you sure you entered a number?";
}
```

As you can see, switch statements have four basic parts:

- The switch—The switch identifies what value or expression is going to be evaluated in each of the cases. In the example above, you tell the switch statement that you are going to evaluate the variable $a in the subsequent cases.
- The case—The case statement evaluates the variable you passed from the switch command. You can use case() the same way you'd use an if statement. If the case holds true, then everything after the case statement is executed, until the parser encounters a break command, at which point execution stops and the switch is exited.
- Breakpoints—Defined by the break command, exit the parser from the switch. Breakpoints are normally put after statements executed when a case() is met.
- Default—The default is a special kind of case. It is executed if none of the other case statements in the switch have been executed.

For Loops

For loops are useful constructions to loop through a finite set of data, such as data in an array:

```
for($i = 0; $i < sizeof($array); $i++) {
    //do something with array[$i];
}
```

For loops require three things when they are defined:

- Counter—In the above example, $i = 0. You can pass in an already assigned variable or assign a value to the variable in the for statement.
- The condition required to continue the for loop—In the above example, while $i is less than the size of the $array, the for loop continues to be executed.
- Statement to modify the counter on each pass of the loop—In the above example, $i++ increments the counter after each loop.

Foreach Loops

Foreach loops allow you to quickly traverse through an array.

```
$array = array("name" => "Jet", "occupation" => "Bounty Hunter" );
foreach ($array as $val) {
    echo "<P>$val";
}
Prints out:
<P>Jet
<P>Bounty Hunter
```

You can also use foreach loops to get the key of the values in the array:

```
foreach ($array as $key => $val) {
    echo "<P>$key : $val";
}
Prints out:
<P>name : Jet
<P>occupation : Bounty Hunter
```

While Loops

While loops are another useful construct to loop through data. While loops continue to loop until the expression in the while loop evaluates to false. A common use of the while loop is to return the rows in an array from a result set. The while loop continues to execute until all of the rows have been returned from the result set:

```
while($row = mysql_fetch_array($result)) {
    // do something with the resulting row
}
```

You can also use the continue command to skip over the current iteration of the loop, then continue. For example:

```
while($row = mysql_fetch_array($result)) {
    if($row['name'] ! = "Jet")) {
      continue;
    } else {
      // do something with the row
    }
}
```

Do While Loops

Do while loops are another useful loop construct. Do while loops work exactly the same as normal while loops, except that the script evaluates the while expression after the loop has completed, instead of before the loop executes, as in a normal while loop.

The important difference between a do while loop and a normal while loop is that a do while loop is always executed at least once. A normal while loop may not be executed at all, depending on the expression. The following do while loop is executed one time, printing out $i to the screen:

```
$i = 0;
do {
    print $i;
} while ($i>0);
```

Whereas the following is not executed at all:

```
$i = 0;
while($i > 0)  {
print $i;
}
```

Quite frankly, I never find much use for do while loops, but you may find an odd problem that requires it.

User-Defined Functions

In addition to PHP's built-in functions, you can create your own functions. Remember that if you want to use variables that exist outside of the function, then you must declare them as global variables or assign them as arguments to the function itself.

```
function check_age($age) {
    if ($age > 21) {
        return 1;
    } else {
        return 0;
    }
}
//usage:
if(check_age($age)) {
    echo "You may enter!";
} else {
    echo "Access Not Allowed!";
    exit;
}
```

The function would be called from within your script at the appropriate time, using the following syntax:

```
$age = 10;
check_age($age);
// prints "Access Not Allowed!" to the screen
```

Object Oriented Programming with PHP

PHP supports Object Oriented Programming (OOP) in the form of classes. Just like in other OOP languages, the classes can be extended for greater reuse of code.

To create an address entry class that contains a person's first and last name and phone number:

```php
class address_book_entry {
    var $first;
    var $last;
    var $number;
    function set_name($first, $last) {
      $this->first = $first;
      $this->last = $last;
    }
    function set_number($number) {
      $this->number = $number;
    }
    function display_entry() {
      echo "<p>Name: " . $this->first . " " . $this-
>last;
      echo "<br>Number: " . $this->number;
    }
}
//Usage:
$entry = &new address_book_entry;
$entry->set_name("Jane","Smith");
$entry->set_number("555-555-5555");
$entry->display_entry();
//displays:
Name: Jane Smith
Number: 555-555-5555
```

Additionally, you can extend an existing class to create a new class that has the same functionality of the old class, plus any new functionality you add:

```php
class address_book_entry2 extends address_book_entry {
var $email;
function set_email($email) {
    $this->email = $email;
  }
  function display_entry2() {
    echo "<p>Name: " . $this->first . " " . $this->last;
    echo "<br>Number: " . $this->number;
    echo "<br>Email: " . $this->email;
  }
}
//Usage:
$entry = &new address_book_entry2;
$entry->set_name("Jane","Smith");
$entry->set_number("555-555-5555");
$entry->set_email("jsmith@com.com");
```

```
$entry->display_entry();
//displays:
Name: Jane Smith
Number: 555-555-5555
Email: smith@com.com
```

phpinfo( )

phpinfo() is a very useful function that allows you to see what version of PHP is running on your Web server, as well as all of the specific settings that are enabled in that version.

Throughout this book, there are sections that ask you to verify your settings. One way to do this is to create a script that includes just the following:

```
<?
    phpinfo();
?>
```

Upon execution of the script, the browser displays the current PHP settings. This function is especially useful if you are working on somebody else's server and are not quite sure of its capabilities.

Additional Resources

If you still need additional information on the basics of PHP, the following books from Prentice Hall provide material suitable for the utmost PHP beginner:

- *Core PHP Programming: Using PHP to Build Dynamic Web Sites* (2nd Edition) by Leon Atkinson. ISBN 0130893986.
- *Essential PHP for Web Professionals* by Christopher Cosentino. ISBN 0130889032.[1]

---

1. Shameless plug for my own book, I know, but I've received a lot of email from nonprogrammers who said the book really helped!

2

Session Management

Introduction to Session Management in PHP4

This chapter introduces you to session management using PHP4's built-in session management techniques.

Session management allows you to track variables associated with a user for a specific Web session. A Web session is the time that a user spends on pages on your site using the same browser instance. If the user closes the browser (or you explicitly end the session), then the session variables are no longer associated with that user, unless you provide for a way that the variables can be saved and later reassociated with the user.

Sessions are typically tracked by PHP by placing a cookie on the user's browser. The cookie references a session ID, which you can view in your scripts by calling the $PHPSESSID variable. However, using cookies is not a foolproof method to track session variables. Some users may set up their browsers so that they do not accept cookies. In these cases, your session variables cannot be tracked using the cookie method.

PHP supports link rewriting, which gets around the problems in using cookies to store session information. With link rewriting, PHP alters any links on your page so that they automatically include the $PHPSESSID variable. This does make the links look a little messy to the user, but in some cases it is the only way to be sure that you are accurately tracking a user's session.

Initial *php.ini* Settings for Session Management

Before you get started with this chapter, you may have to make a couple of minor changes to your *php.ini* file so that sessions work correctly.

On Windows

If you are using a Windows version of PHP, the first thing you need to do is to edit your *php.ini* file. The default session setting in *php.ini* will not work correctly under Windows.

Open your *php.ini* file, which is found in c:\windows or c:\winnt, in a text editor and search for the line:

```
session.save_path = /tmp
```

Change it to a directory in which you keep temporary files, for example:

```
session.save_path = C:/temp
```

You could also leave the value as /tmp and create a directory named "tmp" at the root of the drive on which your Web server resides. For example, if your Web server was located in D:/apache/bin, then you could create the directory d:/tmp and you would not have to change the session.save_path setting in *php.ini*.

A good indication that the session.save_path has not been set correctly on Windows is if Apache crashes when you try to load a session-enabled page.

On Linux

If you are using Linux, you need to make sure that your /tmp directory can be written to by the user who runs the Web processes. Typically this is the user nobody, and most systems, by default, allow the nobody user to write to the /tmp directory.

The rest of the default session settings should work fine for you in the examples in this chapter.

General Considerations

You should not store the session files in any directory which is viewable from your Web server. If you are using Apache, then that would be any directory under the htdocs directory. The reason you do not want to place session files in a directory that is viewable from your Web server is because malicious users may be able to open those files and view individual session data, and even hijack user's sessions in this manner.

Starting a Session

You cannot track variables across a user session unless you start the session on each page on which you want to use or alter those variables. Starting a session uses the session_start() function:

```
session_start();
```

session_start() takes no arguments. If you are starting a new session, then the function initializes the session and creates the necessary temp files to track the session. If a $PHPSESSID is found by the function, either by a cookie or a GET variable, then the function resumes the current session and the page has access to any variables that have been registered to the session.

Once you have started the session, you need to register some variables with it. The session will not track variables until they have been registered using the session_register() function:

```
session_register(STRING);
```

The STRING argument to session_register() should be the name of the variable that you want to register with the session so that it may be accessed across any session-enabled pages.

Once you have started the session and registered one or more variables, you can use those variables across any session enabled pages on your site. Script 2–1, session.php, provides a simple example of starting a session and registering a variable.

SCRIPT 2–1 session.php

```
1.  <?
2.  session_start();
3.  if(!isset($count)) {
4.     session_register("count");
5.     $count = 1;
6.  }
7.  ?>
8.  You have been to this page <?=$count?> times.
9.  <?
10. $count++;
11. ?>
```

Script 2–1 session.php Line-by-Line Explanation

LINE	DESCRIPTION
2	Start the session or continue an existing session.
3	The if statement checks to see if the $count variable has been set. If the $count variable has been set, then the script assumes that this is a continuation of a session and takes no action and the script continues onto line 7.
4	If the $count variable has not been set, then the script assumes that this is the beginning of a new session and registers the variable $count.
5	Since the script has just registered the variable $count in the preceding line, it uses this line to assign a default value of 1 to $count.

Script 2–1 session.php Line-by-Line Explanation (Continued)

LINE	DESCRIPTION
8	Display a line of text stating the number of times the page has been viewed.
10	Increment the $count variable by one.

Run this script and click the reload button several times. Notice that the number of times the page has been viewed increases by one each time you reload the page. Figure 2–1 shows an example of this. Closing the browser then reloading the page in a new browser resets the $count to '1', as closing the browser effectively ends the session.

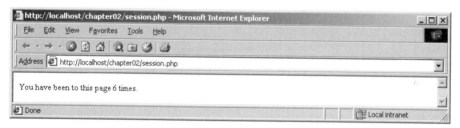

FIGURE 2–1 session.php

The Contents of Session Files

You can view the actual contents of session variables by looking in the directory specified in the session.save_path setting in your *php.ini* file. In that directory, you should see a file named something along the lines of "sess_c4a9722c1745304544dc5cc1 b3e08996." The important part is that the file name begins with "sess_." The random string of characters after that is the unique identifier that PHP assigns to each session. If you are on a shared site or you have run any sessions in the past, then there may be several files that look like PHP session files. Try to find the one with the timestamp closest to when you accessed the example, but opening any of the files will give you an idea of how the session variables are stored. Opening the file in a text editor displays the following:

```
count|i:6;
```

The actual number displayed in the file will be different, depending on how many times you reloaded the page. The contents of the file display the variable name, followed by a pipe symbol, followed by the variable type identifier—in this case "i" for integer—and finally the value of the variable followed by a semicolon. If you have multiple variables registered in the session, then they would be listed in the order they were registered, separated in most cases by semicolons. For example, if you had two integer variables registered in the session, $count and $day, then they would appear as follows:

```
count|i:6;day|i:7;
```

Table 2–1 details some of the common variable types you might see in a typical session. file.

TABLE 2–1 Variable Type Identifiers in Session Files

SYMBOL	VARIABLE TYPE
i	Integer
s	String
b	Boolean
d	Float
a	Array
O	Object
N	NULL

Tracking Variables across Pages during a Session

Now that you know how to start a session and track some variables, how about putting this to some use? There are countless uses for sessions, but the real benefit of sessions is to reduce the amount of work for you and your Web server. Think of a typical site that has registered users. This site may have message boards, feature stories that users can respond to, and various other features that users can choose to enable or disable.

Typically, you'd store these preferences in some sort of database and load the values when the user logs into the site.

You need a way to remember these values across each page that the user views. If users don't want to see a Poll feature on one page, then it's safe to assume they don't want to see it on other pages as well. You could query the database each time the user loads a page to see which features should be enabled, or you could store that information in a cookie, but there are drawbacks to each method. Querying the database each time a page loads can lead to some serious server resource problems for large sites. A cookie can only hold one value, so storing cookies for each feature option quickly turns into a coding nightmare: When you have more than one or two features, you'd need a cookie for each one!

This is where sessions can help. You can store multiple values that can be accessed across many pages. You keep the database queries to a minimum by loading the user preferences at the start of the session, and you only need to worry about storing one cookie on the user's browser, eliminating the worry of exceeding the finite number of cookies any one site can store on a browser. If you use PHP's session link rewriting feature, you don't even have to worry about that one cookie!

In this next example, you'll load some default variables into a session as if they were coming from a database query and then verify that the session variables work in Script 2–3, track-prefs2.php. The result will appear in Figure 2–2.

SCRIPT 2–2 track_prefs1.php

```
1.  <?
2.  session_start();
3.  session_register("first");
4.  session_register("last");
5.  session_register("email");
6.  session_register("news_prefs");
7.  ?>
8.  <html>
9.  <head>
10. <title>Welcome</title>
11. <style type="text/css">
12.     p, ul, h3 {font-family: verdana, helvetica, sans-serif;}
13.     .enabled {font-weight: bold; color: green;}
14.     .disabled {font-weight: bold; color: red;}
15. </style>
```

SCRIPT 2–2 track_prefs1.php (Continued)

```
16.  </head>
17.  <body>
18.  <?
19.  function load_user_data(){
20.     global $first, $last, $email, $news_prefs;
21.     $first = "Faye";
22.     $last = "Valentine";
23.     $email = "faye@bebop.com";
24.     $news_prefs = array(
25.        "Local" => 0,
26.        "Nation" => 1,
27.        "World" => 1,
28.        "Comics" => 0,
29.        );
30.  }
31.  load_user_data();
32.  ?>
33.  <h3>Welcome</h3>
34.  <p>Welcome back <b><?=$first?></b>
35.  <p>Your settings have been loaded.
36.  <p><a href=track_prefs2.php>View Your Settings</a>.
37.  </body>
38.  </html>
```

Script 2–2 track_prefs1.php Line-by-Line Explanation

LINE	DESCRIPTION
2	Start the session or continue an existing session.
3–6	Register session variables for use throughout the session.
8–17	Print out the beginning of the HTML page.
19	Declare a new function, load_user_data().
20	Allow the function to use and modify variables in the global scope of the script. These variables correspond to the session variables that were registered earlier in the script.
21–23	Assign some strings to the session variables.
24	Assign an array to the session variable $news_prefs.
25–29	Assign items to the array.
31	Run the load_user_data() function

Script 2–2 track_prefs1.php Line-by-Line Explanation (Continued)

LINE	DESCRIPTION
33–36	Notify the users that their settings have been loaded and provide a link to view the settings.
37–38	Close out the HTML for the page.

SCRIPT 2–3 track_prefs2.php

```php
1.  <?
2.    session_start();
3.  ?>
4.  <html>
5.  <head>
6.  <title>View Settings</title>
7.  <style type="text/css">
8.    p, ul, h3 {font-family: verdana, helvetica, sans-serif;}
9.    .enabled {font-weight: bold; color: green;}
10.   .disabled {font-weight: bold; color: red;}
11. </style>
12. </head>
13. <body>
14. <h3>View Your Settings</h3>
15. <p>Hello <b><?=$first?> <?=$last?></b>,
16. <p>Email: <?=$email?>
17. <p>Your settings:<ul>
18. <?
19. while(list($key,$value) = each($news_prefs)) {
20.    if($value) {
21.       $value = "Enabled";
22.    } else {
23.       $value = "Disabled";
24.    }
25.    print("<li class=$value>$key: $value</li>");
26. }
27. ?>
28. </ul>
29. </body>
30. </html>
```

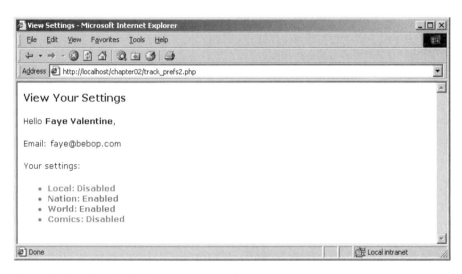

FIGURE 2–2 track_prefs2.php

Script 2–3 track_prefs2.php Line-by-Line Explanation

LINE	DESCRIPTION
2	Start the session or continue an existing session.
4–13	Print out the beginning of the HTML page.
14–17	Greet the users and show some of their current settings.
19–26	Execute a while loop that goes though the user's settings in the $news_prefs session variable. Print the key of the array item to the screen. If the value of the current array item is enabled, then print "Enabled" on the screen; otherwise, print "Disabled" on the screen. In either case, the value determines which CSS class should be used to display the setting.
27–30	End the HTML page.

Unregistering Session Variables

You may find that some of the session variables that you register are only needed on a few pages and not across an entire site. You can unregister these variables so that they are no longer tracked with the session. This is done using the session_unregister() function:

```
session_unregister(STRING);
```

The STRING argument is the name of the variable that you want to unregister from the session. Note that using session_unregister doesn't delete the contents of the variable on the current page. However, the variable value will not be passed to other pages in the session once it has been deleted from the session file.

You may also want to first check to see if the variable is even registered by using the session_is_registered() function:

```
session_is_registered(STRING);
```

For example:

```
//If $name has been registered with the session.
if(session_is_registered("name")) {
unset($name);
    session_unregister("name");
}
```

This has the effect of deleting the variable from the session, as well as deleting the variable from the current page. Also, you don't have to unset the variables one at a time. You can unset all session variables by using the command session_unset():

```
session_unset();
```

session_unset() takes no arguments and simply deletes the values of any variables currently registered with the session. session_unregister() and session_unset() are independent of each other. However, do not call session_unregister() before session_unset() if you also want to unset the value of the variable you are unregistering. Unregistering the variable makes that variable untouchable by session_unset(), for it is no longer a session variable. The proper order to unset the variable $name, as well as unregister it, is:

```
session_unset();
session_unregister("name");
```

You could also do the opposite if you wanted to make sure that a variable was registered and had a value:

```
//If $name has not been registered with the session.
if(!session_is_registered("name")) {
session_register("name");
$name = "Spike";
}
```

Destroying Sessions

If you have been looking at the contents of the session files in your session.save_path directory, you may have noticed that some files have been building up in there, depending on how many session examples you have opened. The reason these files are still there and not deleted when the user ends the session by closing the browser is because we have not made an effort to destroy the session. You have to explicitly destroy sessions for the session files to be deleted. The reason for this is that you have no real way of knowing how long users may be in sessions. It is perfectly feasible for users to start sessions, then go home for the evening (or even a long weekend!) and come back the next day with the browser still sitting open on the desktop. If users have been doing some shopping, you surely wouldn't want to delete their sessions after a set finite amount of time, precisely for the reasons above.

There are two ways to combat the buildup of files in your temporary directory that will not, in most cases, adversely affect your users' sessions.

The first is to make use of the session_destroy() function:

```
session_destroy();
```

session_destroy() takes no arguments. session_destroy() unregisters all session variables associated with the user session and removes any session files created by the session. Remember that even if a variable is unregistered with a session, the variable still exists with its value intact on the *current* page.

This next script demonstrates the use of the session_destroy() function.

SCRIPT 2–4 session2.php

```
1.  <?
2.  session_start();
3.  if(isset($destroy)) {
4.    session_destroy();
5.    unset($name);
6.  } else {
7.    if(!session_is_registered("name")) {
8.      session_register("name");
```

SCRIPT 2-4 session2.php (Continued)

```
9.        $name = "Spike";
10.        }
11.   }
12.   ?>
13.   <p>SESSID: <?=$PHPSESSID?>
14.   <p>Name: <?=$name?>
15.   <form action=session2.php method=post>
16.   <input type="submit" name="reload" value="Reload
      Session"><br>
17.   <input type="submit" name="destroy" value="Destroy
      Session">
18.   </form>
```

Script 2–4 session2.php Line-by-Line Explanation

LINE	DESCRIPTION
2	Start the session or continue an existing session.
3–5	Check to see if the $destroy variable is set. If it is, then the user has pressed the "Destroy" button.
6–10	If $destroy has not been set, then register a session variable named $name and assign that variable the value "Spike".
13–14	Print out the current session ID and the value of the $name variable.
15–18	Display a form to the user that allows him or her to reload the current page or destroy the session variable associated with the current session. If the user reloads the page (by clicking "Reload" or using the browser's reload button), then the session variables are reset and the value for session ID is displayed. If the user clicks the "Destroy" button, then the session file associated with the page is deleted, which in turn deletes the value of the session variable.

Note the files in your temporary directory while clicking the "Reload Session" and "Destroy Session" buttons. Each time you click "Destroy Session," notice that the session file with the corresponding session ID is deleted from your session.save_path directory. Each click of "Reload Session" causes the file to be recreated in that directory.

The other way to manage the orphaned session files is to make use of PHP's automatic "garbage" cleanup of these session files. Open your *php.ini* file in a text editor and scroll down to the [session] settings. Look for the following two settings:

```
; Percentile probability that the 'garbage collection' process
is started
; on every session initialization.
session.gc_probability = 1
; After this number of seconds, stored data will be seen as
'garbage' and
; cleaned up by the garbage collection process.
session.gc_maxlifetime = 1440
```

The first setting, session.gc_probability, sets the percentage probability that the files identified as garbage are deleted. The default of "1" means that there is a one-percent probability that all of the items identified as garbage are deleted for every session started.

The second setting, session.gc_maxlifetime, sets the lifetime, in seconds, that a session file can exist before being labeled as garbage. The default of "1440" means that every session file that is older than 24 minutes is considered junk.

A Simple Session-Based Shopping Cart

The following example is a simple session-based shopping cart that allows users to add or remove items from their cart.

The application, as shown in Figure 2–3, first asks for the user's name and email address. Users are then brought to the main shopping page where they can add or remove items from their cart by modifying the quantity text field for each item and clicking the "Add Items" button.

When the users have added at least one item, they are presented with a "Check Out" button. They can continue shopping or check out. This is shown in Figure 2–4.

When users click "Check Out", they are brought to a confirmation page, which displays the contents of their cart. They then have the choice of finishing the order by clicking the "Finish Order" button or going back and adding additional items to their cart by clicking the "Add More Items" button. This is shown in Figure 2–5.

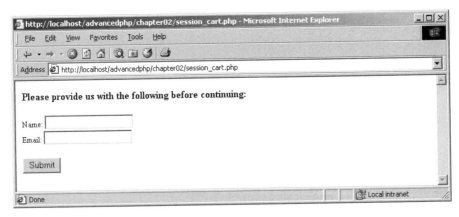

FIGURE 2-3 session_cart.php Sign-In Screen

SCRIPT 2-5 session_cart.php

```
1.   <?
2.   session_start();
3.   $inventory = array(
4.       "001" => "Tooth Paste",
5.       "002" => "Facial Tissue",
6.       "003" => "Cotton Swabs",
7.       "004" => "Shampoo",
8.       "005" => "Conditioner",
9.       "006" => "Deodorant"
10.      );
11.  function populate_cart() {
12.    global $name, $email, $items;
13.    $items = array(0, 0, 0, 0, 0, 0);
14.    session_register("name");
15.    session_register("email");
16.    session_register("items");
17.  }
18.  function get_user_info() {
19.    ?>
20.    <h3>Please provide us with the following before
       continuing:</h3>
21.    <form action=session_cart.php method=post>
22.    <p>Name: <input type="text" name="name">
23.    <br>Email: <input type="text" name="email">
24.    <p><input type="submit" name="infosubmit" value="Submit">
25.    </form>
26.    <?
27.  }
```

```
28.   function shop() {
29.     global $name, $email, $items, $inventory;
30.     ?>
31.     <p>Shop Below:
32.     <form action=session_cart.php method=post><p>
33.     <?
34.     $total = 0;
35.     for($i = 0; $i < sizeof($inventory); $i++) {
36.       ?>
37.       Item ID: <b><?=key($inventory);?></b> Description:
    <b><?=$inventory[key($inventory)]?></b>
38.       Qty: <input type="text" name="items_in[<?=$i?>]"
    value="<?=$items[$i]?>" size="2" maxlength="2"><br>
39.       <?
40.       next($inventory);
41.       $total = $total + $items[$i];
42.     }
43.     ?>
44.     <p>You have <?=$total?> items in your cart.
45.     <p><input type="submit" name="additems">
46.     </form>
47.     <?
48.     if($total > 0) {
49.       ?>
50.       <form action=session_cart_checkout.php>
51.       <input type="submit" name="checkout" value="Check
    Out!">
52.       </form>
53.       <?
54.     }
55.   }
56.   /* MAIN */
57.   if(isset($additems)) {
58.     $items = $items_in;
59.     echo("<h3>Cart Updated!</h3>");
60.     shop();
61.   }elseif(!isset($name)) {
62.     get_user_info();
63.   } elseif(isset($infosubmit)) {
64.     populate_cart();
65.     shop();
66.   } else {
67.     shop();
68.   }
69.   ?>
```

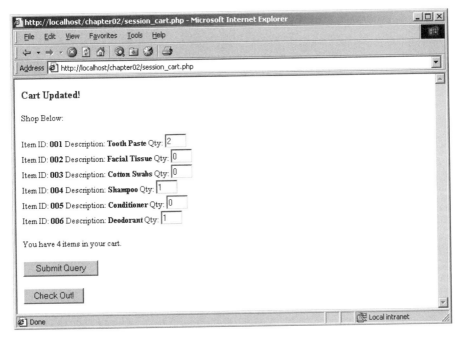

FIGURE 2–4 session_cart.php Shopping Screen

Script 2–5 session_cart.php Line-by-Line Explanation

LINE	DESCRIPTION
2	Start the session or continue an existing session.
3–10	Create an array to be used as the items available in the store.
11	Declare a new function populate_cart(). This function sets up the user's shopping cart.
12	Declare some global variables for the user. The $items variable is the items in the user's shopping cart.
13	Zero out the items in the user's shopping cart.
14–16	Register the variables that have been declared with the session.
18–27	Declare a function to get the user info when the user first arrives at the shopping cart. The function asks for the user's name and email.
28	Declare the shop function. This function does the work of adding and removing items from the user's shopping cart.

Script 2–5 session_cart.php Line-by-Line Explanation (Continued)

LINE	DESCRIPTION
29	Allow the function to access and modify the $name, $email, $items, and $inventory variables.
32	Create the shopping form.
34	Assign a value of 0 to the $totals variable. This variable is used to show how many items are in the user's cart, which is calculated as the user adds or removes items from the cart.
35	Loop through the items in the $inventory array.
37–38	Display the ID (key) and Description (value) for each item in the store's inventory. At the same time, display how many items are in the user's cart in a text input field. If the user has not added any items into the cart, then all values read as 0, which is the value that was used to initialize the cart.
40	Use the next() function so that the next key is available the next time the loop is executed.
41	Add the current total of items in the user's cart for this loop to the running total of items.
42	Exit from the for loop.
44	Display the current item total to the user.
45	Display an "Add Items" button. It is used to execute the additems clause in the main program.
48–54	If the user has at least one item in the cart, then display the "Check Out" button, which brings the user to the session_cart_checkout.php page.
55	End the function.
56	Begin the main program.
57–59	Check to see if the "Add Items" button has been pushed. Display a message to the user that the cart has been updated after the $items session variable is updated.
58	If the "Add Items" button has been pushed, then replace the session variable $items with the items from the form $items_in. The session variable is not automatically updated when you submit variables from a form. You need to explicitly assign a new value to the session variable.
59	Display a message to the user that the cart has been updated after the $items session variable is updated.
60	Run the shop() function so that the user can add or remove additional items.

Script 2–5 session_cart.php Line-by-Line Explanation (Continued)

LINE	DESCRIPTION
61	If the "Add Items" button has not been pushed and the $name variable has not been set, then execute the get_user_info() function, since this is the first time the user has visited the page.
63–65	If none of the above is true, but the $infosubmit variable has been set, then we know the user has just entered the information. Execute the populate_cart() function to initialize the cart.
66–68	If nothing else has happened, just execute the shop function. Since the session variable for $name must be set then, we know the user has entered the information and the cart has been initialized, but no items have been added to the cart.

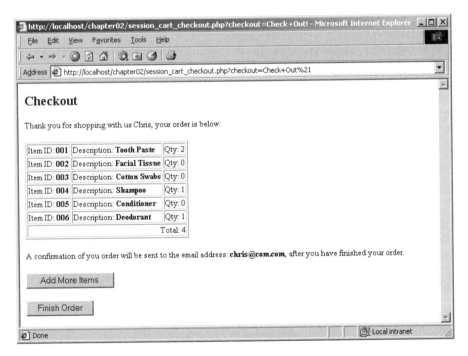

FIGURE 2–5 session_cart_checkout.php

SCRIPT 2-6 session_cart_checkout.php

```php
1.  <?
2.  session_start();
3.  $inventory = array(
4.      "001" => "Tooth Paste",
5.      "002" => "Facial Tissue",
6.      "003" => "Cotton Swabs",
7.      "004" => "Shampoo",
8.      "005" => "Conditioner",
9.      "006" => "Deodorant"
10.     );
11. if(!isset($name)) {
12.     ?>
13.     <h2>Sorry, you need to <a href=session_cart.php>add
    some items</a> before you can check out.
14.     <?
15. }elseif(isset($finish)) {
16.     ?>
17.     <h3>Order Complete!<h3>
18.     <?
19.     // send email confirmation...
20.     // send order to order processing script...
21.     session_unset();
22.     session_destroy();
23. } else {
24.     ?>
25.     <h2>Checkout</h3>
26.     <p>Thank you for shopping with us <?=$name?>, your
    order is below:
27.     <p><table border=1>
28.     <?
29.     $total = 0;
30.     for($i = 0; $i < sizeof($inventory); $i++) {
31.         ?>
32.         <tr><td>Item ID: <b><?=key($inventory);?></b></td>
33.         <td>Description:
    <b><?=$inventory[key($inventory)]?></b></td>
34.         <td>Qty: <?=$items[$i]?></td></tr>
35.         <?
36.         next($inventory);
37.         $total = $total + $items[$i];
38.     }
39.     ?>
40.     <tr><td colspan=3 align=right>Total: <?=$total?></
    td></tr>
41.     </table>
```

SCRIPT 2–6 session_cart_checkout.php (Continued)

```
42.    <p>A confirmation of your order will be sent to the
       email address: <b><?=$email?></b>, after you have
       finished your order.
43.    <p>
44.    <form action=session_cart.php>
45.      <input type="submit" name="continue" value="Add More
       Items">
46.    </form>
47.    <form action=session_cart_checkout.php>
48.      <input type="submit" name="finish" value="Finish
       Order">
49.    </form>
50.    <?
51.  }
52.  ?>
```

Script 2–6 session_cart_checkout.php Line-by-Line Explanation

LINE	DESCRIPTION
2	Start the session or continue an existing session.
3–10	Recreate an array to be used as the items available in the store.
11	Verify that the $name variable is set. If it is, then we know that there is existing session data.
12–14	If the $name variable is not set, then we know that the there is no session data or that it is incomplete. Redirect users back to the shopping cart page so that they can reregister their name and email and add some items to their cart.
15	Check to see if the "Finish Order" has been pushed.
16–20	If the "Finish Order" button has been pushed, then notify the user that the order has been completed. Then do whatever processing is required, such as sending email or sending the order to an order-processing script.
21	Delete all the session variables, since we no longer need the data.
22	Destory the session to remove the session file from the server's disk. This has the added benefit of not allowing the user to click "Reload" or the "Back" button and produce multiple orders for the same thing.
23	If the order has not been finalized and we know the $name variable has been set in the session, then execute the remainder of the script.

Script 2–6 session_cart_checkout.php Line-by-Line Explanation (Continued)

LINE	DESCRIPTION
25–41	Display a table using the data from the $inventory array and from the $items in the user's shopping cart. This table is similar to the one used in the session_cart.php script that displays the shopping form, except that the fields are not editable.
42	Display a message providing details to users of what happens when they click the "Finish Order" button.
43–46	Provide a button so that users can go back and edit items in their cart.
47–49	Display the "Finish Order" button so that users can confirm their order.
51	Close out the if/elseif/else statement started on line 11.

Multiple Database Interaction

Advanced Database Interaction in PHP4

If you have been playing with PHP for a while, you have most likely noticed its excellent support for connecting to MySQL databases. Most of the PHP books on the market describe PHP database support only with MySQL. But PHP supports many more databases with almost the same support it provides for MySQL. As of version 4.1, PHP supports the following databases in one form or another:

- MySQL—*www.mysql.com*
- mSQL—*www.hughes.com.au*
- MS SQL (Microsoft SQL server; on Win32 systems only)
- filePro (Read only)—*www.fptech.com*
- Informix—(from IBM) *www.informix.com*

- InterBase—*www.interbase.com*
- Oracle—*www.oracle.com*
- Ovrimos—*www.ovrimos.com*
- Sybase—*www.sybase.com*
- DB++—experimental—*www.concept-asa.de*
- DBM—flat file databases available on many flavors of *nix
- PostgreSQL—*www.pgsql.com*
- Frontbase—*www.frontbase.com*

Basically, PHP has enough built-in support for a majority of your database needs, especially since it contains support for the commercial heavyweights, such as Oracle, Sybase, Informix, and Microsoft.

Unfortunately, each supported database has different functions to do the same things. For example, to connect to a MySQL database you use the function mysql_connect, and to connect to a MS SQL server you use mssql_connect. The two functions are almost identical, but have different names.

This causes problems as far as code portability goes. Say, for example, you have a killer app that you want to create, but management insists that you use Microsoft's SQL server as the database back-end. However, you know that MySQL or PostgreSQL will do the job just as well, and they are "free" databases that run on the lovely Linux server you have hiding under your desk. Wouldn't it be nice if you could code it once, then run your application using any one of these databases with only the flip of a variable to tell PHP which database it is talking to?

The PHP team has eliminated some of the problems with multiple databases by creating a database abstraction layer called DBX. DBX allows you to use one function that can, for example, connect to different types of databases.

You could also create your own set of custom database "wrappers" to allow you to support multiple databases.

There is also a great database abstraction layer called PEAR::DB. PEAR is a set of libraries for PHP that is similar to the PERL CPAN library, although not as extensive at this time.

This chapter will show you a little bit of all three solutions. The bottom line is that your code will be more portable.

Database-Specific Functions in PHP

This section presents some basics in three of the more prominent databases that you can use with PHP. This book assumes that you have some experience with databases and PHP (notably MySQL). This information is included as a brief overview and to point out some of the differences between the functions across different databases. The databases are:

- MySQL
- PostgreSQL
- MS SQL (Microsoft)

Chances are good that you will have at least one of these databases available to you (very good since MySQL and PostgreSQL are available for free download).

There are four basic concepts in PHP for dealing with databases:

1. Connecting to the database server.
2. Selecting the proper database.
3. Querying the database to insert, read, or delete data.
4. Obtaining the results of your queries to present to the user.

Let's go over these four concepts with the PHP functions used for each database.

Connecting to the Database Server

Before you can do anything in a database-backed application, you need to connect to the database server that contains the actual database that you need to access. For the three databases discussed earlier, this translates into three functions:

- mysql_connect—to connect to a MySQL Server
- mssql_connect—to connect to a MS SQL Server
- pg_connect—to connect to a PostgreSQL Server

mysql_connect() and mssql() connect work identically:

```
mysql_connect(SERVER, USER, PASSWORD);
```

and

```
mssql_connect(SERVER, USER, PASSWORD);
```

In each function, the arguments that need to be defined are:

- SERVER—The host name or IP address of the host on which the database server is running, for example, "mycompany.com" or "192.168.0.1".
- USER—The login of the user who has access to the database server, for example, "Joe".
- PASSWORD—The password of the user.

The connect function for PostgreSQL is much different. pg_connect takes as its argument a single string:

```
pg_connect(STRING);
```

The STRING must contain all of the pertinent information required by your server. The most complete string you could use is:

```
pg_connect("host=localhost port=5432 dbname=test
user=username password=password");
```

It doesn't hurt to use all of the information above, but if the host was localhost, the port was the default port of 5432, and you had no password associated with the user, then you could get by with:

```
pg_connect("dbname=test user=username");
```

Consult your PostgreSQL documentation for your specific implementation. The examples in this chapter assume that you are running your PostgreSQL server on the default port of 5432, so the port is not included in the pg_connect examples.

Selecting the Proper Database

Once you have successfully connected to the database server, you then need to select the database on which you are going to perform your queries.

In the case of PostgreSQL, you have already selected the database in your pg_connect() function, so there is no function to select the database.

However, when using MS SQL or MySQL, you still need to select the database using the respective function:

```
mysql_select_db(STRING)
```

or

```
mssql_select_db(STRING)
```

In each case, STRING refers to the name of the database to which you are connecting.

Querying the Database to Insert, Read, or Delete Data

Once you've connected to the database server and selected the database, the next logical thing is to do *something* with the data in the form of a query. Most databases accept any standard SQL command in a query, as well as their own database-specific commands.

The three databases used in the examples all use the same syntax:

- `mysql_query(STRING);`
- `mssql_query(STRING);`
- `pg_query(STRING);`

where STRING is an SQL statement, such as "SELECT name FROM phonebook WHERE name = 'Sarah'."

Obtaining the Results of Your Queries to Present to the User

Once you have made your query, you need to get the result and show it to the user or perform some other processing on it. One of the simplest ways to accomplish this is using the fetch_array functions included in most PHP supported databases.

- `mysql_fetch_array(RESULT);`
- `mssql_fetch_array(RESULT);`
- `pg_fetch_array(RESULT);`

The data from the result is loaded into a field in the array (that is both associative and indexed). Each column in the result is loaded into a field into the array. The keys of the array correspond to the column names of the data returned.

DBX—PHP Support for Multiple Databases

For applications that don't require complex database-specific queries, you can use PHP's built-in DBX functions.

Before you can use the DBX functions, you must enable support at compile time if you are using Linux or enable the DBX module if you are using Windows.

Enabling DBX in Linux

If you compiled PHP using Apache's APXS functionality (compile --with-apxs=/path/to/apache/bin/apxs), then adding functionality to the PHP module is a breeze.

Before recompiling PHP, I first suggest that you delete the config.cache file and clean up files left over from the previous compile. This can be done like this:

```
cd /path/to/php/source
rm config.cache
make clean
```

After you issue the make clean command, you will notice quite a few files being deleted. Don't worry about it. The make program is just cleaning up files it won't need when you recompile. If you don't run the make clean command, then you may start running into some problems. If you have been compiling PHP with no problems and suddenly it won't compile right, even though you haven't changed anything, it's a good bet that the make clean command will solve your problem.

Once you've cleaned up the mess from the previous compile, you can get started with the new compile.

To compile PHP with DBX support enabled, issue the following command from a shell prompt (replacing paths specific to your install as necessary):

```
./compile --with-apxs=/usr/local/apache/bin/apxs \
--enable-dbx \
```

You should also enable support for any database that you wish to use as well—for example:

```
--with-mssql
```

After the configure runs, issue the command:

```
make
```

Assuming no errors occur, you can then issue the command:

```
make install
```

The final command copies the libphp4.so library file to /path/to/apache/libexec/.

Restart Apache to load the new library:

```
/path/to/apache/bin/apachectl restart
```

You can verify that DBX has been correctly installed by using the phpinfo() function and verifying that DBX is listed under the configuration section.

Enabling DBX in Windows

Enabling DBX support for Windows is very easy, since the DLL file for DBX has been precompiled and included in the basic PHP windows installation. Open your *php.ini* file in a text editor and search for the line that says:

```
extension_dir =  ./
```

This line should point to the place where your PHP extensions reside. If you copied the extensions to the same directory as the *php.ini* file, then you do not need to modify the line. If you did not move the PHP extensions to the same directory as the *php.ini* file, then you need to edit the line to point to the correct directory, for example:

```
extension_dir = C:\Apache\php\extensions
```

Next, find the section in the *php.ini* file that says:

```
;Windows Extensions
```

This line will be followed by many lines of windows .dll extensions for php. To enable DBX support, uncomment (delete the semicolon at the beginning of the line) the line that contains the DBX library DLL:

```
extension=php_dbx.dll
```

After you have uncommented the line, save the file and restart the Apache Web server.

You can verify that DBX has been correctly installed by using the phpinfo() function and verifying that DBX is listed under the configuration section.

DBX Functions

The DBX functions are a single set of functions that allows you to access multiple supported databases without having to write your own wrapper functions.

As of version 4.1, PHP DBX supports the following databases:

- mysql
- odbc
- pgsql
- mssql
- fbsql

The following functions are available in DBX:

```
dbx_close(CONNECTION)
```

The dbx_close() function takes one argument, CONNECTION. CONNECTION is the link identifier created when you call the dbx_connect() function.

```
dbx_connect(MODULE, HOST, DATABASE, USER,
PASSWORD, PERSISTENT)
```

The dbx_connect() function is used to establish a connection to the database server, as well as specify which database is to be used. dbx_connect returns an object that contains the handle of the connection as well as the name of the database to which it is connected. See the example for details. The dbx_connect function accepts six arguments:

- MODULE—The database module that you want to use for this connection. The module is essentially the database type to which you are trying to connect. Values may be:
  - DBX_MYSQL—For MySQL databases.

- DBX_ODBC—For any database which supports an ODBC connection.
- DBX_PGSQL—For PostgreSQL databases.
- DBX_MSSQL—For MS SQL databases.
- DBX_FBSQL—For Frontbase database.
- HOST—The host name or IP address of the database server.
- DATABASE—The name of the database on the database server.
- USER—The username.
- PASSWORD—The password for the user.
- PERSISTENT—Whether or not to make this a persistent connection. If you wish to make the connection persistent, then put DBX_PERSISTENT here. Otherwise, this argument is not required.

Example:

```
$module = DBX_MYSQL; //note the absence of quotes!
$dbconn = dbx_connect($module, "192.168.0.5", "php",
"mysqluser", "password") or DIE ("Unable To
Connect");
//$dbconn->database = "php"
//$dbconn->handle is a resource identifer
```

dbx_error(CONNECTION)

The dbx_error function returns the error from the latest function call to the module. The argument CONNECTION is the link identifier defined when you called dbx_connect().
Example:

```
$result = dbx_query($dbconn, "select something from
non_existing_table");
if ($result == 0) {echo dbx_error($dbconn); }
//responds: Table 'php.non_existing_table' doesn't
exist
```

dbx_query(CONNECTION, SQL STATEMENT, FLAGS)

The dbx_query function lets you send SQL queries to the database. It returns an object if the query does not fail and the query returns one or more rows. A query that returns zero rows does not return an object. Instead it returns 1, for the query was successful, but there was no data returned, such as when you select * from a table that has no data. The arguments are:

- CONNECTION—The link identifier created when you call the dbx_connect() function.
- SQL STATEMENT—A standard SQL statement.
- FLAGS—You can specify how much information is returned by the query by specifying one or more of the following flags. By default, all flags are turned on. When specifying the flags, you must use a | symbol to separate them—for example "DBX_RESULT_INDEX | DBX_RESULT_INFO". The flags are:
  - DBX_RESULT_INDEX—Always returned. All results in the result array are indexed by a number, i.e., $result[0], $result[1], etc.
  - DBX_RESULT_INFO—Returns information about the columns returned, such as field name and field type.
  - DBX_RESULT_ASSOC—Sets the keys of the returned array to the column names.

The object returned by dbx_query contains the following properties:

- handle—The same handle that is available from $dbconn->handle. Accessed as $result->handle.
- cols—The number of columns in the result set. Accessed by $result->col.
- rows—The number of rows in the result set. Accessed by $result->rows.
- info—Returned only if either DBX_RESULT_INFO or DBX_RESULT_ASSOC is specified in the flag's parameter. Provides a two-dimensional array containing the name of the column and its type. Accessed by $result['info'][$x] and $result['name'][$x], where $x is the index of the particular row.
- data—Contains the actual data from result. Accessed by $result->data[$x]['field name'] where $x is the index of the particular row.

Example:

```
$result = dbx_query($dbconn, "select something from
some_table", DBX_RESULT_INFO);
```

```
dbx_sort(RESULT, SORT FUNCTION)
```

The dbx_sort function allows you to sort the results of a query using your own custom sort function. However, it is more efficient to use the "ORDER BY" clause in your SQL statement. The arguments the dbx_sort accepts are:

- RESULT—The result of a previous dbx_query statement.
- SORT FUNCTION—Your custom sort function.

Example:

```
function my_sort {
        //your custom sort definition
}
dbx_sort($result, "my_sort");
//$result is now sorted according to my_sort()
```

```
dbx_compare(ROW1, ROW2, COLUMN KEY, FLAGS)
```

The dbx_compare function allows you to compare two result sets, ROW1 and ROW2. If ROW1 = ROW2, then dbx_compare returns 0. If ROW1 > ROW2, then dbx_compare returns 1. If ROW1 < ROW2, then dbx_compare returns –1. The arguments that dbx_compare accepts are:

- ROW1—A result from a dbx_query function call.
- ROW2—A result from a dbx_query function call.
- COLUMN KEY—The name of the column on which the comparison should be made.
- FLAGS—You can specify several flags to compare the rows in ascending or descending order, and what type of comparison should be made. Separate the order of any type by a pipe.
  - DBX_CMP_ASC—(default) Compare in ascending order.
  - DBX_CMP_DESC—Compare in descending order.
  - DBX_CMP_NATIVE—(default) Compare the items "as is."
  - DBX_CMP_TEXT—Compare the items as strings.
  - DBX_CMP_NUMBER—Compare the items as numbers.

Example:

```
$comp = dbx_compare ($r1, $r2, "income");
//$comp = 0 if $r1 = $r2
//$comp = 1 if $r1 > $r2
//$comp = -1 if $r < $r2
```

Using DBX

Now that you have some idea of how the DBX functions work, let's create a small URL database to keep track of some of your favorite links. Since you are using DBX, you can use this application with any database that is supported by DBX. Figure 3–1 shows dbx_urls.php in action.

SCRIPT 3–1 dbx_urls.php

```
1.   <html>
2.   <head>
3.   <title>A PHP-DBX URL Organizer</title>
4.   <style type=text/css>
5.     p, ul, td, h1, h2, h3 {font-family: verdana, helvetica,
     sans-serif;}
6.   </style>
7.   </head>
8.   <body>
9.   <?
10.  /*****
11.  * TABLE DEFINITION FOR THIS EXAMPLE:
12.  * create table URLS (
13.  * url VARCHAR(128) not null,
14.  * description TEXT,
15.  * primary key (url));
16.  *****/
17.  //define $MODULE as DBX_MYSQL, DBX_MSSQL, DBX_PGSQL, or
     your supported database
18.  $MODULE = DBX_PGSQL;
19.  $server = "192.168.0.5";
20.  $user = "psqluser";
21.  $password = "password";
22.  $database = "php";
23.  /* FUNCTIONS */
24.  function get_urls($dbconn, $sql) {
25.    $result = @dbx_query($dbconn, $sql);
26.    if ( $result == 0 ) {
```

```
27.        echo dbx_error($dbconn);
28.      } else {
29.        return $result;
30.      }
31.    }
32.    function url($action, $dbconn, $url, $description) {
33.      if($action == "add") {
34.        $sql = "insert into URLS values('$url',
       '$description')";
35.      }elseif($action == "delete") {
36.        $url = urldecode($url);
37.        $sql = "delete from URLS where URL = '$url'";
38.      }
39.      $result = @dbx_query($dbconn, $sql);
40.      if ( $result == 0 ) {
41.        echo "<P>ERROR ADDING URL: " . dbx_error($dbconn);
42.      } else {
43.        print("<p>$action : $url succeeded!<p>");
44.      }
45.    }
46.    /*** MAIN ***/
47.    $dbconn = dbx_connect($MODULE, $server, $database, $user,
       $password) or die("CANNOT CONNECT TO DATABASE");
48.    ?>
49.    <h1>PHP DBX URL Organizer</h1>
50.    <form action=dbx_urls.php method=post>
51.    <p><b>Add a URL:</b>
52.    <br>URL: <input type="text" name="url" maxlength="128"
       value="http://"> Description: <input type="text"
       name="description"> <input type="submit" name="addurl"
       value="Add URL!">
53.    </form>
54.    <?
55.    if(isset($addurl)) {
56.      url("add", $dbconn, $url, $description);
57.    }
58.    if(isset($delete)) {
59.      url("delete", $dbconn, $delete, "");
60.    }
61.    $sql = "select * from URLS";
62.    $result = get_urls($dbconn, $sql);
63.    if(sizeof($result->data) == 0) {
64.      ?>
65.      <h3>Sorry, there are no URLs in the database. You
       should add some.
```

SCRIPT 3–1 dbx_urls.php (Continued)

```
66.    <?
67.    } else {
68.      ?>
69.      <p>
70.      <table border=1 cellpadding=5 cellspacing=0 width=600>
71.      <tr><td><b>URL</b></td><td><b>Description</b></
       td><td> </td></tr>
72.      <?
73.      for($i = 0; $i < sizeof($result->data); $i++) {
74.        ?>
75.        <tr><td><a href=<?=$result-
       >data[$i]['url']?>><?=$result->data[$i]['url']?></a></td>
76.        <td><?=$result->data[$i]['description']?></td>
77.        <td width=1><a
       href=dbx_urls.php?delete=<?=urlencode($result-
       >data[$i]['url'])?>>delete</a></tr>
78.        <?
79.      }
80.      ?></table><?
81.    }
82.    ?>
83.    </body>
84.    </html>
```

Script 3–1 dbx_urls.php Line-by-Line Explanation

LINE	DESCRIPTION
1–8	Print out normal HTML to start the page.
10–16	The SQL statement required to create the table for this example.
18	The $MODULE definition for the type of database the script will access. Valid choices are defined in line 17.
19	Define the database server host name or IP.
20	Define the database user's username.
21	Define the database user's password.
22	Define the database name on the database server.
24	Define a function to query the database and return the URLs in the database.
25	Issue the query. Note the "@" sign before the call to the dbx_query() function. The "@" sign suppresses any warning that may be issued if something goes awry with the function—for example, if the database is down. More information on handling these errors is available in Chapter 8.

Script 3–1 dbx_urls.php Line-by-Line Explanation (Continued)

LINE	DESCRIPTION
26	If the $result == 0, then there was an error, because upon success, the dbx_query is supposed to return an object.
27	Print out the error if line 26 is true.
28–30	If there was no error, then return the result object.
30	End the function declaration.
32	Define a function to add or remove URLs from the database called url(). The function takes the following arguments: • $action—either "add" or "delete" • $dbconn—the connection link to the database • $url—the URL to be added or removed • $description—the description of the URL
33	If the $action argument is "add", then we are adding a URL.
34	Generate the SQL to add the URL.
35	If $action is not "add", then check to see if it is "delete".
36	Decode the encoded URL.
37	Generate the SQL to delete the URL.
38	End the if/else statement started on line 33.
39	Query the database with the generated SQL.
40	If the $result == 0, then there was an error, because upon success, the dbx_query is supposed to return an object.
41	Display an error to the user including the specific DBX error message.
42–44	If there wasn't an error querying the database, then display a success message to the user.
45	End the function.
46	Start the man program.
47	Generate the database connection string with the variables defined at the beginning of the script.
49–53	Print out the HTML for the page that displays the heading, as well as the form to add URLs.
55–57	If the "Add URL!" button has been pushed, then run the url() function.
58–60	If a "Delete" link has been clicked next to any of the URLs, then run the url() function.

Script 3–1 dbx_urls.php Line-by-Line Explanation (Continued)

LINE	DESCRIPTION
61	Generate an SQL statement to retrieve the URLs.
62	Run the get_url() function using the SQL generated above to retrieve the URLs from the database.
63	Check to make sure there was data in the result set that was returned from the get_urls() function. If there was no data, then the database is empty.
65	Display a message to the user that the database was empty.
67	If the database was not empty, then execute the rest of the script.
70–71	Create a table to display the URLs.
73	Start a for loop to loop through the data returned from the get_url() function.
75	Print out the URL to the table and include a hyperlink to the URL.
76	Print out the description of the URL to the table.
77	Print a delete link for the URL.
79	End the for loop.
81	End the if/else statement started on line 63.
83–84	Close out the HTML for the page.

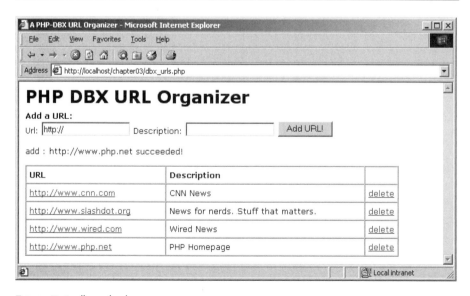

FIGURE 3–1 dbx_urls.php

Creating Your Own Support for Multiple Databases

If you have a simple application that doesn't require complex database interaction, but you still want it to work with multiple databases, then you can create your own set of database wrapper functions.

You have to take into account the different database-specific limitations that may arise and code to the lowest common denominator. That is, you can't use the useful "AUTO_INCREMENT" column feature that is supported in MySQL if you also want to support MS SQL or PostgreSQL databases, since they do not implement that feature. Similarly, MySQL doesn't support secondary keys, so you cannot use that convention.

This next example provides a sample database wrapper that supports MySQL, MS SQL, and PostgreSQL databases. It is called DBlib and contains the following functions listed in Table 3–1:

TABLE 3–1 DBlib.php Functions

FUNCTION	DESCRIPTION
connectDB(DB_ID)	Connects to the database server and returns a DB_CONNECTION.
selectDB(DB_ID)	Selects which database should be used on the server.
queryDB(DB_ID, QUERY)	Sends an SQL query to the database. Returns a RESULT set.
returnDBarray(DB_ID, RESULT)	Returns an array of a row in the RESULT set.
numrowsDB(DB_ID, RESULT)	Returns the number of affected rows from the last query.
closeDB(DB_ID, DB_CONNECTION)	Closes the connection to the database.

The first part of the example is the DBlib.php file, which you include in your own application.

SCRIPT 3-2 DBlib.php

```php
1. <?
2. function connectDB($db) {
3.    global $host, $database, $username, $password;
4.    switch($db) {
5.       case ("psql"):
6.          $conn_string = "host=" . $host . " dbname=" . $database . " user=" . $username . " password=" . $password;
7.          $dbconn = pg_connect($conn_string) or die ("Error Connecting to PostgreSQL DB");
8.          return $dbconn;
9.          break;
10.      case ("mysql"):
11.         $dbconn = mysql_connect($host, $username, $password) or die ("Error Connecting to MySQL DB");
12.         return $dbconn;
13.         break;
14.      case("mssql"):
15.         $dbconn = mssql_connect($host, $username, $password) or die ("Error Connecting to MS SQL DB");
16.         return $dbconn;
17.         break;
18.      default;
19.         echo "<P>Invalid Database: $db";
20.         return 0;
21.   }
22. }
23.
24. function selectDB($db) {
25.    global $database;
26.    switch($db) {
27.       case ("psql"):
28.          return 1;
29.          break;
30.       case ("mysql"):
31.          mysql_select_db($database) or die ("Error Connecting to MySQL DB");
32.          return 1;
33.          break;
34.       case("mssql"):
35.          mssql_select_db($database) or die ("Error Connecting to MS SQL DB");
36.          return 1;
37.          break;
38.       default;
```

```
39.          echo "<P>Invalid Database: $db";
40.          return 0;
41.      }
42. }
43.
44. function queryDB($db, $query) {
45.    switch($db) {
46.       case ("psql"):
47.          if(!$result = @pg_exec($query)){
48.             $result = 0;
49.          }
50.          break;
51.       case ("mysql"):
52.          if(!$result = @mysql_query($query)){
53.             $result = 0;
54.          }
55.          break;
56.       case("mssql"):
57.          if(!$result = @mssql_query($query)){
58.             $result = 0;
59.          }
60.          break;
61.       default;
62.          echo "<P>Invalid Database: $db";
63.          $result = 0;
64.       }
65.    return $result;
66. }
67.
68. function returnDBarray($db, $result) {
69.    if($result != "error") {
70.       switch($db) {
71.          case ("psql"):
72.             if(!$array = @pg_fetch_array($result)){
73.                $array = 0;
74.             }
75.             break;
76.          case ("mysql"):
77.             if(!$array = @mysql_fetch_array($result)){
78.                $array = 0;
79.             }
80.             break;
81.          case("mssql"):
82.             if(!$array = @mssql_fetch_array($result)){
83.                $array = 0;
```

```
84.              }
85.              break;
86.          default;
87.              echo "<P>Invalid Database: $db";
88.              $array = 0;
89.          }
90.          return $array;
91.      }
92. }
93.
94. function closeDB($db,$dbconn) {
95.      switch($db) {
96.          case ("psql"):
97.              if(!@pg_close($dbconn)){
98.                  return 0;
99.              } else {
100.                 return 1;
101.             }
102.             break;
103.         case ("mysql"):
104.             if(!@mysql_close($dbconn)){
105.                 return 0;
106.             } else {
107.                 return 1;
108.             }
109.             break;
110.         case("mssql"):
111.             if(!@mssql_close($dbconn)){
112.                 return 0;
113.             } else {
114.                 return 1;
115.             }
116.             break;
117.         default;
118.             echo "<P>Invalid Database: $db";
119.             return 0;
120.         }
121. }
122.
123. function numrowsDB($db, $result) {
124.     switch($db) {
125.         case ("psql"):
126.             if(!$rows = @pg_numrows($result)){
127.                 return 0;
128.             } else {
```

SCRIPT 3–2 DBlib.php (Continued)

```
129.        return $rows;
130.      }
131.      break;
132.    case ("mysql"):
133.      if(!$rows = @mysql_numrows($result)){
134.        return 0;
135.      } else {
136.        return $rows;
137.      }
138.      break;
139.    case("mssql"):
140.      if(!$rows = @mssql_num_rows($result)){
141.        return 0;
142.      } else {
143.        return $rows;
144.      }
145.      break;
146.    default;
147.      echo "<P>Invalid Database: $db";
148.      return 0;
149.    }
150. }
151.
152. ?>
```

Script 3–2 DBlib.php Line-by-Line Explanation

LINE	DESCRIPTION
2	Declare the connectDB function. The function requires the type of database ($db) as an argument.
3	Declare global variables that can be accessed by this function. The variables are required to connect to the database.
4	Start a switch statement that checks to see which of the cases should be run, depending on the value of $db.
5	If $db = "psql", then the user wants to use a PostgreSQL database.
6	Generate a connection string for a PostgreSQL database.
7	Execute the pg_connect() function to connect to the PostgreSQL server. If there is an error, then kill the script and provide an error message.

Script 3–2 DBlib.php Line-by-Line Explanation (Continued)

LINE	DESCRIPTION
8	If there is not an error, then return the $dbconn variable, which is the database connection handler and is required for many of the other functions.
9	Break out of the switch statement, since the case has been satisfied.
10	If $db = "mysql", then the user wants to use a MySQL database.
11	Execute the mysql_connect() function to connect to the MySQL server. If there is an error, then kill the script and provide an error message.
12	If there is not an error, then return the $dbconn variable, which is the database connection handler and is required for many of the other functions.
13	Break out of the switch statement, since the case has been satisfied.
14	If $db = "mssql", then the user wants to use a MS SQL database.
15	Execute the mssql_connect() function to connect to the MS SQL server. If there is an error, then kill the script and provide an error message.
16	If there is not an error, then return the $dbconn variable, which is the database connection handler and is required for many of the other functions.
17	Break out of the switch statement, since the case has been satisfied.
18–19	If none of the cases have been satisfied, then display a message that the $db value sent to the function was not valid.
20	Return 0 (false), so that any functions using this function know that the function failed.
21	End the switch statement.
22	End the function declaration.
24	Declare the selectDB function. The function requires the type of database ($db) as an argument.
25	Declare a global variable that can be accessed by this function. The variable is required to select the database.
26	Start a switch statement that checks to see which of the cases should be run, depending on the value of $db.
27	If $db = "psql", then the user wants to use a PostgreSQL database.

Script 3–2 DBlib.php Line-by-Line Explanation (Continued)

LINE	DESCRIPTION
28	Return 1 (true), so that the function accessing this function knows that the call to the SelectDB function was successful. PostgreSQL syntax specifies which database to use during pg_connect(), which should have been run before this function.
29	Break out of the switch statement, since the case has been satisfied.
30	If $db = "mysql", then the user wants to use a MySQL database.
31	Execute the mysql_select_db() function to select the proper database on the MySQL server. If there is an error, then kill the script and provide an error message.
32	If there is not an error, then return 1 (true), so that the function accessing this function knows that the call to the SelectDB function was successful.
33	Break out of the switch statement, since the case has been satisfied.
34	If $db = "mssql", then the user wants to use a MS SQL database.
35	Execute the mssql_select_db() function to select the proper database on the MS SQL server. If there is an error, then kill the script and provide an error message.
36	If there is not an error, then return 1 (true), so that the function accessing this function knows that the call to the SelectDB function was successful.
37	Break out of the switch statement, since the case has been satisfied.
38–39	If none of the cases have been satisfied, then display a message that the $db value sent to the function was not valid.
40	Return 0 (false), so that any functions using this function know that the function failed.
41	End the switch statement.
42	End the function declaration.
44	Declare the queryDB function. The function requires the type of database ($db) and the SQL query ($query) as arguments.
45	Start a switch statement that checks to see which of the cases should be run, depending on the value of $db.
46	If $db = "psql", then the user wants to use a PostgreSQL database.
47	Run the query using pg_exec() and check if there is an error.
48	If there was an error, then set $result to 0.

Script 3–2 DBlib.php Line-by-Line Explanation (Continued)

LINE	DESCRIPTION
49	End the if statement.
50	Break out of the switch statement, since the case has been satisfied.
51	If $db = "mysql", then the user wants to use a MySQL database.
52	Run the query using mysql_query() and check if there is an error.
53	If there was an error, then set $result to 0.
54	End the if statement.
55	Break out of the switch statement, since the case has been satisfied.
56	If $db = "mssql", then the user wants to use a MS SQL database.
57	Run the query using mssql_query() and check if there is an error.
58	If there was an error, then set $result to 0.
59	End the if statement.
60	Break out of the switch statement, since the case has been satisfied.
61–62	If none of the cases have been satisfied, then display a message that the $db value sent to the function was not valid.
63	Return 0 (false), so that any functions using this function know that the function failed.
64	End the switch statement.
65	Return the value of $result to the function calling this function. If the $result = 0, then the calling function knows an error has occurred.
66	End the function declaration.
68	Declare the returnDBarray function. The function requires the type of database ($db) and the result set from the previous query ($result) as arguments.
69	Verify that the result does not equal 0. If it does, then there was an error with the previous query. If there was no error, then continue.
70	Start a switch statement that checks to see which of the cases should be run, depending on the value of $db.
71	If $db = "psql", then the user wants to use a PostgreSQL database.
72	Fetch the array using pg_fetch_array() and check if there is an error.
73	If there was an error, then set $array to 0.

Script 3–2 DBlib.php Line-by-Line Explanation (Continued)

LINE	DESCRIPTION
74	End the if statement.
75	Break out of the switch statement, since the case has been satisfied.
76	If $db = "mysql", then the user wants to use a MySQL database.
77	Fetch the array using mysql_fetch_array() and check if there is an error.
78	If there was an error, then set $array to 0.
79	End the if statement.
80	Break out of the switch statement, since the case has been satisfied.
81	If $db = "mssql", then the user wants to use a MS SQL database.
82	Fetch the array using mssql_fetch_array() and check if there is an error.
83	If there was an error, then set $array to 0.
84	End the if statement.
85	Break out of the switch statement, since the case has been satisfied.
86–87	If none of the cases have been satisfied, then display a message that the $db value sent to the function was not valid.
88	Set $array to 0 (false), so that any functions using this function know that the function failed.
89	End the switch statement.
90	Return the value of $result to the function calling this function. If the $result = 0, then the calling function knows an error has occurred.
91	End the if statement that checked to make sure that $result did not equal 0.
92	End the function declaration.
94	Declare the closeDB function. The function requires the type of database ($db) and the database connection ($dbconn) as arguments.
95	Start a switch statement that checks to see which of the cases should be run, depending on the value of $db.
96	If $db = "psql", then the user wants to use a PostgreSQL database.
97	Run pg_close() and check if there is an error.
98	If there was an error, then return 0, notifying the calling function that the close failed.

Script 3–2 DBlib.php Line-by-Line Explanation (Continued)

LINE	DESCRIPTION
99–100	If there was not an error, then notify the calling function that the close succeeded.
101	End the if statement.
102	Break out of the switch statement, since the case has been satisfied.
103	If $db = "mysql", then the user wants to use a MySQL database.
104	Run mysql_close() and check if there is an error.
105	If there was an error, then return 0, notifying the calling function that the close failed.
106–107	If there was not an error, then notify the calling function that the close succeeded.
108	End the if statement.
109	Break out of the switch statement, since the case has been satisfied.
110	If $db = "mssql", then the user wants to use a MS SQL database.
111	Run mssql_close() and check if there is an error.
112	If there was an error, then return 0, notifying the calling function that the close failed.
113–114	If there was not an error, then notify the calling function that the close succeeded.
115	End the if statement.
116	Break out of the switch statement, since the case has been satisfied.
117–118	If none of the cases have been satisfied, then display a message that the $db value sent to the function was not valid.
119	Return 0 to notify the calling function that the function failed.
120	End the switch statement.
121	End the function declaration.
123	Declare the numrowsDB function. The function requires the type of database ($db) and the result set from the previous query ($result) as arguments.
124	Start a switch statement that checks to see which of the cases should be run, depending on the value of $db.
125	If $db = "psql", then the user wants to use a PostgreSQL database.

Script 3–2 DBlib.php Line-by-Line Explanation (Continued)

LINE	DESCRIPTION
126	Run pg_numrows() and check if there is an error.
127	If there was an error, then return 0, notifying the calling function that the close failed.
128–129	If there was not an error, then notify the calling function that the close succeeded.
130	End the if statement.
131	Break out of the switch statement, since the case has been satisfied.
132	If $db = "mysql", then the user wants to use a MySQL database.
133	Run mysql_num_rows() and check if there is an error.
134	If there was an error, then return 0, notifying the calling function that the close failed.
135–136	If there was not an error, then notify the calling function that the close succeeded.
137	End the if statement.
138	Break out of the switch statement, since the case has been satisfied.
139	If $db = "mssql", then the user wants to use a MS SQL database.
140	Run mssql_num_rows() and check if there is an error.
141	If there was an error, then return 0, notifying the calling function that the close failed.
142–143	If there was not an error, then notify the calling function that the close succeeded.
144	End the if statement.
145	Break out of the switch statement, since the case has been satisfied.
146–147	If none of the cases have been satisfied, then display a message that the $db value sent to the function was not valid.
148	Return 0 to notify the calling function that the function failed.
149	End the switch statement.
150	End the function declaration.

The next part of the example is the SQL required to create the table for the sample application:

SCRIPT 3-3 addressbook.sql

```
1.   CREATE TABLE addressbook (
2.   first VARCHAR(32),
3.   last VARCHAR(32),
4.   home VARCHAR(16),
5.   cell VARCHAR(16),
6.   work VARCHAR(16));
```

The final bit is the example application, which uses the DBlib.php file as its database wrapper, allowing the application to be used with three different database back-ends without having to change any of the code. See Figure 3–2 for the output produced by this script:

SCRIPT 3-4 customDB.php

```
1.   <?
2.   $page = "customDB.php";
3.
4.   require_once("DBlib.php");
5.   /* REQUIRED FOR DBlib.php */
6.   //$db = "psql"; //PostgreSQL Database
7.   //$db = "mysql"; //MySQL Database
8.   $db = "mssql"; // MS SQL Database
9.   $host = "192.168.0.1";
10.  $database = "php";
11.  $username = "mssqluser";
12.  $password = "password";
13.  /***********************/
14.
15.  function display_addresses ($db) {
16.     global $dbconn;
17.     selectDB($db, $dbconn);
18.     $sql = "select * from addressbook";
19.     if(!$result = queryDB($db, $sql)) {
20.        echo "<P>Error with query!";
21.     }
22.     $rows = numrowsDB($db, $result);
23.     if($rows == 0) {
24.        echo "There are entries in your addressbook.";
25.     } else {
26.        ?><table border=1><?
```

```
27.        while($row = returnDBarray($db, $result)) {
28.          ?>
29.          <tr><td colspan=2><b><?=$row['first'];?>
      <?=$row['last'];?></b></td></tr>
30.          <tr><td>Home: </td><td><?=$row['home'];?></td></tr>
31.          <tr><td>Cell: </td><td><?=$row['cell'];?></td></tr>
32.          <tr><td>Work: </td><td><?=$row['work'];?></td></tr>
33.          <?
34.        }
35.      ?></table><?
36.      }
37.  }
38.
39.  function add_address($db, $HTTP_POST_VARS) {
40.    global $dbconn;
41.    selectDB($db, $dbconn);
42.    $query = "insert into addressbook values ('" .
43.      $HTTP_POST_VARS['first'] . "','" .
44.      $HTTP_POST_VARS['last'] . "','" .
45.      $HTTP_POST_VARS['home'] . "','" .
46.      $HTTP_POST_VARS['cell'] . "','" .
47.      $HTTP_POST_VARS['work'] . "')";
48.    if(!queryDB($db, $query)) {
49.      echo $query;
50.      return 0;
51.    } else {
52.      return 1;
53.    }
54.  }
55.
56.  function add_address_form(){
57.    global $page;
58.    ?>
59.    <h3>Add An Address:</h3>
60.    <form action=<?=$page?> method=post>
61.    <p>First Name: <input type="text" name="first">
62.    <br>Last Name: <input type="text" name="last">
63.    <br>Home: <input type="text" name="home">
64.    <br>Cell: <input type="text" name="cell">
65.    <br>Work: <input type="text" name="work">
66.    <p><input type="submit" name="add_address" value="Add
      Entry!">
67.    </form>
68.    <?
69.  }
```

SCRIPT 3–4 customDB.php (Continued)

```
70.   /***** MAIN *****/
71.   ?>
72.   <h3>Address Book</h3>
73.   <p><a href=<?=$page?>?action=add>Add An Entry</a>
74.   <p>
75.   <?
76.   $dbconn = connectDB($db);
77.   if(isset($add_address)) {
78.     if(!add_address($db, $HTTP_POST_VARS)) {
79.       echo "<h3>ERROR ADDING ENTRY!</h3>";
80.     } else {
81.       echo "<h3>ENTRY ADDED!</h3>";
82.     }
83.   } elseif(isset($action) && $action == "add") {
84.     add_address_form();
85.   }
86.   ?>
87.   <h4>Current Addresses:</h4>
88.   <?
89.   display_addresses ($db);
90.   if(!closeDB($db, $dbconn)) {
91.     echo "<p>ERROR CLOSING DB CONNECTION";
92.   }
93.   ?>
```

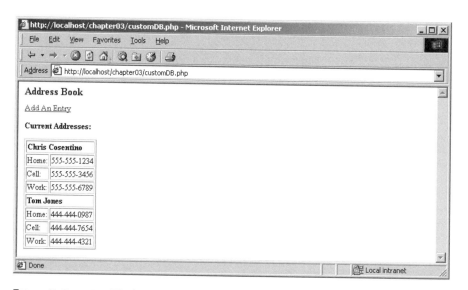

FIGURE 3–2 customDB.php

Script 3–4 customDB.php Line-by-Line Explanation

LINE	DESCRIPTION
2	Declare the name of the page so that it can be used in a function that prints out a form action. This is useful when testing the script if you want to quickly give it a new name.
4	Require the DBlib.php file so that this script has access to the database wrapper.
6–8	The different databases that this script can access. Uncomment only one.
9–12	Database connection information required to connect to the database server and access the specific database.
15	Declare the display_addresses function. This function takes one argument, $db, which is defined above.
16	Make the $dbconn variable, the connection handler to the database, available to this function.
17	Run the selectDB function from DBlib.php.
18	Generate an SQL statement to select all of the entries in the address book table.
19	Query the database using the queryDB function from DBlib.php. If there is not an error, then $result should contain a valid database query result.
20	If there was an error, display an error message to the screen.
22	Execute the numrowsDB function from DBlb.php.
23–24	If there are no rows in the result set, then the database is empty. Notify the user that there are no entries in the address book.
25	If there are rows in the result set, then continue executing the function.
26	Create a table to display the results.
27	Loop through each row in the result set using the returnDBarray function from DBlib.php.
29–34	Display the data in the current row.
35	Close the table.
36	End the if statement started on line 23.
37	End the function declaration.
39	Declare the add_address function. It takes as arguments the database type ($db) and the variables sent from the add_address_form, which is defined later in the script.

Script 3–4 customDB.php Line-by-Line Explanation (Continued)

LINE	DESCRIPTION
40	Make the $dbconn variable accessible to this function.
41	Select the database using the selectDB function from DBlib.php.
42–47	Generate an SQL statement that inserts the data from the form into the database.
48–49	If the query fails, then echo the query to help debug.
50	Return 0, since the query failed.
51–53	If the query didn't fail, then return 1.
56–69	Declare a function that prints a standard form to the browser that allows the user to enter a new address book entry.
70	Start the main part of the script.
72	Print a heading for the page.
73	Create a link that, when clicked, displays the form so the user can add another entry.
76	Create a connection to the database using the connectDB function from DBlib.php.
77	If the $add_address variable is set, then run the add_address() function to add a new entry to the address book.
78–79	If the query fails, then print an error message.
80–82	If the query is successful, then print a message telling the user.
87	Print a heading for the current addresses in the database.
89	Run the display_addresses function to print out.
90	Close the database connection using the closeDB function fromDBlib.php.
91	If there is an error closing the database connection, then notify the user.
92	End the if statement that began on line 77.

Using Pear::DB

Although PHP's DBX functions are useful on simple sites, there is a more feature-rich solution available for sites that require greater complexity in their database use. This solution is PEAR::DB.

PEAR—PHP Extension and Application Repository

PEAR is a "framework and distribution system for reusable PHP components."[1] PEAR provides "modules" along the lines of the PERL CPAN module set. Think of the modules as libraries of prebuilt components that you can use to make your PHP coding easier. PEAR is currently in beta and is under heavy development, but it already contains many useful modules that you can use in your own projects. PEAR provides open-source modules, distribution and maintenance for those modules, and a coding standard for said modules.

PEAR is distributed with PHP. If you've installed PHP recently, you may have noticed the "pear" directory and the many files that it contains. Since PEAR is still in beta, it hasn't been widely advertised, but it has begun to get a lot of attention from PHP developers, especially those who have been using third-party libraries, such as PHPLIB and ADOdb. Although there are good third-party libraries available, there is not yet a standard as far as coding guidelines, distribution, and maintenance. PEAR looks to be the solution to this problem.

One of the modules that is starting to gain a lot of popularity is PEAR DB "a unified API for accessing SQL-databases." PEAR DB greatly exceeds the functionality of the DBX library and is almost purely object oriented. PEAR DB supports a decent subset of the core PHP-supported databases and is being extended to support even more. PEAR DB is a great tool to code database-independent PHP applications.

Downloading PEAR

You can download recent versions of PEAR from the PEAR Web site at *pear.php.net*. Type "DB" into the "search for" box in the upper right corner of the site.

Click on the first search result that comes up, "DB," then download the latest stable version from the list of releases.

---

1. From the PEAR Web site at *pear.php.net*.

Downloading PEAR from Concurrent Versions System (CVS)

Although PEAR is included with all recent versions of PHP and you can download later stable versions from the PEAR Web site, the latest and greatest version of PEAR with the latest features is probably still sitting in the CVS repository. **Note that you should not use CVS versions on production Web sites!** If you have access to CVS (*www.cvshome.org*), then you should take advantage of it and download the latest PEAR source code from the PHP CVS repository. You can find out all the specifics on the PHP CVS repository at *http://cvs.php.net/*.

To download the latest PEAR source:

1. Change directory to the location that you want to place the source (or a convenient place from which you can copy the files).
2. Execute the command: `cvs -d :pserver:cvsread@cvs .php.net:/repository login`
   You are prompted for a password. Enter "**phpfi**".
3. Execute the command: `cvs -d :pserver:cvsread@cvs .php.net:/repository export -D "last week" php4/pear`
   Thomas V. V. Cox, one of the main contributors to the PEAR DB documentation, recommends using the "last week" flag. Sometimes the latest is a little buggy, but most bugs are fixed in a week.[2]
4. Copy the pear folder over your existing pear folder in your PHP installation.

Installing PEAR

Once you have downloaded the source, you should modify your include_path setting in *php.ini* to point to the pear directory, or you could use the following function at the top of each script that requires access to PEAR:

```
ini_set("include_path", "path/to/pear");
```

---

2. Thomas has an excellent quick start guide, from which the current PEAR DB documentation is written, at *http://vulcanonet.com/soft/?pack=pear_tut*.

Once you have the latest PEAR source, you are ready to begin. If you don't have the latest, you can still try out the examples, but your mileage may vary.

Back to the Basics

Now that you are ready to code a PEAR DB application, you have to learn the basics of connecting to and querying a database once again. Like any database-backed PHP application, you first have to connect to the database. PEAR DB uses the DB::connect() function for this purpose (notice the similarity to PERL's CPAN module syntax).

```
$dbconn = DB::connect(DSN);
```

DB::connect() takes one argument, a DSN. DSN stands for data source name, and it is a way to specify all the necessary settings needed to connect to the database in one neat package. A DSN is typically comprised of the following:

- type—The type of database server to which you are connecting. See below for examples.
- host—The host name of the database server to which you are connecting, optionally followed by the port.
- database—The name of the database to which you are connecting.
- username—The login of the user with access rights to the database.
- password—The user's password.

The type of databases can be one of the following:

- mysql—MySQL
- pgsql—PostgreSQL
- ibase—InterBase
- msql—mSQL
- mssql—Microsoft SQL Server
- oci8—Oracle 7/8/8i
- odbc—ODBC
- sybase—Sybase
- ifx—Informix
- fbsql—FrontBase

All of this information is formatted in a single string:

```
$dsn = "type://username:password@host:port/database";
```

If your database doesn't require an option, such as the password, or if it is running on the standard port, then you can omit those from the DSN. If the connection is successful, then DB::connect() returns a valid connection object. If there was a failure, then it returns a DB Error object.

A PEAR DB-enabled page starts like this:

```
ini_set("include_path", "path/to/pear");
require_once('DB.php');
$type = "mssql";
$user = "mssqluser";
$pass = "password";
$host = "192.168.0.1";
$database = "php";
$dsn = "$type://$user:$pass@$host/$database";
$dbconn = DB::connect($dsn);
```

Once you have attempted to make the connection, you should verify that it worked. PEAR DB provides the DB::isError() function to check if there was an error.

```
DB::isError(OBJECT)
```

DB::isError() takes one argument, OBJECT, the object that was created by a previous PEAR DB function. In the example above, you would check for an error like this:

```
if (DB::isError($db)) {
        die ($dbconn->getMessage());
}
```

Wait a second, it looks like something sneaked in there! $dbconn->getMessage() is a method that, when an error is produced, allows you to display any message associated with the error object. If the connection attempt doesn't work, the $dbconn turns into a DB Error object. If there is no error, then getMessage() won't work on $db, since it is a valid connection object.

Okay, so you've got a connection set up and a way to trap an error if the connection fails. The next thing you need to know how to do is send queries to your database. This is done using the query() method.

```
$result = $dbconn->query(QUERY);
```

query() takes one argument, QUERY, which is an SQL statement. You assign the result of that query to a variable, such as $result, which is a result object.

Once you have a valid result object, you can use one of the "fetch" methods to fetch the data from the result and then format and display it to the user or perform some other processing on it. There are two fetch methods that you can use: fetchRow() and fetchInto(). Both of these functions do essentially the same thing; however, their syntax is slightly different.

```
$row = $result->fetchRow();
```

and

```
$result->fetchInto($row);
```

produce exactly the same thing, a variable called $row that has the current row data from the result object.

You can specify the format of the data retrieved by the fetch methods by assigning an additional argument to the method. The fetch methods support three formats of data that they can retrieve. These are:

- DB_FETCHMODE_ORDERED—(default) Data is formatted as an ordered array.
- DB_FETCHMODE_ASSOC—Data is formatted as an associative array.
- DB_FETCHMODE_OBJECT—Data is formatted as an object, with the column names as properties.

As an example, suppose you have the following information in a table (Table 3–2) called "crew":

TABLE 3–2 Sample Data

ID	NAME	ORIGIN
0	Spike	MA
1	Jett	AZ
2	Faye	FL
3	Ed	NM
4	Ein	CO

You query the database and get a result:

```
$sql = "select name, origin from crew";
$result = $dbconn->query($slq);
```

The three formats would be:

```
//using the default format of DB_FETCHMODE_ORDERED
$row = $result->fetchRow();
$name = $row[0]; // $name = "Spike";
$origin = $row[1]; //$origin = "MA";

//using an associative array as the format
$row = $result->fetchRow(DB_FETCHMODE_ASSOC);
$name = $row['name']; // $name = "Spike";
$origin = $row['origin']; //$origin = "MA";

//using an object as the format
$result->fetchInto($row, DB_FETCHMODE_OBJECT);
$name = $row->name; // $name = "Spike";
$origin = $row->origin; //$origin = "MA";
```

These formats provide for a lot of flexibility. Also notice that the different fetch methods would produce the same expected result.

Since it can be a real drag having to type out DB_FETCHMODE_ASSOC or DB_FETCHMODE_OBJECT as an argument to every fetch method in your script (if you choose to use those formats), PEAR DB provides a nifty method called setFetchMode().

```
$dbconn->setFetchMode(MODE);
```

setFetchMode is a method for the connection object that sets the default fetch mode for all fetch functions. The argument, MODE, can be any one of the three fetch modes specified earlier. Note that it is pointless to set the fetch mode to DB_FETCHMODE_ORDERED if you haven't already set the fetch mode to one of the other values, since it is already the default. Once you use this method, all of the fetch methods that you call use the mode specified by setFetchMode(), unless you have specified a different fetch mode in the fetch method itself.

You should also check your results for errors using the same method as when checking the connection for errors. If a query() results in an error, then it returns an error object:

```
$result = $dbconn->query($sql);
if (DB::isError($result)) { die ($result->getMessage());}
```

After you have finished with your result set, you should free the result object by using the free() method. This will "free" the memory associated with the result set and reduce the load on your Web server:

```
$result->free();
```

Finally, when you have completed your script, you should close the connection to the server. This is done using the disconnect method of the connection object:

```
$dbconn->disconnect();
```

You now have the building blocks to create a simple script. This next script illustrates the different fetch methods and errors.

SCRIPT 3–5 peardb1.php

```
1.   <?
2.   ini_set("include_path", "/path/to/php/pear");
3.   require_once('DB.php');
4.   $type = "mssql";
5.   $user = "mssqluser";
6.   $pass = "password";
7.   $host = "192.168.0.1";
8.   $database = "php";
9.   $dsn = "$type://$user:$pass@$host/$database";
10.  $dbconn = DB::connect($dsn);
11.  if (DB::isError($dbconn)) { die ($dbconn->getMessage()); }
12.  /*
13.  create table bebop (
14.      id INT,
15.      name VARCHAR(8),
16.      origin CHAR(2));
17.  */
18.  $values = array (
19.      "insert into bebop values ('0','Spike','MA')",
20.      "insert into bebop values ('1','Jett','AZ')",
21.      "insert into bebop values ('2','Faye','FL')",
22.      "insert into bebop values ('3','Ed','NM')",
```

```
23.      "insert into bebop values ('4','Ein','CO')"
24.      );
25.
26.   $result = $dbconn->query("select * from bebop");
27.   if(DB::isError($result)) { die ($result->getMessage());}
28.   if($result->numRows() == 0) {
29.      echo "<P>Populating the DB!<p>";
30.      for($i = 0; $i < sizeof($values); $i++) {
31.         $result2 = $dbconn->query($values[$i]);
32.         if (DB::isError($result2)) { die ($result2-
   >getMessage());}
33.      }
34.      echo "<P>Done the DB! Reload Page<p>";
35.   } else {
36.      $result = $dbconn->query("select name, origin from
   bebop");
37.      if (DB::isError($result)) { die ($result-
   >getMessage());}
38.      echo "<P>Default Fetch Mode
   (DB_FETCHMODE_ORDERED):";
39.      while($result->fetchinto($row)){
40.         echo "<br>" . $row[0] . " " . $row[1];
41.      }
42.      $result = $dbconn->query("select name, origin from
   bebop");
43.      $dbconn->setFetchMode(DB_FETCHMODE_ASSOC);
44.      echo "<HR>DB_FETCHMODE_ASSOC Fetch Mode:";
45.      while($row = $result->fetchRow()){
46.         echo "<br>" . $row['name'] . " " . $row['origin'];
47.      }
48.      $result = $dbconn->query("select name, origin from
   bebop");
49.      $dbconn->setFetchMode(DB_FETCHMODE_OBJECT);
50.      echo "<HR>DB_FETCHMODE_OBJECT Fetch Mode:";
51.      while($result->fetchinto($row)){
52.         echo "<br>" . $row->name . " " . $row->origin;
53.      }
54.   }
55.   $result->free();
56.   $dbconn->disconnect();
57.   ?>
```

Script 3–5 peardb1.php Line-by-Line Explanation

LINE	DESCRIPTION
2	Set the include path so that the PEAR library is accessible to your script.
3	Require the DB.php library from the PEAR distribution.
4–8	Define the require properties so that your script can connect to your database.
9	Build the DSN using the properties defined above.
10	Establish a connection to the database server.
11	If there is an error connecting to the database, then kill the script and display any message associated with the error.
13–16	Define the SQL statement needed to create the table used in this example.
18–24	Create an array of SQL statements that will be used to create entries in the database.
26	Query the database to see if anything exists in the table.
27	Check to see if the query from line 26 is an error. If it is, then kill the script and display the error message to the user.
28	If the number of rows returned in the result set is 0, then execute lines 29–34.
29	Notify the user that the script is populating the database.
30	Start a for loop to loop through the items in the $values array.
31	Execute a query for each of the items in the $value array.
32	If there is an error with the query, kill the script and display any error messages.
34	If no errors occur, notify users that the database has been populated and that they should reload the page.
35	If there are rows in the table (checked in line 28), then execute the rest of the script.
36–37	Query the database. If there is an error with the query, kill the script and display any error messages.
38–41	Display the results using DB_FETCHMODE_ORDERED. Note how the results are displayed on line 40.
42	Query the database.
43	Set the fetch mode.
44–47	Display the results using DB_FETCHMODE_ASSOC. Note how the results are displayed on line 46.

Script 3–5 peardb1.php Line-by-Line Explanation (Continued)

LINE	DESCRIPTION
48	Query the database.
49	Set the fetch mode.
50–52	Display the results using DB_FETCHMODE_OBJECT. Note how the results are displayed on line 52.
54	End the if statement started on line 28.
55	Free the result.
56	Close the database connection.

4

Better Form Processing

Introduction to Better Forms

This chapter covers forms. Forms are the most fundamental method of interaction for your users. Users must use a form to enter information into a site. Think about it, every bulletin board, shopping cart, feedback form, and poll is a type of form. Without forms, the Web is nothing more than a publishing medium for those who can FTP Web pages up to a server.

Since forms are the basis for much of the user interaction on your site, it behooves you to make it easier for users to enter information. How many times have you filled in a long form only to have it tell you that you filled something out wrong and to click "Back" to fix it? Upon clicking the "Back" button you find the entire form empty, forcing you to fill in all of the information again! Or how about forms that tell you that you filled in *something* incorrectly, but upon closer inspection you cannot tell what is wrong, and the script does not provide any more clues. Wouldn't it be better if you *didn't* have to enter all of the information again, and the fields that you filled out incorrectly were highlighted some way so that you could easily make corrections?

You can check data before the form is submitted by using JavaScript, but not all browsers treat JavaScript the same way, so you might run into compatibility problems with some browsers. With PHP, you can be sure to send only pure HTML to the browser, reducing cross-browser compatibility errors. Checking for errors using PHP instead of JavaScript does increase the load on the server slightly, depending on the complexity of your code.

Post and Get

There are two methods that you can use when creating a form in HTML. They are *post* and *get*, as in:

```
<form action=submit.php method=post>
```

or:

```
<form action=submit.php method=get>
```

If you don't specify a method, then the Web server assumes that you are using the get method. So what's the deal? They do the same thing right? Well, almost. You may have noticed that the URL looks a lot longer after you submit a form that uses the get method. For example, you may see something like:

```
http://web.com/form.php?name=fred&age=20&comments
=This+site+rocks
```

That's because the get method puts the contents of the form right in the URL. There are a few disadvantages to this. First, depending on your Web server's operating system and software, there is a limit to how much data you can send through a form using the get method. On many systems, this limit is 256 characters. Also, the individual get queries may be stored in your Web server logs. If you are using space on a shared server, then other people may be able to decipher data sent from your forms that use the get method.

The post method was created to correct the inadequacies of the get method. The information sent using the post method is not visible in the URL, and form data cannot be deciphered by looking in the Web server logs. There also isn't such a small limit on the amount of data that can be sent from a form. Again, it depends on your server, but you probably won't ever hit the limit of sending data using the *post* method for a text-based form.

I use the post method for my scripts unless I need to debug something. When you need to debug something on a form, it is easy enough to switch to the get method (by changing the action line in your script) and then check the URL after you submit your buggy form. You can usually pick up typos and such with a quick look.

Making Forms Friendly

The first script in this chapter, form1.php, shows you how you can make a simple script to determine if the user filled in all of the fields. If the user fails to fill in all the fields, then the script prints out the form again, printing out the field names in red for the fields that the user missed. It also saves any text that the user previously entered and automatically populates the form fields with those values.

The script contains three functions:

- print_form()
- check_form()
- error_flag()

The complete script and explanation follows:

```
1.  <?
2.  $page = "form1.php";
3.  ?>
4.  <html>
5.  <head>
6.  <style type="text/css">
7.    .error {color:red;}
8.  </style>
9.  </head>
10. <body bgcolor="#FFFFFF" text="#000000">
11. <?
12. function error_flag($error, $field) {
13.    if($error[$field]) {
14.       print("<td class=error>");
15.    } else {
16.       print("<td>");
17.    }
18. } //end function error_flag
19.
20. function print_form() {
21.    global $error, $print_again, $first, $last, $page;
22.    ?>
23.    <form action="<? echo $page ?>" method="post">
24.    <?
25.    if($print_again) {
26.       ?><h3>You missed some fields. Please correct the
    <span class=error>red</span> fields.<?
27.    } else {
28.       ?><h3>Please fill-in the following fields.</h3><?
29.    }
30.    ?>
31.    <table border="0">
32.       <tr><td <? error_flag($error, "first"); ?>First
    Name:</td>
33.          <td><input type="text" name="first"
    value="<?=$first ?>"></td></tr>
34.          <tr><td <? error_flag($error, "last"); ?>Last
    Name:</td>
35.          <td><input type="text" name="last" value="<?=$last
    ?>"></td></tr>
36.       <tr><td colspan="2" align="center">
37.          <input type="submit" name="submit" value="Submit
    Form"></td></tr>
38.    </table>
39.    </form>
```

SCRIPT 4–1 form1.php (Continued)

```
40.    <?
41.  } // end function print_form
42.
43.  function check_form() {
44.     global $error, $print_again, $first, $last;
45.     $error['first'] = false;
46.     $error['last'] = false;
47.     $print_again = false;
48.     if($first == "") {
49.        $error['first'] = true;
50.        $print_again = true;
51.     }
52.     if($last == "") {
53.        $error['last'] = true;
54.        $print_again = true;
55.     }
56.     if($print_again) {
57.        print_form();
58.     } else {
59.        print("<h3>Thank you for completing the form!</
     h3>");
60.     }
61.  } // end function check_form
62.
63.  /***** MAIN *****/
64.  if(isset($submit)) {
65.     check_form();
66.  } else {
67.     print_form();
68.  }
69.  ?>
70.  </body>
71.  </html>
```

Script 4–1 form1.php Line-by-Line Explanation

LINE	DESCRIPTION
2	Set the $page variable to the script name.
12	Define the error_flag() function. It takes two arguments, $error and $field. The $error variable is actually an array, which contains all of the errors that were found in the form. The $field variable is the current field for which the script is generating an error.

Script 4–1 form1.php Line-by-Line Explanation (Continued)

LINE	DESCRIPTION
13–17	Check to see if there is an error for this particular field. If there is an error, then the script prints <td class=error>, which causes that field name to be printed in red. Otherwise, the script prints out a normal <td> tag.
18	End the error_flag function.
20	Declare the print_form() function.
21	Define some global variables so that they can be easily used in the function. The variables are: • $error—An array of errors (if any) returned from the check_form() function. • $print_again—A boolean variable returned from the check_from() function. • $first and $last—Variables returned from the forms in this field. • $page—We use this variable in the form action=... line. Useful so that we can easily change the name of the page and not worry about breaking our scripts. All of these variables are empty if this is the first time that this script is being run.
22–24	Print out the form tag. Note that we include the $page variable. Also note the post method.
25–30	The if/then/else statement checks to see if the $print_again variable is set to true. If it is, then we print a message saying that some of the fields were missed previously. If the $print_again variable is not set, then we just print a message asking the user to fill in the form.
31–40	Print out the form fields. This is a pretty standard form except for two things: 1. Each field label is preceded by the function error_flag instead of a normal <td> tag. This is because we want to check to see if the users previously screwed up entering information into this field. If they did (and they do at one time or another), then the error_flag() function prints out <td class=error> instead of <td>. The *error* Cascading Style Sheets (CSS) class simply makes the text in that cell red. 2. Each text input has a value associated with it—for example, *value="<?=$first ?>"*. If this is the first time that the user is filling in the form, then these values are blank. However, if the user previously made an error and this is the second or subsequent time that he or she is filling out the form, then the previously entered value is shown in the form. That way, the user doesn't have to re-enter information into the form.
41	End the print_form() function.
43	Define the check_form() function.
44	Allow the function to use the global variables listed. Note that these are the same variables used in the print_form() function.
47	Initialize the $print_again variable to false. Assuming all goes well with the data that the user entered, then this should remain false.

Script 4–1 form1.php Line-by-Line Explanation (Continued)

LINE	DESCRIPTION
48–51	Check the $first variable (representing the user's first name) to see if the user entered a value. If he or she did not enter anything into this field, then we generate an error by setting the *first* element in the $error array to true and also setting the $print_again variable to true.
52–55	These three lines do the same thing as lines 48–51, except that this time we are checking the $last variable (representing the user's last name).
56–60	If an error was encountered and the $print_again variable is set to 1 (true), then print the form again, else print a message to the user.
61	End the check_form() function.
64–65	If the Submit button was pressed, then execute the check_form() function.
66–68	If the Submit button was not pressed, then execute the print_form() function.
70–71	Close out the HTML page.

Souping Up the Script

You can soup up this script to be smarter:

Check for Spaces

This script as it currently is can be easily fooled if a user just enters spaces in each of the fields. In the check_form script on lines 46 and 50, we check to see if the user entered *anything*. This includes spaces. If we want to make sure the users enter characters (not just spaces), we could check like this:

```
if(ereg("^ +", $last)) {
    $error[last] = true;
    $print_again = true;
}
```

Basically, the ereg() function is checking the $last variable to see if it starts with one or more spaces. We'll take a closer look at the ereg() function a little later in this chapter.

Check for Minimum Number of Characters

Sometimes you may want to make sure the user enters a minion the *maximum* number of characters that a user can enter, by using the *maxlength* attribute on an HTML input tag—for example, `<input type="text" maxlength="24">`.

```
if(strlen($first) < 3) {
      $error[first] = true;
      $print_again = true;
   }
```

Here we use the strlen() function (**string length**) to see if the $first variable contains at least three characters. If it has zero, one, or two characters then we throw an error.

Add More Error Information

It's also useful to add a little extra error information. We can modify our examples above slightly:

```
if(strlen($first) < 3) {
     $error['first'] = "Please enter more than two
characters in this field. ";
     $print_again = true;
   }
   if(ereg("^ +", $last)) {
     $error['last'] = "Please enter characters in
this field, not spaces. ";
     $print_again = true;
   }
```

Here, instead of assigning the $error variable a true value, we can add a short description of the error. Then if we modify our error_flag function as follows, we can print this message out to the users when we display the form to them again:

```
function error_flag($error, $field) {
      if($error[$field]) {
        print("<td class=error>$error[$field]");
      } else {
        print("<td>");
      }
   } //end function error_flag
```

Form-Field Checking

As you can see, it isn't too hard to make a form a little more user-friendly. You can make the task of entering information easier on the user, but to make it worthwhile for yourself, you should check to see that the user has entered data that is actually useful. Otherwise, why collect it? Just checking to make sure that they filled in a field is not always adequate.

That's where ereg() comes in. ereg() is a built-in PHP function. It means Evaluate a **Reg**ular Expression. There is also a PERL-compatible function that works the same as ereg() (and may be a little faster) called preg_match(). The syntax for both functions is very similar, if not exactly the same in most instances. The syntax is:

```
ereg(search, string)
```

where *search* is the regular expression search criteria, and *string* is the string that you wish to search. The ereg function returns a boolean value of either true or false. If the search criteria matches the string, then ereg() returns true; otherwise, it returns false.

Now, regular expressions are one of those things that all programmers who spend a lot of time wading around in text should really get to know. The different *search* criteria used in regular expressions can be cryptic, but they really get the job done.

Take a look at the example we used earlier:

```
if(ereg("^ +", $last)) {
    $error['last'] = true;
    $print_again = true;
}
```

The search criteria, "^ +", literally means, "A string starting with a space and followed by zero or more spaces." We search for this because we do not want users to fool the form into being accepted by entering spaces for the last name instead of characters.

However, we can get a lot more detailed about analyzing the data entered into a form using other regular expression operators. A list of common regular expression operators can be found in Table 4–1.

TABLE 4–1 Common Regular Expression Operators

SYMBOL	DESCRIPTION	EXAMPLES
*	Match zero or more occurrences.	Just like the UNIX wildcard symbol, * matches everything. Use this for groups of symbols.
+	Match one or more occurrences.	"e+" matches a string that has one or more occurrences of the character "e" in it.
^	Placed at the beginning of a string, matches that string at the start.	"^Hello" matches any string that starts with the word "Hello".
$	Placed at the end of a string, matches that string at the end.	"$goodbye!" matches any string that ends with "goodbye!"
|	Used to separate searches.	"a|b" matches a string that contains the character "a" or the character "b".
[ ]	Matches range of characters.	"[a-z]" matches a string that contains a lowercase character from a through z. "[A-D]" matches a string that contains an uppercase character from A through D. "[0-9]" matches a string that contains a numeral from 0 through 9. "[1-5]" matches a string that contains a numeral from 1 to 5.
( )	Group operators in a sequence.	Parentheses work similarly to how they do in most programming operations. You can group items together. For example, (5[0-9]+) matches a string that contains a 5 followed by one or more numerals. "5" does not match, while "55" does.

TABLE 4–1 Common Regular Expression Operators (Continued)

Symbol	Description	Examples
.	Matches any single character.	"[0-9].[0-9]" matches a string that contains a numeral followed by any other character, followed by a numeral.
\	Escape an operator so that it is taken literally.	You must escape the following operators if you want to search for that particular operator literally: [* \ + ? { } .]

Checking for Valid Email Addresses

One of the most common things for a user to enter into a form is an email address. Having users' email addresses lets you do things like send users their password if they happen to forget it. This saves users from having to create a new account on your site, and it also saves you some space on your database.

But sometimes a user will fill out a form and not put in a valid email. Have you ever received a form submission with something along the lines of "qwert" in the email field? Using regular expression matching, you can at least check the user's email address entry to see if it is technically valid.

A technically valid email address consists of a username, the "@" sign, and a server name. Valid usernames can contain letters, numbers, the underscore ("_"), the minus sign ("-"), and periods ("."). Valid server names are *almost* the same, except that server names cannot contain an underscore. Finally, the end of the domain name must have a "." in it followed by two or more letters, such as ".com", ".it", or ".info". Using our regular expression operators from Table 4–1, we can build a regular expression that matches against valid email addresses.

Let's state that a valid username must start with at least one letter or one number:

```
^[a-z0-9]+
```

This is followed by zero or more letters or numbers, under-scores "_", or minus signs "-":

```
[a-z0-9_-]*
```

Then it can be followed by zero or one "."s, followed by any number of letters or numbers, underscores "_", or minus signs "-":

```
(\.[a-z0-9_-]+)*
```

then followed by the @ sign:

```
@
```

which is then followed by at least one letter or number:

```
[a-z0-9]+
```

Then it can be followed by zero or one "."s, followed by any number of letters or numbers, underscores "_", or minus signs "-":

```
(\.[a-z0-9_-]+)*
```

Finally, it can be followed by another ".", then two or more letters (the end of the domain name), and then the email string must end:

```
\.([a-z]+){2,}$
```

Put it all together and you get:

```
^[a-z0-9]+(\.[a-z0-9_-]+)*@[a-z0-9_-]+(\.[a-z0-9-
]+)*\.([a-z]+){2,}$
```

But we haven't taken into account the case of the letters! The expressions above only allow for lowercase letters in the email address, but uppercase letters are valid as well. To save some time, we didn't include the "A–Z" ranges in our expressions, because we can use a slightly different form of ereg(), which is called eregi(). eregi() works exactly the same as ereg() except that it is not case-sensitive. That way you don't have to search for both uppercase and lowercase characters in your expressions, using the [a-zA-Z] syntax. You only need to use [a-z].

Our eregi() function now looks like this:

```
eregi("^[a-z0-9]+[a-z0-9_-]*(\.[a-z0-9_-]+)*@[a-z0-
9_-]+(\.[a-z0-9_-]+)*\.([a-z]+){2,}$", $email);
```

It's very ugly, but it does a very good job of checking for valid email addresses.

Here is a short script that demonstrates the prowess of this function:

SCRIPT 4–2 checkemail.php

```
1.  <?
2.  $email = array ("chris_2@company.com", "-
    fred@broken.org", "joe.smith@works.it", "Busted@bad.a",
    "strange@44.44", "works.fine.all_day@x.y.z.com","is-
    dashed-line@d-a-s-h-e-d.com", "CC@c.com",
    "this.works.fine@also.ok");
3.
4.  for($i = 0; $i < sizeof($email); $i++) {
5.    if(eregi("^[a-z0-9]+[a-z0-9_-]*(\.[a-z0-9_-]+)*@[a-z0-
      9_-]+(\.[a-z0-9_-]+)*\.([a-z]+){2,}$", $email[$i])) {
6.      echo "<p>$email[$i] is valid.";
7.    } else {
8.      echo "<p>$email[$i] is <b>not</b> valid.";
9.    }
10. }
11. ?>
```

Script 4–2 checkemail.php Line-by-Line Explanation

LINE	DESCRIPTION
1	Tell the server to start parsing as PHP code.
2	Create an array of valid and invalid email addresses.
4	Create a for loop to loop through each email address in the array.
5	Test the email address received from the array against the eregi() function to check for valid email addresses. If the email is valid, line 6 executes. Otherwise, the script executes line 8.
6	Executed if the email address matches the eregi() expression.
7–9	Executed if the email address does not match the eregi() expression.
10	End the for loop.
11	Tell the server to stop parsing the page as PHP code.

There is also an additional syntax that you can use with ereg() and eregi() to search strings. See Table 4–2 below.

TABLE 4-2 Portable Regular Expression Operators

SYMBOL	DESCRIPTION
[[:alpha:]]	equal to [a-zA-Z]
[[:alnum:]]	equal to [a-zA-Z0-9]
[[:digit:]]	equal to [0-9]
[[:lower:]]	equal to [a-z]
[[:upper:]]	equal to [A-Z]
[[:space:]]	equal to a blank space (" ")
[[:print:]]	matches any printable character, except that /n (newline) and /t (tab) do not match
[[:graph:]]	matches a string with any graphical character except a space
[[:xdigit:]]	hexidecimal, equal to [a-fA-F0-9]
[[:punct:]]	matches a string with any punctuation

The same expression that we used for the email syntax checking:

```
eregi("^[a-z0-9]+[a-z0-9_-]*(\.[a-z0-9_-]+)*@[a-z0-
9_-]+(\.[a-z0-9_-]+)*\.([a-z]+){2,}$", $email);
```

is written like this using the portable syntax:

```
eregi("^[[:alpha:]]+[[:alnum:]_-]*(\.[[:alnum:]_-
]+)*@[[:alnum:]_-]+(\.[[:alnum:]_-]+)*\.([[:alpha:]_-
]+){2,}$", $email);
```

Using $HTTP_GET_VARS and $HTTP_POST_VARS

PHP automatically registers[1] any variables passed from a form into the $HTTP_GET_VARS or $HTTP_POST_VARS array. If the form is submitted with the post method, then any values in the form are assigned to the $HTTP_POST_VARS array. If the form is submitted using the get method (the default method if

---

1. Your *php.ini* file is automatically enabled for this feature if you are using PHP 4.0.3 or greater. If it is not turned on, then you have to edit the line in *php.ini* for *track_vars* and set it to true.

no method is specified), then the values of the form are assigned to the $HTTP_GET_VARS array.

For example, when the following form is submitted to a PHP script:

```
<form action=script.php method=post>
<input type=hidden name=firstname value="Edward">
<input type=hidden name=occupation value="Computer Specialist">
</form>
```

PHP automatically creates an array that can be accessed associatively:

```
$PHP_POST_VARS['name'] = "Edward";
$PHP_POST_VARS['occupation'] = "Computer Specialist";
```

This functionality makes it easier to create and manage form functions, as you don't have to either globalize each variable or list each variable when you call the form handler function.

If you had a form that called for the input of 15 separate fields and did not use $HTTP_POST_VARS or $HTTP_GET_VARS, then your function definition might look something like:

```
function my_form_handler($var1, $var2, $var3, $var4,
..., $var19, $var 20){
```

or:

```
function my_form_handler(){
   global $var1, $var2, $var3, $var4, ..., $var19, $var 20;
```

Using $HTTP_POST_VARS or $HTTP_GET_VARS, your code is more manageable:

```
function my_form_handler($HTTP_POST_VARS) {
```

or:

```
function my_form_hander() {
   global $HTTP_POST_VARS;
```

This also makes it easier to add (or subtract) additional fields to your forms without having to search through your code for the function calls that handle the form and the additional variables to the function call line.

An example:

SCRIPT 4–3 form2.php

```php
1.  <?
2.  function print_form() {
3.    ?>
4.    <form action="form2.php" method=post>
5.    <p>First Name: <input type="text" name="first">
6.    <br>Last Name: <input type="text" name="last">
7.    <br>Number: <input type="text" name="number">
8.    <br><input type="submit" name="submit" value="Submit">
9.    </form>
10.   <?
11. }
12.
13. function form_handler($first, $last, $number) {
14.   $sql = "insert into phonelist values ('$first',
      '$last', '$number')";
15.   echo "<P>$sql";
16. }
17.
18. function form_handler2($HTTP_POST_VARS) {
19.   $sql = "insert into phonelist values('" .
      $HTTP_POST_VARS['first'] .
20.                         "','" . $HTTP_POST_VARS['last'] .
21.                         "','" . $HTTP_POST_VARS['number']
      . "')";
22.   echo "<P>$sql";
23. }
24.
25. if(isset($submit)) {
26.   form_handler($first, $last, $number);
27.   form_handler2($HTTP_POST_VARS);
28. } else {
29.   print_form();
30. }
31. ?>
```

Script 4–3 form2.php Line-by-Line Explanation

LINE	DESCRIPTION
2–11	Declare a function, print_form(). This function simply prints a form so that the user can enter a first name, a last name, and a phone number.
13	Declare a function, form_hander(), that requires three arguments, the items returned when the user submits the form from the print_form() function.

Script 4–3 form2.php Line-by-Line Explanation (Continued)

LINE	DESCRIPTION
14	Generate the SQL using the values provided by the user.
15	Print out the generated SQL.
16	End the function.
18	Declare a function, form_handler2(), that requires only one argument, HTTP_POST_VARS.
19–21	Generate the SQL using the values provided by the user.
22	Print out the generated SQL.
23	End the function.
25	If the user has pressed the "Submit" button, then execute the script until line 27.
26	Call the form_handler() function with the three required variables.
27	Call the form_handler2() function with just $HTTP_POST_VARS.
28–30	If the "Submit" button has not been pushed, then execute the print_form() function.

Putting It All Together

Now that we have the building blocks to build smart, friendly, and easy form processing, let's take a look at a real-world example. This example, shown in Figure 4–1, provides a way for a user to register for a typical community site.

Some of the fields are required and some are not. The script deems fields to be required if the field name ends with "_required".

The script also checks to make sure that a valid email address is entered and that the user enters two identical passwords.

SCRIPT 4–4 register.php

```html
1. <html>
2. <head>
3.    <title>Register</title>
4. <style type="text/css">
5.    .error {color:red; font-weight: bold;}
6. </style>
```

```
 7. </head>
 8. <body>
 9. <?
10. $page = "register.php";
11.
12. function print_form() {
13.    global $page, $error, $print_again, $HTTP_POST_VARS;
14.    $fields = array("first" => "text",
15.            "last" => "text",
16.            "age" => "text",
17.            "email_required" => "text",
18.            "login_required" => "text",
19.            "password1_required" => "password",
20.            "password2_required" => "password");
21.    $labels = array("first" => "First Name",
22.            "last" => "Last Name",
23.            "age" => "Age",
24.            "email_required" => "Email",
25.            "login_required" => "Desired Username",
26.            "password1_required" => "Password",
27.            "password2_required" => "Confirm Password");
28.    ?>
29.    <form action="<? echo $page ?>" method="post">
30.    <?
31.    if($print_again) {
32.       ?><h3>You missed or incorrectly entered some fields.
    Please correct the <span class=error>red</span> fields.
    Passwords must match.<?
33.    } else {
34.       ?><h3>Please fill-in the following fields.</h3><?
35.    }
36.    ?>
37.    <table border="0">
38.    <?
39.    foreach($fields as $key => $value) {
40.       ?>
41.       <tr><td <? error_flag($error, $key);
    ?><?=$labels[$key]?>: </td>
42.          <td><input type="<?=$value?>" name="<?=$key?>"
    value="<? @print($HTTP_POST_VARS[$key])?>"></td></tr>
43.       <?
44.    }
45.    ?>
46.    <tr><td colspan="2"><input type="submit" name="submit"
    value="Submit"></td></tr>
```

```
47.   </table>
48.   </form>
49.   <?
50. } // end function print_form
51.
52. function error_flag($error, $field) {
53.   if($error[$field]) {
54.      print("<td class=error>");
55.   } else {
56.      print("<td>");
57.   }
58. } //end function error_flag
59.
60. function check_form() {
61.   global $error, $print_again, $HTTP_POST_VARS;
62.   $print_again = false;
63.   //Check Required Fields Have Been Entered
64.   foreach($HTTP_POST_VARS as $key => $value) {
65.      if(($value == "") && eregi("_required$", $key)){
66.         $error[$key] = true;
67.         $print_again = true;
68.      } else {
69.         $error[$key] = false;
70.      }
71.   }
72.   //Verify Email
73.   if(!eregi("^[a-z0-9]+[a-z0-9_-]*(\.[a-z0-9_-]+)*@[a-z0-
   9_-]+(\.[a-z0-9_-]+)*\.([a-z]+){2,}$",
   $HTTP_POST_VARS['email_required'])) {
74.         $error['email_required'] = true;
75.         $print_again = true;
76.         $HTTP_POST_VARS['email_required'] = "ENTER A VALID
   EMAIL";
77.   }
78.   //Verify Desired User Name Is Available
79.   $available = true;
80.   if(!$available) {
81.      $error['login_required'] = true;
82.      $print_again = true;
83.      $HTTP_POST_VARS['login_required'] = "Name Not
   Available: " . $HTTP_POST_VARS['login_required'];
84.   }
85.   //Verify Passwords Match
86.   if($HTTP_POST_VARS['password1_required'] !=
   $HTTP_POST_VARS['password2_required']) {
```

```
87.      $error['password1_required'] = true;
88.      $error['password2_required'] = true;
89.      $HTTP_POST_VARS['password1_required'] = NULL;
90.      $HTTP_POST_VARS['password2_required'] = NULL;
91.      $print_again = true;
92.    }
93.    //Print Again If Errors Are Found
94.    if($print_again) {
95.      print_form();
96.    } else {
97.      print("<h3>Thank you for completing the form!</h3>");
98.      // Do database insert, email, etc. Since Data Is OK
99.    }
100. } // end function check_form
101.
102. /***** MAIN *****/
103. if(isset($submit)) {
104.   check_form();
105. } else {
106.   print_form();
107. }
108. ?>
109. </body>
110. </html>
```

Script 4–4 register.php Line-by-Line Explanation

LINE	DESCRIPTION
1–8	Create the beginning of the HTML page.
10	Create a $page variable for use in the function to print the forms.
12	Create a print_form() function used to print the form to the screen.
14–20	Create an array to be used as input for the form-field names and types.
21–27	Create an array to be used as input for the form-field labels.
29	Start printing the form to the browser.
31	Check to see if the $print_again variable is set. If it is, then the user made a mistake entering information on his or her previous try filling in the form.
32	Print a message to the user notifying him or her that he or she made an error when filling out the form.

Script 4–4 register.php Line-by-Line Explanation (Continued)

LINE	DESCRIPTION
33	If there were no previous errors, then print out a simple message asking the user to fill out the form.
37	Begin printing the table for the form fields.
39	Loop though the $fields array and create the form. Notice how the keys for the $fields array are the same as the keys for the $labels array.
41	If there was an error, then highlight the label using the error_flag() function. Print the label for the field.
42	Print the field name and type (from the $fields array). If there was an existing value that the user entered, then print it out. The "@" sign suppresses any warnings that occur if the user is filling out the form for the first time or failed to enter a value previously. If you omit the "@" sign, then a warning is printed because the $HTTP_POST_VARS[$key] variable has not been declared.
46	Print the submit button for the form.
50	End the function.
52	Declare the error_flag function. The error_flag() function takes two arguments: • $error—A boolean value of 0 or 1. 1 means an error occurred with this field. Either it was not filled in or the user's entry was invalid. • $field—The key of the field in which the error occurred.
53	If the $error is 1 (true), then apply some formatting to the field label using CSS.
56	If there was no error, then just print a normal <td> tag.
58	End the function.
60	Declare the function check_form().
61	Allow the check_form() function to use and modify the variables listed.
64–71	These lines check to see if any fields ending with "_required" are not filled in. If they are not, then an error is generated for each field that is not filled in. Additionally, the $print_again variable is set to true.
73–77	These lines verify that the email address is the proper format. If it is not, then an error is generated for the email field and an error message is inserted into the form the next time it is printed.

Script 4—4 register.php Line-by-Line Explanation (Continued)

LINE	DESCRIPTION
79–84	These lines pseudo-check if a login name is available. You can change the setting on line 79 to false to see what happens when the name is not available. Normally, you would query your database or text-file list of users to verify whether a name was available or not. If the name is not available, then an error is generated for the login_required field.
86–92	These lines check if the password fields match. If they do not, then an error is generated and the existing passwords are set to NULL so that they are not reinserted into the form when it is printed again.
94	If the $print_again variable is set, then print the form again.
97	If the $print_again variable is not set, then all went well and you can insert the user registration into a database, or email the contents to an email address.
102	Begin the main program. If the submit button is pressed, then go to line 104. Otherwise, go to line 106.
104	Run check_form(), since we know the user has pressed the submit button.
106	The user has not yet filled out the form because the Submit button hasn't been pushed. Print the form using print_form().

FIGURE 4—1 register.php

Variable Variables

One thing that I've found incredibly useful in some of my form-based applications is variable variables. Variable variables allow you to have variable names for variables. This way you can generate variable names on the fly for whatever purposes your script requires.

Example:

```
$name =   "integer";
$$name = 10;
//results in $integer = 10;
```

Note that when you echo these values to the screen, you get different results from those which you may expect. In the above example, if you want to print the value out to the screen, you cannot enclose the variable variable name in quotes as you might normally:

```
echo "<p>$$name";
// results in "$integer" being printed to the screen
echo "<p>" . $$name;
//results in "10" being printed to the screen
```

Variable variable names can also be created using expressions such as the following:

```
$name = "integer";
${$name . "_1"} = 10;
// results in $integer_1 = 10;
```

When coupled with a for loop, this helps create dynamic forms that can be easily changed to include more or fewer fields.

The example below, shown in Figure 4–2, allows you to upload files to a server. You just need to specify how many files you would like to upload, and the script automatically creates the necessary variables.

SCRIPT 4–5 upload.php

```
1.   <?
2.   $page = "upload.php";
3.   ?>
4.   <html>
5.   <head>
6.     <title>Upload Files</title>
7.   </head>
8.   <body>
9.   <?
10.
11.  function specify_number() {
12.    global $page;
13.    ?>
14.    <form action=<?=$page?> method=post>
15.    Enter number of fields to display for upload and press
     Enter: <input type="text" name="fields" size="2"
     maxlength="2">
16.    </form>
17.    <?
18.  }
19.
20.  function print_form($fields) {
21.    global $page
22.    ?>
23.    <form action=<?=$page; ?> method=post
     enctype="multipart/form-data">
24.    <table border=1>
25.    <?
26.    for($i = 0; $i < $fields; $i++) {
27.    ?>
28.    <tr><td>File:</td>
29.    <td>
30.      <input type="hidden" name="MAX_FILE_SIZE"
     value="1024000">
31.      <input type="file" name="file_<?=$i?>">
32.    </td></tr>
33.    <?
34.    }
35.    ?>
36.    </table>
37.      <input type="hidden" name="fields"
     value="<?=$fields?>">
38.      <input type="submit" name="submit" value="Upload!">
39.    </form>
40.    <?
```

SCRIPT 4–5 upload.php (Continued)

```
41.  } // end print_form
42.
43.  $uploaddir = "/tmp/"; //make sure you include the
     trailing slash.
44.  if(isset($submit)) {
45.    for($i = 0; $i < $fields; $i++) {
46.      if(is_uploaded_file(${"file_".$i})) {
47.        $newfile = $uploaddir . $_FILES['file_' .
     $i]['name'];
48.        if(!@copy(${"file_".$i}, $newfile)) {
49.          echo "<p>Error Uploading <i>" . $_FILES['file_'
     . $i]['name'] . "</i>.";
50.        } else {
51.          echo "<p>Upload OK for " . $_FILES['file_' .
     $i]['name'];
52.        }
53.      }
54.      flush();
55.    }
56.  } elseif(isset($fields)) {
57.    print_form($fields);
58.  } else {
59.    specify_number();
60.  }
61.  ?>
62.  </body>
63.  </html>
```

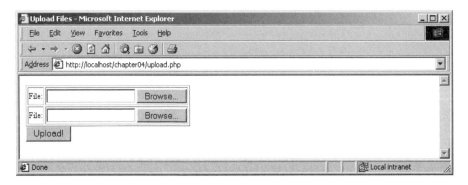

FIGURE 4–2 upload.php

Script 4–5 upload.php Line-by-Line Explanation

LINE	DESCRIPTION
2	Define the name of the page so that it can be used in functions that submit forms.
4–8	Print out the beginning HTML for the page.
11	Declare the specify_number() function. This function simply allows the users to enter the number of files that they wish to upload.
12	Allow this function to access the global $page variable.
14–16	Print the form that asks the users how many files they want to upload.
20	Declare the print_form() function. This function takes one argument, $fields, which is the number of fields the user entered into the specify_number function's form.
23	Create the form.
24	Create a table to display the form fields.
26–32	Create a form field for a file upload. Do this as many times as the user entered for the number of fields. Note how the field is named on line 31.
36–39	Close the table and the form. Add a hidden variable for the number of fields that were requested.
41	End the function.
43	Specify an upload directory for the files.
44	If the submit button has been pressed, then execute through line 56.
45	Create a for loop that goes through the same number of iterations as specified by the user for files to be uploaded.
46	Verify that a file has been uploaded by the user. Note the variable variable.
47	Create a variable that contains the path and filename for the uploaded file.
48	Attempt to copy the file from PHP's temporary file space to the location you have specified in the $newfile variable.
49	Notify the user if there is an error.
51	Notify the user if the upload was successful.
54	Flush the notification to the user.
56	If the submit button has not been pressed but the $fields variable has been set, then we know the user just entered how many files uploaded.
57	Execute the print_form() function, since the above statement is true.

Script 4–5 upload.php Line-by-Line Explanation (Continued)

LINE	DESCRIPTION
58	If the submit button has not been pressed and $fields is not set…
59	Execute the specify_number() function.
60	End the if/else statement started on line 44.
62–63	Close out the HTML for the page.

5

Using What You Have Learned—A Simple Shopping Cart

Introduction

This chapter provides a simple shopping cart application that highlights the topics covered in the previous chapters, namely database interaction, session management, and form processing.

This shopping cart contains features that I would consider to be a bare minimum. You should add additional features as you see fit, making sure to be conscious of security issues surrounding the user's credit cards and personal information.

Features of the Shopping Cart

This shopping cart was designed to be easy to use, easy to administer, and easy to set up. It has several features that I have found have frustrated many users of some of the existing shopping carts that are available.

Simple Shopping Interface

This shopping cart provides a simple interface, shown in Figure 5–1, for users. They can browse through different categories of items with a single mouse click. All categories can be accessed from a dropdown menu at the top of the page.

When users select a category, all of the items in that category appear on the page. If they know what they want, they can simply click on the "Add" button to add an item to their cart. Each click of the "Add" button adds one of the items; multiple clicks mean multiple items are added.

If users wish to find out more information on a specific item, they can click on the item name. This presents users with a more detailed view of the item, as well as a picture of the item if one is provided for them to look at.

Once again, they can click the "Add" button to add one or more items to their cart; multiple clicks mean multiple items.

Users are also presented with a link to return to the category that they were just browsing, or they can choose a new category from the dropdown list at the top of the page.

Another feature that makes the shopping cart simple is the cart interface. Users are able to see their cart and the items it contains on each page that they are on while shopping. A running total of the cost of their purchases is also displayed.

Users have the option to remove items from their cart by clicking the "Remove" button next to an item. Each click removes one unit of the item, until there are no more items.

Users also have the option to modify "bulk" quantities of items in their cart by clicking on the bulk-modification link in the cart. This presents users with text-entry fields next to each one of the items that they can use to specify the exact quantity of an item in their cart. This saves users from clicking "Add" 50 times if they want 50 units of a particular item.

Finally, there is a "Check Out" link that appears whenever there are items in the user's cart. Clicking "Check Out" brings the users to a standard checkout form where they enter Name, Address, Credit Card Information, etc.

FIGURE 5–1 The Shopping Interface

Simple Administration and Management Interfaces

The shopping cart also comes with simple administration and management interfaces. One interface is used to manage the categories and inventory of the store (see Figure 5–2), while the other manages orders (see Figure 5–3).

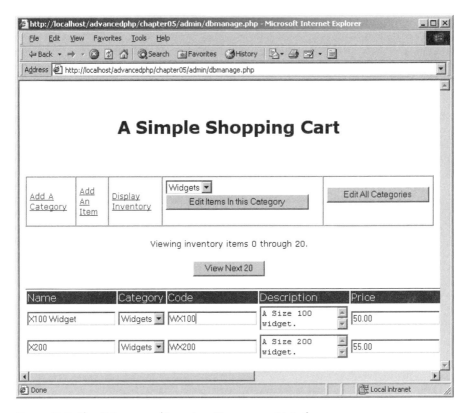

FIGURE 5–2 The Category and Inventory Management Interface

To manage the categories and inventory of the store, you use the dbmanage.php script. This script contains the following:

- Add a Category—Allows you to add a category.
- Add an Item—Allows you to add an item within a category.
- Display Inventory—Allows you to display all the items in the store.
- Edit Items in a Specific Category—Allows you to edit or delete items within one specific category.
- Edit All Categories—Allows you to edit or delete existing categories. If you delete a category, then all inventory items associated with that category are also deleted.

To manage the order received from the shopping cart, you use the administration script. The script contains the following:

- View All Orders—View all orders regardless of their state.
- View Open Orders—View orders that are in the (default) open status.
- View Shipped Orders—View orders that have been shipped.
- View Backorder Orders—View orders that have been placed on backorder.
- View Hold Orders—View orders that have been placed on hold.

You are able to change the state of any of the orders from any of the order status screens. Changing states causes an email to be sent to the customer notifying him or her of the state change. You can also optionally add a tracking number to the email so that a customer can check the ship status of the package with your shipping company.

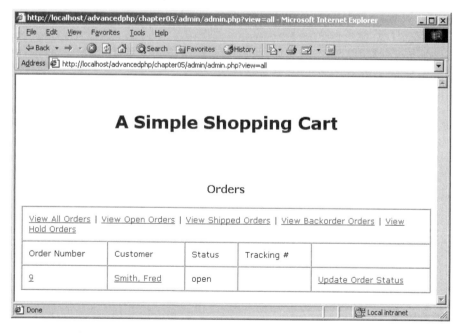

FIGURE 5–3 The Order Management Interface

Setting It Up

Setting up this shopping cart is fairly straightforward, but keep in mind the initial setup is not secure, and you must also customize the checkout form so that it correctly interfaces with your credit card authorization service. This shopping cart has been designed with the Authorize.net (*www.authorize.net*) credit card authorization service in mind, but may work with other credit card authorization services.

Before using this script, you should thoroughly test it!

The general layout of the installation is shown in Table 5–1:

TABLE 5–1 Directory Structure for the Shopping Cart

FOLDER	CONTAINS
Top Level	• cart.php • checkout.php • finishorder.php • admin directory • images directory • include directory
Admin Directory[a]	• admin.php • dbmanage.php
Images Directory	• add.gif • remove.gif • any images for products
Include Directory	• cart_inc.php

a. This directory must be password protected!

Once you have the scripts installed and your database set up, the next thing you need to do is go into the dgmanage.php page and add a category. Once you have created a category, you can create a few items. If you add a picture to the item, place the image file in the directory that you defined for IMAGE_URL.

Once you have a minimum of one category and one item, you can test out the script.

The Code

This section details the code involved in the script. The descriptions are of a high level, as most of the topics have already been covered. Additional descriptions are provided when new topics are introduced.

cart.sql

cart.sql is the SQL statement required to set up the database for use with this application.

SCRIPT 5-1 cart.sql

```
1.   create table customers (
2.   id INT NOT NULL,
3.   first VARCHAR(32),
4.   mi CHAR(2),
5.   last VARCHAR(32),
6.   address1 VARCHAR(64),
7.   address2 VARCHAR(64),
8.   city VARCHAR(32),
9.   state CHAR(2),
10.  zip VARCHAR(10),
11.  country VARCHAR(32),
12.  shiptobilling VARCHAR(5),
13.  ship_address1 VARCHAR(64),
14.  ship_address2 VARCHAR(64),
15.  ship_city VARCHAR(32),
16.  ship_state CHAR(2),
17.  ship_zip VARCHAR(10),
18.  ship_country VARCHAR(32),
19.  ship_phone VARCHAR(32),
20.  email VARCHAR(128),
21.  PRIMARY KEY(id));
22.
23.  create table order_details (
24.  id int not null,
25.  orderid INT,
26.  code VARCHAR(32),
27.  qty INT,
28.  PRIMARY KEY(id));
29.
30.  create table orders (
31.  id INT not null,
```

SCRIPT 5-1 cart.sql (Continued)

```
32.  customer INT,
33.  status VARCHAR(16),
34.  tracking_number VARCHAR(128),
35.  PRIMARY KEY(id));
36.
37.  create table inventory (
38.  id INT not null,
39.  name VARCHAR(32),
40.  category INT,
41.  code VARCHAR(32),
42.  description TEXT,
43.  price VARCHAR(8),
44.  picture VARCHAR(128),
45.  qty INT,
46.  PRIMARY KEY(id));
47.
48.  create table category (
49.  id INT not null,
50.  name VARCHAR(128),
51.  description TEXT,
52.  PRIMARY KEY(id));
```

Script 5-1 cart.sql Line-by-Line Explanation

LINE	DESCRIPTION
1–21	Create a table to store customer data.
23–28	Create a table to store details of an order. Each item in an order has its own row in this table. The orderid column acts as a foreign key to the orders table.
30–35	Create a table to store the order. This table references the customer table for customer information, and holds that status and tracking information for the order.
37–46	Create a table to hold the data for each of the items in the inventory. The category column acts as a foreign key to the category table.
48–52	Create a table to store the category information.

cart.php

cart.php is the main script for the application. It references cart_inc.php for some additional shared functions.

SCRIPT 5–2 cart.php

```php
1.  <?
2.  require_once("include/cart_inc.php");
3.  session_start();
4.  session_register("items");
5.  session_register("category_choice");
6.  session_register("total");
7.
8.  if(!isset($items)) {
9.     $items = array();
10. }
11. if(!isset($category_choice)) {
12.    $category_choice=1;
13. }
14.
15. /*************** MAIN ***************/
16. head();
17. $dbconn = connect();
18. select_cat();
19. $status = "shopping";
20.
21. ?>
22. <table width="58%" border="1" cellspacing="10"
    cellpadding="10" height="371" bordercolor="#0000FF"
    bgcolor="#999999">
23. <tr align="left" valign="top">
24. <td bgcolor="#CCCCCC" bordercolor="#0000FF">
25. <table border="0" cellpadding="10"><tr><td valign=top>
26. <?
27. if(isset($category_choice_in)) {
28.    $category_choice = $category_choice_in;
29. }
30.
31. if(isset($update_cart)) {
32.    foreach($items_in as $cat => $val) {
33.       foreach($items_in[$cat] as $id => $qty) {
34.          if($qty < 1) {
35.             unset($items_in[$cat][$id]);
36.          }
37.       }
```

```
38.      }
39.      $items = $items_in;
40.  }
41.
42.  if(isset($itemview)) {
43.      full_item($itemview);
44.  } else {
45.      display_items($category_choice,$items);
46.  }
47.
48.  if(isset($action)) {
49.      $items = alter_cart($cat, $items, $item, $action);
50.  }
51.
52.  ?>
53.  </td><td valign=top>
54.  <h3>Your Cart:</h3>
55.  <?
56.  if(isset($modify)) {
57.      edit_cart($items);
58.  } else {
59.      display_cart($items);
60.  }
61.  ?>
62.  <p>
63.  <?
64.
65.  if(sizeof($items) > 0) {
66.      $total = calculate_total($items);
67.      //print_r($items);
68.      ?>
69.      <p>Do you want to <a
     href="<?=SECURE_URL?>checkout.php"><b>Checkout</b></a>?
70.      <?
71.  }
72.  ?>
73.  </td></tr></table>
74.  </td>
75.  </tr>
76.  </table>
77.  </div>
78.  </body>
79.  </html>
```

Script 5–2 cart.php Line-by-Line Explanation

LINE	DESCRIPTION
2	Require the cart_inc.php file to use the functions that it contains.
3	Start a session.
4–6	Register session variables to store the items in the cart, the current category that the user is browsing, and the total amount of the user's cart.
8–10	If the $items array has not been set yet, then initialize it.
11–13	If the user has not yet selected a category, then show the first category by default.
16	Call the head() function to display the opening HTML for the page. We do this now so that the session variables can be registered correctly.
17	Establish the connection to the database.
18	Execute the select_cat() function from cart_inc.php. This function lists the available categories to browse.
19	Set the $status variable to shopping. Later, we will change it to checkout.
21–25	Print out a table to hold the items and shopping cart.
27–29	Update the session variable $category_choice with the category the user is currently browsing.
31–40	If the user has updated the cart, then add or subtract the changes to the $items_in array. Then update the session variable $items with the current items in the user's cart.
42–46	If the user clicked on an item name in the item list, then display the full information for that item using the full_item() function from cart_inc.php. Else, display all the items in the category.
48–50	If one of the actions was taken (add or remove an item), then execute the alter_cart() function from cart_inc.php.
52–55	Print out some normal HTML for the page.
56–60	If the user clicked the bulk modify link on the cart, then execute the edit_cart() function from cart_inc.php, else display the cart using the display_cart() function.
61–63	Print out a <p> to make some space on the page.

Script 5–2 cart.php Line-by-Line Explanation (Continued)

LINE	DESCRIPTION
65–71	If there are one or more items in the cart, then calculate the total by calling the calculate_total() function from cart_inc.php. Also, provide a checkout link. For testing, you can uncomment line 67 to see what items are stored in the items array.
72–79	Close out the table and end the HTML for the page.

cart_inc.php

cart_inc.php holds the functions that do all the grunt work for cart.php. I've separated them out in this file to make it easier to customize the appearance of cart.php.

SCRIPT 5–3 cart_inc.php

```
1. <?
2. define(SECURE_URL, "http://localhost/advancedphp/
   chapter05/");
3. define(IMAGE_URL, "http://localhost/advancedphp/chapter05/
   images/");
4. define(SHIPPING_COST, "7.00");
5. define(COMPANY_NAME, "Widget Industrial Inc.");
6. define(CREDIT_AUTH_URL, "finishorder.php");
7. define(COMPANY_EMAIL, "company@example.com");
8.
9. function connect() {
10.    ini_set("include_path", "G:\apache\Apache\php\pear");
11.    require_once("DB.php");
12.    $type = "mysql";
13.    $username = "php";
14.    $password = "password";
15.    $host = "localhost";
16.    $database = "cart";
17.    $dsn = $type . "://" . $username . ":" . $password . "@"
       . $host . "/" . $database;
18.    $dbconn = DB::connect($dsn);
19.    errortrap($dbconn);
20.    $dbconn->setFetchMode(DB_FETCHMODE_ASSOC);
21.    return $dbconn;
22. }//end connect
23.
24. function errortrap($result) {
```

```php
25.    if(DB::isError($result)) {
26.        ?><h3>There was an error!</h3><?
27.        die($result->getMessage());
28.    }
29. } //end errortrap
30.
31. function alter_cart($cat, $items, $item, $action) {
32.    global $dbconn;
33.    $sql = "select * from inventory where id = '$item' AND
    category = '$cat'";
34.    $result = $dbconn->query($sql);
35.    errortrap($result);
36.    if($result->numRows() > 0) {
37.        switch($action) {
38.            case("add"):
39.                if(!isset($items[$cat][$item])) {
40.                    $items[$cat][$item] = 0;
41.                }
42.                $items[$cat][$item]++;
43.                break;
44.            case("remove"):
45.                if(isset($items[$cat][$item])) {
46.                    $items[$cat][$item]--;
47.                }
48.                if($items[$cat][$item] < 1) {
49.                    unset($items[$cat][$item]);
50.                }
51.                break;
52.            default:
53.                break;
54.        }
55.    }
56.        return $items;
57. } //end alter_cart
58.
59. function full_item($item, $items) {
60.    global $dbconn;
61.    $sql = "select * from inventory where id = $item";
62.    $result = $dbconn->query($sql);
63.    errortrap($result);
64.    $result->fetchinto($r);
65.    ?>
66.    <table border=1 cellpadding=5 cellspacing=0>
67.    <tr><td class=tablehead><?=$r["name"]?></td></tr>
68.    <tr><td><?=$r["name"]?><br><?=$r["description"]?>
```

```php
69.   <br><b>Price</b>: <?=$r["price"]?>
70.   <p>
71.   <?
72.   if($r["picture"] != "") {
73.      ?><div align="center"><img src="<? echo IMAGE_URL .
      $r["picture"]?>"></div><?
74.   }
75.   if($r["qty"] > 1) {
76.      ?>
77.      <p><div align=center><a
      href="<?=SECURE_URL?>cart.php?cat=<?=$r["category"]?>&item
      =<?=$item?>&itemview=<?=$item?>&action=add"><img
      src="<?=IMAGE_URL?>add.gif" border=0></a>
78.      <?
79.   } else {
80.      ?>
81.      <p>Sorry, Out Of Stock</p>
82.      <?
83.   }
84.   ?>
85.   <br><a href="<?=SECURE_URL?>cart.php">Return To List Of
      Items In This Category</a></div></td></tr>
86.   </table>
87.   <?
88. } //end function full_item
89.
90. function build_menu ($ref, $table) {
91.      global $dbconn;
92. $sql = "select * from $table order by id";
93. $result = $dbconn->query($sql);
94.      errortrap($result);
95.      if($result->numRows() > 0) {
96.         $x = 0;
97.            while($result->fetchInto($r)){
98.               if($x == 0) {
99.                     echo '<option value="' . $r["id"] . '"
      selected>' . $r[$ref] . '</option>';
100.                 $x++;
101.              } else {
102.                 echo '<option value="' . $r["id"] . '">' .
      $r[$ref] . '</option>';
103.              }
104. }
105. } else {
```

```
106.          echo '<option value="">NO CATEGORIES DEFINED</
      option>';
107. }
108. } //end build_menu
109.
110. function head() {
111.    ?>
112.    <html>
113.    <head>
114.    <style type=text/css>
115.    h1, h2, h3, p, td {font-family: verdana, sans-serif; }
116.    .tablehead {font-size: 12pt; color: #FFFFFF; background-
      color: #000099; }
117.    .required {font-weight: bold; color: red; }
118.    .smalli {font-size: 8pt; font-style: italic;}
119.    </style>
120.    </head>
121.    <body bgcolor="#FFFFFF">
122.    <div align=center>
123.    <table width="74%" border="0" cellspacing="0"
      cellpadding="0" height="128" bgcolor="#FFFFFF">
124. <tr>
125. <td height="134" align="center"><h1>A Simple Shopping
      Cart</h1></td>
126. </tr>
127. </table>
128.    <?
129. }
130.
131. function calculate_total($items) {
132.    global $dbconn;
133.    $shipping = SHIPPING_COST;
134.    $total = 0;
135.    foreach($items as $key => $val) {
136.      foreach($items[$key] as $key2 => $val2) {
137.        $sql = "select * from inventory where id = '$key2'";
138.        $result = $dbconn->query($sql);
139.        errortrap($result);
140.        $result->fetchinto($r);
141.        $total+= ($r["price"] * $val2);
142.      }
143.    }
144.    if($total != 0) {
145.      $total = $total + $shipping;
146.    }
```

Script 5-3 cart_inc.php (Continued)

```php
147.    return $total;
148. } //end calculate_total
149.
150. function display_cart($items) {
151.    global $dbconn;
152.    global $items, $status;
153.    $shipping = SHIPPING_COST;
154.    $count = 0;
155.    ?>
156.    <table border=1 cellpadding=5 cellspacing=0>
157.    <tr><td class=tablehead>Name</td><td
    class=tablehead>Qty</td><td class=tablehead>Price Each</
    td><td class=tablehead> </td></tr>
158.    <?
159.    foreach($items as $cat => $val) {
160.      foreach($items[$cat] as $item => $qty) {
161.        $sql = "select * from inventory where id = '$item'";
162.        $result = $dbconn->query($sql);
163.        errortrap($result);
164.        $result->fetchinto($r);
165.        ?>
166.        <tr><td><?=$r["name"]?></td><td><?=$qty?></
    td><td><?=$r["price"]?></td>
167.        <?
168.        if($status == "checkout") {
169.          echo "<td> </td>";
170.        } else {
171.          ?>
172.          <td><a
    href="<?=SECURE_URL?>cart.php?cat=<?=$r["category"]?>&item
    =<?=$r["id"]?>&action=remove">
173.          <img src="<?=IMAGE_URL?>remove.gif" border=0></
    a></td>
174.        <?
175.        }
176.        ?>
177.        </tr>
178.        <?
179.        $count++;
180.      }
181.    }
182.    if($count == 0) {
183.      $items= array();
184.      ?>
```

```
185.      <tr><td colspan=4><h3>Your Cart Is Empty!</h3></
     td><tr>
186.    <?
187.
188.    }
189.    $total = calculate_total($items);
190.    ?>
191.    <tr><td colspan=3>Shipping and Handling</
     td><td><?=$shipping?></td></tr>
192.    <tr><td class=smalli>
193.    <?
194.    if($status != "checkout") {
195.       if($count > 0) {
196.          ?>Click <a
     href=<?=SECURE_URL?>cart.php?modify=bulk">HERE</a> to
     modify bulk<br>quantities in your cart.<?
197.       }
198.    }
199.    ?>
200.     </td><td colspan="2" align="right">Total:</td><td>
201.    <?
202.    printf("%.2f", $total);
203.    ?></td></tr></table><?
204. }//end display_cart
205.
206. function cart2form($items) {
207. foreach($items as $cat => $val) {
208. foreach($val as $item => $qty) {
209. ?>
210. <input type="hidden" name="cart[<?=$item; ?>]"
     value="<?=$qty; ?>">
211. <?
212. }
213. }
214. }//end cart2form
215.
216. function display_items($cat, $items) {
217.    global $dbconn;
218.    $sql = "select * from inventory where category =
     '$cat'";
219.    $result = $dbconn->query($sql);
220.    errortrap($result);
221.    if($result->numRows() > 0) {
222.       ?>
223.       <h2>Available Items In This Category:</h2>
```

```
224.      <table border=1 cellpadding=5 cellspacing=0>
225.      <tr><td class=tablehead>Name <div class=smalli>click
     name for details</div></td><td class=tablehead>Price</
     td><td class=tablehead> </td></tr>
226.      <?
227.      while($result->fetchinto($r)) {
228.          ?>
229.      <tr><td><a
     href="<?=SECURE_URL?>cart.php?itemview=<?=$r["id"]?>"><?=$
     r["name"]?></a></td>
230.      <td><?=$r["price"]?></td>
231.      <td>
232.      <?
233.      if($r["qty"] > 1) {
234.          ?>
235.      <a
     href="<?=SECURE_URL?>cart.php?cat=<?=$r["category"]?>&item
     =<?=$r["id"]?>&action=add"><img
     src="<?=IMAGE_URL?>add.gif" border=0></a>
236.          <?
237.      } else {
238.          ?>
239.      Out Of Stock
240.          <?
241.      }
242.      ?>
243.      </td></tr>
244.      <?
245.      }
246.      ?>
247.      </table>
248.      <?
249.   } else {
250.      echo "<h3>Select A Category Above</h3>";
251.   }
252. } //end display_items
253.
254. function edit_cart($items) {
255.      global $dbconn;
256.      ?>
257.   <form action=cart.php method=post>
258.   <table border=1 cellpadding=5 cellspacing=0>
259.   <tr><td class=tablehead>Name</td><td
     class=tablehead>Price Each</td><td class=tablehead>Qty</
     td></tr>
```

```
260.  <?
261.  foreach($items as $cat => $val) {
262.     foreach($items[$cat] as $item => $qty) {
263.        $sql = "select * from inventory where id = '$item'";
264.        $result = $dbconn->query($sql);
265.        errortrap($result);
266.        $result->fetchinto($r);
267.        ?>
268.        <tr><td><?=$r["name"]?></td><td><?=$r["price"]?></
      td>
269.        <td>
270.        <input type="text"
      name="items_in[<?=$cat?>][<?=$item?>]" value="<?=$qty?>"
      size="3">
271.        </td></tr>
272.        <?
273.     }
274.  }
275.  ?>
276.  </table>
277.  <input type="submit" name="update_cart" value="Update
      Cart">
278.  </form>
279.  <?
280. } //end edit_cart
281.
282. function select_cat() {
283.    ?>
284.    <form action=cart.php method=post>
285.    <p>Select Category to Shop: <select
      name="category_choice_in">
286.    <? build_menu("name","category"); ?>
287.    </select>
288.    <input type="submit" name="submit" value="Submit">
289.    </form>
290.    <?
291. } //end select_cat
292. ?>
```

Script 5–3 cart_inc.php Line-by-Line Explanation

LINE	DESCRIPTION
2–7	Create some constants. Fill in the values as applicable to your site. Since this cart assumes a flat shipping rate, I've also specified the shipping cost here so that it can be easily changed.
9–22	Use a PEAR DB connect function to create a connection to the database.
24–29	Create a short error trapping function to check for PEAR DB errors after every query. This can be customized to suit your reporting needs. Error reporting is covered in detail in Chapter 8.
31–57	Define a function, alter_cart(), to add and remove items from the user's shopping cart. The items array is actually a two-dimensional array. Each element in the items array is an array itself. The top-level arrays are categories. The arrays within them are item arrays. The structure looks like this: • items[category[cat1], category[cat2], category[cat3]] • cat1[item1[qty], item2[qty], item3[qty]] • cat2[item1[qty], item2[qty], item3[qty]] • cat3[item1[qty], item2[qty], item3[qty]]
59–88	Define a function, full_item(), to display the full description and option picture of an item. Users are also able to add items to the cart when they are viewing the full description.
90–108	Define a function, $build_menu, to use as a "helper function." This function simply creates a drop-down menu for use in other functions.
110–129	Define a function, head(), to display the opening HTML for a page.
131–141	Define a function, calculate_total(), to determine the total cost of the items in the shopping cart.
150–204	Define a function, $display_cart(), that displays the items in the shopping cart to the users. This function serves a couple of purposes. First, users can easily see what items are in their shopping cart. Second, users can easily remove items with the click of a button.
206–214	Define a function, cart2form(), that extracts the items in the user's cart and places them in hidden form fields. This is used on the checkout.php page.
216–252	Define a function, display_items(), to display the list of items in a given category. In addition to displaying the items, this function also provides a button to add items to a user's cart and a link to see the full description of an item.

Script 5–3 cart_inc.php Line-by-Line Explanation (Continued)

LINE	DESCRIPTION
254–280	Define a function, edit_cart(), that allows the users to "bulk modify" items in their carts by specifying a quantity of items instead of having to click the "Add" button numerous times.
282–291	Define a function, select_cat(), that prints out a short form so that the user may select a category to browse.
292	End the PHP for the page.

dbmanage.php

dbmanage.php is used to manage the categories and items in the inventory.

SCRIPT 5–4 dbmanage.php

```
1. <?
2. require_once("../include/cart_inc.php");
3.
4. function add($item, $HTTP_POST_VARS) {
5.    global $dbconn;
6.    if($item == "cat") {
7.       $id = $dbconn->nextID('category',true);
8.       $sql = "insert into category values ('$id', '" .
       $HTTP_POST_VARS["name"] . "','" .
       $HTTP_POST_VARS["description"] . "')";
9.    } elseif($item == "item") {
10.      $id = $dbconn->nextID('inventory',true);
11.      $sql = "insert into inventory VALUES('$id', '" .
12.         $HTTP_POST_VARS["name"] . "','" .
13.         $HTTP_POST_VARS["category"] . "','" .
14.         $HTTP_POST_VARS["code"] . "','" .
15.         $HTTP_POST_VARS["description"] . "','" .
16.         $HTTP_POST_VARS["price"] . "','" .
17.         $HTTP_POST_VARS["picture"] . "','" .
18.         $HTTP_POST_VARS["qty"] . "')";
19.   } else {
20.      return 0;
21.   }
22.   $result = $dbconn->query($sql);
23.   errortrap($result);
24.   return 1;
```

```
25. } //end add
26.
27. function display($item, $cat) {
28.    global $dbconn;
29.    if($item == "cat") {
30.       $sql = "select * from categories order by name";
31.    } elseif($item == "item") {
32.       $sql = "select * from inventory order by category,
    name";
33.    } else {
34.       return 0;
35.    }
36.    $result = $dbconn->query($sql);
37.    errortrap($result);
38.    ?>
39.    <p>
40.    <table border=1 cellpadding=5>
41.    <?
42.    if($item == "item") {
43.       ?><tr class=tablehead><td>Name</td><td>Code</
    td><td>Description</td><td>Price</td><td>Picture</
    td><td>Qty</td></tr><?
44.    } else {
45.       ?><tr class=tablehead><td>Name</td><td>Description</
    td></tr><?
46.    }
47.    while($result->fetchinto($r)) {
48.       if($item == "cat") {
49.          ?>
50.          <tr><td><?=$r["name"]?></
    td><td><?=$r["description"]?></td></tr>
51.          <?
52.       } elseif($item == "item") {
53.          ?>
54.          <tr><td><?=$r["name"]?></td><td><?=$r["code"]?></
    td><td><?=$r["description"]?></td>
55.          <td><?=$r["price"]?></
    td><td><?=$r["picture"]?> </td>
56.          <td><?=$r["qty"]?></td>
57.          </tr>
58.          <?
59.       }
60.    }
61.    ?></table><?
62. }// end display
```

```php
63.
64. function item_edit($cat, $limit) {
65.     global $dbconn;
66.         $sql = "select * from inventory where category =
    '$cat' order by id limit $limit,20";
67.     $result = $dbconn->query($sql);
68.     errortrap($result);
69.     if($result->numRows() > 0) {
70.         ?>
71.         <p>Viewing inventory items <?=$limit?> through
    <?=($limit+=20) ?>.
72.         <form action=dbmanage.php method=post>
73.         <input type=hidden name="category"
    value="<?=$cat?>">
74.         <input type=hidden name=limit value="<?=$limit ?>">
75.         <input type="submit" name="choose_cat" value="View
    Next 20">
76.         </form>
77.             <table>
78.             <tr class=tablehead><td>Name</td><td>Category</
    td><td>Code</td><td>Description</td><td>Price</
    td><td>Picture</td><td>Qty</td><td>Action</td>
79.             <?
80.         while($result->fetchinto($r)){
81.                 ?>
82.                 <form action=dbmanage.php method=post>
83.                 <input type=hidden name=id
    value="<?=$r["id"]?>">
84.             <input type=hidden name=limit value="<?=$limit
    ?>">
85.                 <tr>
86.                 <td><input type=text name=name
    value="<?=$r["name"]?>"></td>
87.                     <td>
88.                         <select name="category">
89.                         <?
    build_menu("name","category"); ?>
90.                         </select>
91.                     </td>
92.                     <td><input type=text name=code
    value="<?=$r["code"]?>"></td>
93.                     <td><textarea name=description
    cols=15 rows=2><?=$r["description"]?></textarea></td>
94.                     <td><input type=text name=price
    value="<?=$r["price"]?>"></td>
```

```
95.                      <td><input type=text name=picture
      value="<?=$r["picture"]?>"></td>
96.                      <td><input type=text name=qty
      value="<?=$r["qty"]?>"></td>
97.                      <td><input type="submit"
      name="submit" value="Update Item"><input type="submit"
      name="submit" value="Delete Item"></td>
98.                  </form>
99.                  <?
100.            }
101.            ?></table><?
102.     } else {
103.        ?>
104.        <h2>There are no more items in this category</h2>
105.        <?
106.     }
107. }//end item_edit
108.
109. function process_item_edit ($HTTP_POST_VARS) {
110.     global $dbconn;
111.     $delete_cat_items = "false";
112.         if($HTTP_POST_VARS["submit"] == "Delete Item") {
113.             $sql = "delete from inventory where id = '"
      . $HTTP_POST_VARS["id"] . "'";
114.          } elseif($HTTP_POST_VARS["submit"] == "Update
      Item") {
115.              $sql = "update inventory set name='" .
      $HTTP_POST_VARS["name"] . "', category='"
      .$HTTP_POST_VARS["category"] .
116.                      "', code='" .
      $HTTP_POST_VARS["code"] ."', description='" .
117.
      $HTTP_POST_VARS["description"] . "', price='" .
      $HTTP_POST_VARS["price"]   .
118.                      "', picture ='" .
      $HTTP_POST_VARS["picture"] . "', qty='" .
      $HTTP_POST_VARS["qty"] .
119.                      "' where id='" .
      $HTTP_POST_VARS["id"] . "'";
120.          } elseif($HTTP_POST_VARS["submit"] == "Delete
      Category") {
121.         $sql = "delete from category where id = '" .
      $HTTP_POST_VARS["id"] . "'";
122.         $delete_cat_items = "true";
```

```
123.     } elseif($HTTP_POST_VARS["submit"] == "Update
    Category") {
124.        $sql = "update category set name='" .
    $HTTP_POST_VARS["name"] ."', description='" .
125.
    $HTTP_POST_VARS["description"] . "' where id='" .
    $HTTP_POST_VARS["id"] . "'";
126.    }
127.        $result = $dbconn->query($sql);
128.        errortrap($result);
129.            echo "<h2>" . $HTTP_POST_VARS["submit"] . "
    Successful!</h2>\n";
130.    if($delete_cat_items == "true") {
131.            $sql2 = "delete from inventory where category =
    '" . $HTTP_POST_VARS["id"] . "'";
132.            $result = $dbconn->query($sql2);
133.            errortrap($result);
134.            //}
135.    }
136. } //end process_item_edit
137.
138. function cat_edit() {
139.    global $dbconn;
140.        $sql = "select * from category order by id ";
141.    $result = $dbconn->query($sql);
142.    errortrap($result);
143.    if($result->numRows() > 0) {
144.        ?>
145.        <p>Viewing Categories:
146.            <table>
147.            <tr class=tablehead><td>Name</
    td><td>Description</td><td>Action</td></tr>
148.            <?
149.            // while($r = mysql_fetch_array($result)) {
150.        while($result->fetchinto($r)) {
151.                ?>
152.                <form action=dbmanage.php method=post>
153.                <input type=hidden name=id
    value="<?=$r["id"]?>">
154.                <tr>
155.                    <td><input type=text name=name
    value="<?=$r["name"]?>"></td>
156.                    <td><textarea name=description
    cols=25 rows=5><?=$r["description"]?></textarea></td>
```

```
157.                              <td><input type="submit"
      name="submit" value="Update Category"><input type="submit"
      name="submit" value="Delete Category"></td>
158.                    </form>
159.                    <?
160.           }
161.        } else {
162.          ?>
163.          <h2>There are no categories to edit!</h2>
164.             </table>
165.          <?
166.        }
167. }//end cat_edit
168.
169. function add_cat_form() {
170.    ?>
171.    <form action=dbmanage.php method=post>
172.       <table border="1" cellspacing="0" cellpadding="5">
173.       <tr class=tablehead> <td colspan="2"><h2>Add A
      Category</h2></td></tr>
174.       <tr><td>Name</td><td><input type="text" name="name"
      size="32" maxlength="32"></td></tr>
175.       <tr><td>Description</td><td><textarea
      name="description" cols=30 rows=5></textarea></td></tr>
176.       <tr><td colspan="2"> <input type="submit"
      name="add_cat" value="Add Category"></td></tr>
177.       </table>
178.     </form>
179.     <?
180. }//end add_cat_form
181.
182. function add_item_form() {
183.    ?>
184.    <form action=dbmanage.php method=post>
185.       <table border="1" cellspacing="0" cellpadding="5">
186.       <tr class=tablehead> <td colspan="2"><h2>Add An
      Inventory Item</h2></td></tr>
187.       <tr><td>Name</td><td><input type="text" name="name"
      size="32" maxlength="32"></td></tr>
188.       <tr><td>Category</td><td><select name="category"> <?
      build_menu("name","category"); ?></select></td></tr>
189.       <tr><td>Code</td><td><input type="text" name="code"
      size="32" maxlength="32"></td></tr>
190.       <tr><td>Description</td><td><textarea
      name="description" cols=30 rows=5></textarea></td></tr>
```

```
191.        <tr><td>Price</td><td><input type="text" name="price"
       size="8" maxlength="8"></td></tr>
192.        <tr><td>Picture</td><td><input type="text"
       name="picture"></td></tr>
193.        <tr><td>Qty In Stock</td><td><input type="text"
       name="qty" size="5"></td></tr>
194.        <tr><td colspan="2"> <input type="submit"
       name="add_item" value="Add Item"></td></tr>
195.        </table>
196.    </form>
197.    <?
198. }//end add_item_form
199.
200. function choose_cat_form() {
201.    ?>
202.    <form action=dbmanage.php method=post>
203.       <select name="category">
204.            <? build_menu("name","category"); ?>
205.       </select>
206.        <input type="submit" name="choose_cat" value="Edit
       Items In This Category">
207.    </form>
208.    <?
209. }//end choose_cat_from
210.
211.
212. function edit_cats_form() {
213.    ?>
214.    <form action=dbmanage.php method=post>
215.        <input type="submit" name="edit_cat" value="Edit All
       Categories">
216.    </form>
217.    <?
218. }
219.
220.
221. function choices() {
222.    ?>
223.    <table border=1 cellpadding=5 cellspacing=0>
224.       <tr valign="middle"><td><a
       href=dbmanage.php?action=addcat>Add A Category</a></
       td><td><a href=dbmanage.php?action=additem>Add An Item</
       a></td><td>
```

```
225.      <a href=dbmanage.php?action=display>Display
     Inventory</a></td><td><?=choose_cat_form()?></
     td><td><?=edit_cats_form()?></td></tr>
226.   </table>
227.   <?
228. }//end_choices
229.
230. /***** MAIN *****/
231. head();
232. $dbconn = connect();
233. if(isset($submit)) {
234.   process_item_edit($HTTP_POST_VARS);
235. }
236. if(isset($add_cat)) {
237.   if(!add("cat", $HTTP_POST_VARS)) {
238.     echo "Error adding cat!";
239.   } else {
240.     echo "<h2>Added New Category</h2>";
241.   }
242. }
243. if(isset($add_item)) {
244.   if(!add("item", $HTTP_POST_VARS)) {
245.     echo "Error adding item!";
246.   } else {
247.     echo "<h2>Added New Item</h2>";
248.   }
249. }
250. choices();
251. if(isset($action)) {
252.   if($action == "addcat") {
253.     add_cat_form();
254.   }elseif($action == "additem") {
255.     add_item_form();
256.   }elseif($action == "display") {
257.     display("item","1");
258.   }
259. }
260. if(isset($choose_cat)) {
261.   if(!isset($HTTP_POST_VARS["limit"])) {
262.     $HTTP_POST_VARS["limit"] = 0;
263.   }
264.   item_edit($category, $HTTP_POST_VARS["limit"]);
265. }
266. if(isset($edit_cat)) {
267.   cat_edit();
```

268. }
269. ?>
270. </body>
271. </html>

Script 5–4 dbmanage.php Line-by-Line Explanation

LINE	DESCRIPTON
2	Require cart_inc.php because it contains some functions used by this script.
4–25	Define a function, add(), which adds a category or an item to the inventory. This function uses the PEAR DB function nextID() to generate an auto-increment ID:

```
$dbconn->nextID($table, $create);
```

nextID takes two arguments:

- $table—The table for which the ID is to be generated.
- $create—A boolean value, set to true if it should start an ID sequence if one does not already exist.

The nextID() function solves the problem for those of us who like to use the auto_increment feature to create IDs in MySQL, but who also want the application to be used on different databases, some of which do not use the auto_increment feature for IDs.

LINE	DESCRIPTON
27–62	Define a function, display(), that displays the items in the inventory.
64–107	Define a function, item_edit(), to print a form to edit an existing item in the inventory. This function displays multiple items at once, 20 items at a time.
109–136	Define a function, process_item_edit(), to process the changes made by using the item_edit() function. If a category is deleted, then all of the items associated with that category are also deleted.
138–167	Define a function, cat_edit(), to print a form to edit an existing category.
169–180	Define a function, add_cat_form, to print a form to add a new category.
182–198	Define a function, add_item_form(), to print a form to add a new item.
200–218	Define a function, choose_cat_form(), to print a form allowing the user to choose a category to edit.
221–228	Define a function, choices(), that displays the different actions the user can take to manage the inventory.
230	Begin the main program.
231	Use the head() function to print out the beginning HTML for the page.

Script 5–4 dbmanage.php Line-by-Line Explanation (Continued)

LINE	DESCRIPTON
232	Establish a connection to the database.
233–235	If the "Submit" button has been pushed, then execute the process_item_edit() function. The $submit button is mapped to all of the edit features on this page.
236–242	If the $add_item variable is set, then attempt to add a new item. If there was an error, then print out a message to the screen (most likely the script will die before this, because the error trap should catch it). If there was no error, then inform the user that the new item was added.
243–249	If the $add_cat variable is set, then attempt to add a new category. If there was an error, then print out a message to the screen (most likely the script will die before this, because the error trap should catch it). If there was no error, then inform the user that the new category was added.
250	Execute the choices() function to display these features to the user.
251–259	If the $action variable is set, then we know the user has pushed one of the buttons for "Add Category," "Add Item," or "Display All Items," as defined in the choices() function. Execute the proper function for the button (or link) that was clicked.
260–265	If the $choose_cat variable is set, then we know the user wished to view or edit the items in a particular category. Display the items in the category. Limit is used to view only 20 items at a time. If $limit is not set, then we know the user is on the first page, so set $limit to zero. The item_edit() function will increment limit each time the user views a subset of the data.
266–268	If the $edit_cat variable is set, then we know the user wishes to edit a category, so execute the cat_edit() function.
269	Close out the PHP and HTML for the page.

admin.php

admin.php is used to manage the orders that have been sub-mitted.

SCRIPT 5–5 admin.php

```php
1. <?
2. function display_orders($mode) {
3.    global $dbconn;
4.    switch($mode) {
```

```
5.      case("all"):
6.          $sql = "select * from orders order by id";
7.          break;
8.      case("open"):
9.          $sql = "select * from orders where status = 'open'
   order by id";
10.         break;
11.     case("shipped"):
12.         $sql = "select * from orders where status =
   'shipped' order by id";
13.         break;
14.     case("backorder"):
15.         $sql = "select * from orders where status =
   'backorder' order by id";
16.         break;
17.     case("hold"):
18.         $sql = "select * from orders where status = 'hold'
   order by id";
19.         break;
20.     default:
21.         $sql = "select * from orders order by id";
22.         break;
23.     }
24.     $result = $dbconn->query($sql);
25.     errortrap($result);
26.     ?>
27.     <h3>Orders</h3>
28.     <table border=1 cellpadding=10 cellspacing=0>
29.     <tr><td  colspan=5><a href="admin.php?view=all">View All
   Orders</a> | <a href="admin.php?view=open">View Open
   Orders</a> | <a href="admin.php?view=shipped">View Shipped
   Orders</a> | <a href="admin.php?view=backorder">View
   Backorder Orders</a>  | <a href="admin.php?view=hold">View
   Hold Orders</a></td></tr>
30.     <tr><td>Order Number</td><td>Customer</td><td>Status</
   td><td>Tracking #</td><td> </td></tr>
31.     <?
32.     while($result->fetchinto($r)) {
33.         $r2 = get_customer($r["customer"]);
34.     ?>
35.     <tr>
36.         <td><a
   href="admin.php?display=orderdetails&id=<?=$r["id"]?>"><?=
   $r["id"]?></a></td>
```

```
37.         <td><a
   href="admin.php?display=customer&id=<?=$r2["id"]?>"><?=$r2
   ["last"]?>, <?=$r2["first"]?></a></td>
38.         <td><?=$r["status"]?></td>
39.         <td><?=$r["tracking_number"]?>  </td>
40.         <td><a
   href="admin.php?display=update&id=<?=$r["id"]?>">Update
   Order Status</a></td>
41.     </tr>
42.     <?
43.   }
44.   ?>
45.   </table>
46.   <?
47. } //end display_orders
48.
49. function display_order_details($id) {
50.   global $dbconn;
51.   $sql = "select * from order_details where orderid =
   '$id'";
52.   $result = $dbconn->query($sql);
53.   errortrap($result);
54.   ?>
55.   <h2>Order Details For Order <?=$id?></h2>
56.   <h3>Items In Order</h3>
57.   <table border=1 cellpadding=10 cellspacing=0>
58.   <tr><td>Qty</td><td>Description</td></tr>
59.   <?
60.   while($result->fetchinto($r)) {
61.     ?>
62.     <tr>
63.       <td><?=$r["qty"]?>  </td>
64.       <?
65.       $sql2 = "select * from inventory where id='" .
   $r["code"] . "'";
66.       $result2 = $dbconn->query($sql2);
67.       errortrap($result2);
68.       $result2->fetchinto($r2);
69.       ?>
70.       <td>
71.       name: <?=$r2["name"]?>
72.       <br>code: <?=$r2["code"]?>
73.       <br>description: <?=$r2["description"]?>
74.       <br>price: <?=$r2["price"]?>
75.       </td>
```

```
76.      </tr>
77.      <?
78.    }
79.    ?>
80.    </table>
81.    <?
82.    $sql = "select customer from orders where id = '$id'";
83.    $result = $dbconn->query($sql);
84.    errortrap($result);
85.    $result->fetchinto($r);
86.    $cust = get_customer($r["customer"]);
87.    display_customer($cust);
88. } //end display_order_details
89.
90. function update_order_status($id) {
91.    global $dbconn;
92.    $sql = "select * from orders where id = '$id'";
93.    $result = $dbconn->query($sql);
94.    errortrap($result);
95.    $result->fetchinto($r);
96.    ?>
97.    <form action=admin.php method=post>
98.    <P>When changing status to "Shipped" you can include an
    optional tracking number that is sent to the customer by
    email.
99.    <table border=1 cellpadding=5 cellspacing=0>
100.   <tr><td>Order ID</td><td><?=$r["id"]?></td></tr>
101.   <tr><td>Status (current status is <b><?=$r["status"]?></
    b>)</td>
102.      <td>
103.      <select name="status">
104.         <option value="open">Open</option>
105.         <option value="shipped">Shipped</option>
106.         <option value="backorder">Backorder</option>
107.         <option value="hold">Hold</option>
108.      </select>
109.      </td></tr>
110.   <tr><td>Tracking Number</td><td><input type="text"
    name="tracking" value="<?=$r["tracking"]?>"></td></tr>
111.   <input type=hidden name="id" value="<?=$r["id"]?>">
112.   <input type=hidden name="customer"
    value="<?=$r["customer"]?>">
113.   <tr><td colspan=2><input type="submit" name="update"
    value="Update Order!"></td></tr>
114.   </table>
```

```
115.  </form>
116.  <?
117.  } //end update_order
118.
119.  function update_order_process($HTTP_POST_VARS) {
120.     global $dbconn;
121.     $sql = "update orders set status= '" .
      $HTTP_POST_VARS["status"] . "', tracking_number='" .
      $HTTP_POST_VARS["tracking"] ."' where id='" .
      $HTTP_POST_VARS["id"] . "'";
122.     $result = $dbconn->query($sql);
123.     errortrap($result);
124.     $message = "Your order from " . COMPANY_NAME . " has
      been processed. It's current status is:\n";
125.     $message .= "Status: " . $HTTP_POST_VARS["status"] .
      "\n";
126.     if($HTTP_POST_VARS["tracking"] != "") {
127.        $message .= "The tracking number for your shipment is
      " . $HTTP_POST_VARS["tracking"] . "\n";
128.     }
129.     $r_cust = get_customer($HTTP_POST_VARS["customer"]);
130.     $to = $r_cust["email"];
131.     mail($to, COMPANY_NAME . " Order!", $message, "From: " .
      COMPANY_NAME . " <" . COMPANY_EMAIL . ">");
132.  ?>
133.     <h3>Status Changed!</h3>
134.     <p>The status has been updated and an email has been sent
      to the customer.
135.     <p>Click <a href="admin.php">here</a> to return to the
      administration page.
136.  <?
137.  } //end update_order_process
138.
139.  function get_customer($id) {
140.     global $dbconn;
141.     $sql = "select * from customers where id = '$id'";
142.     $result = $dbconn->query($sql);
143.     errortrap($result);
144.     $result->fetchinto($row);
145.     return $row;
146.  } //end get_customer
147.
148.  function display_customer($r_cust) {
149.  ?>
150.     <h3>Customer Details</h3>
```

```
151.    <table border=1 cellpadding=5 cellspacing=0>
152.    <tr><td>Customer ID</td><td><?=$r_cust["id"]?></td></tr>
153.    <tr><td>First Name </td><td><?=$r_cust["first"]?></td></tr>
154.    <tr><td>Middle Initial </td><td><?=$r_cust["mi"]?></td></tr>
155.    <tr><td>Last Name </td><td><?=$r_cust["last"]?></td></tr>
156.    <tr><td>Address </td><td><?=$r_cust["address1"]?></td></tr>
157.    <tr><td>Address 2 </td><td><?=$r_cust["address2"]?></td></tr>
158.    <tr><td>City </td><td><?=$r_cust["city"]?></td></tr>
159.    <tr><td>State </td><td><?=$r_cust["state"]?></td></tr>
160.    <tr><td>Zip </td><td><?=$r_cust["zip"]?></td></tr>
161.    <tr><td>Country </td><td><?=$r_cust["country"]?></td></tr>
162.    <tr><td>Ship to Billing Address? </td><td><?=$r_cust["shiptobilling"]?></td></tr>
163.    <tr><td>Ship to Address </td><td><?=$r_cust["ship_address1"]?></td></tr>
164.    <tr><td>Ship to Address 2 </td><td><?=$r_cust["ship_address2"]?></td></tr>
165.    <tr><td>Ship to City </td><td><?=$r_cust["ship_city"]?></td></tr>
166.    <tr><td>Ship to State </td><td><?=$r_cust["ship_state"]?></td></tr>
167.    <tr><td>Ship to Zip </td><td><?=$r_cust["ship_zip"]?></td></tr>
168.    <tr><td>Ship to Country </td><td><?=$r_cust["ship_country"]?></td></tr>
169.    <tr><td>Ship to Phone </td><td><?=$r_cust["ship_phone"]?></td></tr>
170.    <tr><td>Email </td><td><?=$r_cust["email"]?></td></tr>
171.    </table>
172.    <?
173.    } //end display_customer
174.
175.    /***** MAIN *****/
176.    require_once("../include/cart_inc.php");
177.    $dbconn = connect();
178.    head();
179.
180.    if(isset($view)) {
181.        display_orders($view);
```

Script 5–5 admin.php (Continued)

```
182. } elseif(isset($update)) {
183.    update_order_process($HTTP_POST_VARS);
184. } elseif(isset($display)) {
185.    switch($display) {
186.      case("orderdetails"):
187.        display_order_details($id);
188.        break;
189.      case("customer"):
190.        $r_cust = get_customer($id);
191.        display_customer($r_cust);
192.        break;
193.      case("update"):
194.        update_order_status($id);
195.        break;
196.      default;
197.        break;
198.    } //end switch
199. } else {
200.    display_orders("all");
201. }
202. ?>
```

Script 5–5 admin.php Line-by-Line Explanation

LINE	DESCRIPTION
2–47	Define a function, display_orders(), that displays orders based on the mode selected. The modes are: • All (every order regardless of state) • Open • Shipped • Backorder • Hold
49–88	Define a function, display_order_details(), that displays the details for a particular order. This function is called when the user clicks on an order number. The following information is displayed: • Items Ordered • Quantity of Items • Customer Information
90–137	Define a function, update_order_status(), that allows an administrator to change the status of an order. An email is sent to the customers notifying them of the status change.

Script 5–5 admin.php Line-by-Line Explanation (Continued)

LINE	DESCRIPTION
139–146	Define a function, get_customer(), that is used to get the information for a customer and return it to the calling function for display.
148–173	Define a function, display_customer(), that displays the information returned from get_customer(). Both of these functions are helper functions used within get_order_details().
175	Begin the main program.
176	Require the cart_inc.php script so that this script can use those functions defined in cart_inc.php.
177	Establish a connection to the database.
178	Print out the beginning HTML for the page.
180–181	If the $view variable is set, then display the orders according to the $view variable—for example, $view = "open".
182–183	If the $update variable is set, then process the update using the update_order_process() function.
184–198	If the $display variable is set, then switch to the proper function based on the contents of $display.
199–201	If nothing else has been set, then display all the orders.
202	End the PHP for the page.

checkout.php

checkout.php is used to gather the customer's details and send all of the information to the credit card authorization service. In this case, it sends the information directly to finishorder.php. Normally, you would submit this page to an authorization service and the authorization service would redirect to finishorder.php. Figure 5–4 displays the checkout screen.

SCRIPT 5–6 checkout.php

```
1. <?
2. require_once("include/cart_inc.php");
3. session_start();
4. head();
5. $dbconn = connect();
```

```
6.  $response = "1";
7.  //$response = "2"; //Declined Credit Card
8.  //$response = "3"; //General Error
9.
10. if(sizeof($items) == 0) {
11.    ?>
12.    <h3>There are no items in your cart! Click your
    browser's Back button and add some items to your cart.</h3>
13.    <?
14. } else {
15. ?>
16. <h2>Here are the items that you are ordering:</h2>
17. <?
18. $status = "checkout";
19. display_cart($items);
20. ?>
21. <p>Please fill in the following information to proceed.<p>
22.    <FORM METHOD=POST ACTION="<?=CREDIT_AUTH_URL?>">
23.       <INPUT TYPE=HIDDEN NAME="Amount" VALUE="<?=$total?>">
24.       <INPUT TYPE=HIDDEN NAME="x_Description" VALUE="Order
    From <?=COMPANY_NAME?>">
25.       <INPUT TYPE=HIDDEN NAME="x_Invoice_Num"
    VALUE="<?=time()?>">
26.    <INPUT TYPE=HIDDEN NAME="x_response_code"
    VALUE="<?=$response?>">
27.    <?cart2form($items);?>
28.    <table border="1" cellspacing="1" cellpadding="5">
29.       <tr>
30.          <td colspan="2" class="tablehead"><b>BILLING
    ADDRESS</b>:</td>
31.       </tr>
32.       <tr>
33.          <td>Credit Card Number<span class="required">*</
    span></td>
34.          <td>
35.             <input type="text" name="x_card_num">
36.          </td>
37.       </tr>
38.       <tr>
39.          <td>Expiration Date<span class="required">* <br>
40.             (MMYY - for example 0402 for April 2002)</span></
    td>
41.          <td>
42.             <input type="text" name="x_exp_date" maxlength="4"
    size="4">
```

```
43.        </td>
44.      </tr>
45.      <tr>
46.        <td>First Name<span class="required">*</span></td>
47.        <td>
48.          <input type="text" name="x_first_name">
49.        </td>
50.      </tr>
51.      <tr>
52.        <td>Middle Initial</td>
53.        <td>
54.          <input type="text" name="x_mi">
55.        </td>
56.      </tr>
57.      <tr>
58.        <td>Last Name<span class="required">*</span></td>
59.        <td>
60.          <input type="text" name="x_last_name">
61.        </td>
62.      </tr>
63.      <tr>
64.        <td>Address Line 1:<span class="required">*</span></
    td>
65.        <td>
66.          <input type="text" name="x_address">
67.        </td>
68.      </tr>
69.      <tr>
70.        <td>Address Line 2:</td>
71.        <td>
72.          <input type="text" name="x_address_2">
73.        </td>
74.      </tr>
75.      <tr>
76.        <td>City<span class="required">*</span></td>
77.        <td>
78.          <input type="text" name="x_city">
79.        </td>
80.      </tr>
81.      <tr>
82.        <td>State (two letter abbreviation)<span
    class="required">*</span></td>
83.        <td>
84.          <input type="text" name="x_state" size="2"
    maxlength="2">
```

```
85.        </td>
86.      </tr>
87.      <tr>
88.        <td>Zip/Postal Code<span class="required">*</span></
    td>
89.        <td>
90.          <input type="text" name="x_zip" size="10"
    maxlength="10">
91.        </td>
92.      </tr>
93.      <tr>
94.        <td>Country<span class="required">*</span></td>
95.        <td>
96.          <select name=x_country>
97.            <option> Canada
98.            <option> United Kingdom
99.            <option selected> United States
100.         </select>
101.       </td>
102.     </tr>
103.     <tr>
104.       <td>Daytime Phone Number</td>
105.       <td>
106.         <input type="text" name="x_phone">
107.       </td>
108.     </tr>
109.     <tr>
110.       <td>Email<span class="required">*</span></td>
111.       <td>
112.         <input type="text" name="x_email">
113.       </td>
114.     </tr>
115.     <tr>
116.       <td>Shipping Address Is The Same As Billing Address:
    </td>
117.       <td>
118.         <input type="checkbox" name="shiptobilling"
    value="true">
119.         <br>
120.         <font size="-2"> (Check To Ship To Your Billing
    Address)</font></td>
121.     </tr>
122.     <tr>
123.       <td colspan="2" class="tablehead">
124.         <p><b>SHIPPING ADDRESS </b><br>
```

```
125.               (Fill this out if your shipping address is
     different from your billing
126.               address):</p>
127.          </td>
128.      </tr>
129.      <tr>
130.        <td>Address Line 1:</td>
131.        <td>
132.          <input type="text" name="x_ship_to_address">
133.        </td>
134.      </tr>
135.      <tr>
136.        <td>Address Line 2:</td>
137.        <td>
138.          <input type="text" name="x_ship_to_address2">
139.        </td>
140.      </tr>
141.      <tr>
142.        <td>City</td>
143.        <td>
144.          <input type="text" name="x_ship_to_city">
145.        </td>
146.      </tr>
147.      <tr>
148.        <td>State (two letter abbreviation)</td>
149.        <td>
150.          <input type="text" name="x_ship_to_state" size="2"
     maxlength="2">
151.        </td>
152.      </tr>
153.      <tr>
154.        <td>Zip</td>
155.        <td>
156.          <input type="text" name="x_ship_to_zip" size="10"
     maxlength="10">
157.        </td>
158.      </tr>
159.      <tr>
160.        <td>Country</td>
161.        <td>
162.          <select name=x_ship_to_country>
163.            <option> Canada
164.            <option> United Kingdom
165.            <option selected> United States
166.          </select>
```

SCRIPT 5–6 checkout.php (Continued)

```
167.          </td>
168.        </tr>
169.      </table>
170.      <p>
171.        <INPUT TYPE=SUBMIT VALUE="Submit Order">
172.      </p>
173. </FORM>
174. <?
175. session_unset();
176. session_destroy();
177. }
178. ?>
```

Script 5–6 checkout.php Line-by-Line Explanation

LINE	DESCRIPTION
2	Require cart_inc.php (we need the information contained in the define statements).
3	Start the session. We'll be using information from the $items session variable.
4	Print out the beginning HTML for the page.
5	Establish a connection to the database.
6–8	Normally, these are sent by the authorization service. Uncomment one of these to see the results in the finishorder.php script.
10–14	Check to see if there is anything in the cart. If there is not, then there is no need to present this page.
15–20	Print out a short table displaying the items that have been ordered. Set the $status variable to $checkout.
21–173	Display the form to the user.
174–176	Unset the session variables and destroy the session.
177	End the if statement started on line 10.
178	End the PHP for the page.

FIGURE 5–4 checkout.php

finishorder.php

finishorder.php is used to place the authorized order into the database. If the order is not authorized by the server (defined by a response code sent by the authorization service), then a message is displayed to the users notifying them of a problem.

If the order goes through, the order, customer, and order_details tables are updated with the new order information and a confirmation email is sent to the customer.

SCRIPT 5-7 finishorder.php

```php
1.  <?
2.  require_once("include/cart_inc.php");
3.  head();
4.  $dbconn = connect();
5.
6.  switch($x_response_code) {
7.    case("1"):
8.      if(!isset($shiptobilling)) {
9.        $shiptobilling = "false";
10.     }
11.     $id = $dbconn->nextID('customers',true);
12.     $sql = "insert into customers values ('$id',
    '$x_first_name', '$x_mi', '$x_last_name', '$x_address',
    '$x_address_2', '$x_city', '$x_state', '$x_zip',
    '$x_country', '$shiptobilling', '$x_ship_to_address',
    '$x_ship_to_address2', '$x_ship_to_city',
    '$x_ship_to_state', '$x_ship_to_zip',
    '$x_ship_to_country', '$x_phone', '$x_email')";
13.     $result = $dbconn->query($sql);
14.     errortrap($result);
15.     $id2 = $dbconn->nextID('orders',true);
16.     $sql = "insert into orders values ('$id2', '$id',
    'open', NULL)";
17.     $result = $dbconn->query($sql);
18.     errortrap($result);
19.     foreach($cart as $code => $qty) {
20.       $id3 = $dbconn->nextID('order_details',true);
21.       $sql = "insert into order_details values ('$id3',
    '$id2', '$code', '$qty')";
22.       $result = $dbconn->query($sql);
23.       errortrap($result);
24.       $sql2 = "update inventory set qty = qty-'$qty'
    where id = '$code'";
25.       $result2 = $dbconn->query($sql2);
26.       errortrap($result2);
27.     }
28.     $mail = "Thank you for your order from " .
    COMPANY_NAME . "!\n";
29.     $mail .= "We have received your order and we will
    notify you when the order ships.";
```

```
30.       mail($x_email, "Your order from " . COMPANY_NAME,
     $mail, "From: " . COMPANY_NAME . " <" . COMPANY_EMAIL .
     ">");
31.       ?>
32.       <h2>Thank You!</h2>
33.       <p>Your order has been accepted. You should receive
     an email receipt in your email address in a few minutes.
34.       <h3>DO NOT RELOAD THIS PAGE OR YOU MAY BE DOUBLE-
     BILLED FOR YOUR ORDER</h3>
35.       <?
36.       break;
37.    case("2"):
38.       ?>
39.       <h3>Your Credit Card Was Declined</h3>
40.       <p>The reason given was:
     <?=$x_response_reason_text?>
41.       <?
42.       break;
43.    case("3"):
44.       ?>
45.       <h3>There Was An Error Processing Your Request</h3>
46.       <p>The reason given was:
     <?=$x_response_reason_text?>
47.       <?
48.       break;
49.    default:
50.       ?>
51.       <h3>There Was An Error Processing Your Request</h3>
52.       <?
53.    break;
54. } //end switch
55. ?>
56. <hr>
57. </body>
58. </html>
```

Script 5–7 finishorder.php Line-by-Line Explanation

LINE	DESCRIPTION
2	Require cart_inc.php so you can use some of the functions that it contains.
3	Print out the beginning HTML for the page.
4	Establish a connection to the database.

Script 5–7 finishorder.php Line-by-Line Explanation

LINE	DESCRIPTION
6	Switch on the response code.
7–36	If the response code was "1", then the authorization was successful. Insert the customer and order information into the database and send a confirmation email to the customer.
37–42	If the response code was "2", then the credit card was denied. Display a message informing the user.
43–48	If the response code was "3", then there was an unspecified error. Notify the user.
49–54	If the response code was anything else, then assume a general unspecified error occurred and display a message to the user.
55	End the PHP for the page.
57–58	Close out the HTML for the page.

6

Working with Files

Overview

P HP is a very useful language for working with files. Although it may not be as robust as other languages, such as PERL, when it comes to parsing files, PHP still provides great power and flexibility when it comes to working with text files.

This chapter covers reading from, manipulating, and writing to text files. You can use the features covered in this chapter to create applications that can read in text from a file (locally or over the Internet using HTTP or FTP), then use the data gathered in a manner more suited to your needs.

Opening and Closing Files

Opening Files

Before you can use PHP to read a file, you must first open it. To open a file, you use the fopen() function.

```
$file_handler = fopen($file, $mode)
```

You must assign the function to a variable, as above. This is referred to as a file pointer. You use the file pointer to reference the open file throughout your script.

The fopen() function takes two arguments:

- $file is the name (and path, if required) of the file.
- $mode is one of a list of available modes:
  - r—Open the file as read-only. You cannot write anything to the file. Reading begins at the beginning of the file.
  - r+—Open the file for reading and writing. Reading and writing begin at the beginning of the file. You will delete existing contents if you write to the file without first moving the internal pointer to the end of the file.
  - w—Open the file for write-only. You cannot read data from the file. Writing begins at the beginning of the file. You will again delete contents if you write to the file without first moving the pointer to the end of the file. If the file specified by the $fie argument does not exist, then PHP attempts to create the file. Make sure your permissions are set correctly!
  - w+—As above, but the file may also be read.
  - a—This mode is the same as the 'w' mode, with the exception that the internal pointer is placed at the end of the file. Existing contents will not be overwritten unless you rewind the internal pointer to the beginning of the file.
  - a+—As above, but the file may also be read.

Additionally, if the file is a binary file, you must include a "b" in the mode if your OS is Windows. This chapter only deals with ASCII text files, so you will not require the "b: mode in the following example. If you do need to open a binary file, an example is below:

```
$file_handle = fopen($filename, "rb+")
```

Note the differences between the "w" and "a" modes. Using "w" to open a file effectively deletes the contents of the file, while using the "a" mode retains the contents of the file and allows you to append additional data to the end of the file.

Once you have the file opened, you can then read from or write to the file.

Reading Files

There are multiple functions available to read from a file.

You can read data from the file using the fread() function:

```
$file_contents = fread($file_pointer, $length_to_read);
```

You must assign the value of fread() to a variable, which will contain the data that has been read. The fread() function takes two arguments:

- $file_pointer is the file pointer to which you assigned the value from the fopen() function.
- $length is the amount of bytes that you wish to read.

When using fread() to read a file, you can read in the entire file. To do this, you need to know the byte-size of the file. You can easily find the total byte-size of a file using the filesize() function:

```
$bytes = filesize($filename);
```

The following script demonstrates how to open a short text file and display its contents:

```
$file = "/path/to/text.txt";
$filepointer = fopen($file, "r");
$contents = fread($filepointer, filesize($file));
echo "<pre>" . htmlentities($contents) . "</pre>";
```

There is a slight problem when reading files from the Internet: You cannot easily determine the size of the file, since it does not exist on the local server. An easy fix for this is to attempt to read many more bytes than you think exist in the file. Since fread() stops when it reaches the end of the file (EOF), you don't have to worry about PHP wasting processing on the extra bytes you specified for the $length argument in fread(). For example:

```
$file = "http://www.example.com/text.txt";
$filepointer = fopen($file, "r");
$contents = fread($filepointer, 9999999);
```

Closing Files

When you have finished reading from or writing to a file that has been opened using the fopen() function, you should always close it using the fclose() function:

```
fclose($filepointer);
```

Closing the file allows you to clean up any memory that was used to open it and also prevents possible file corruption that sometimes (rarely) occurs when a file is left open.

Putting It to Use

This next script shows how to open a file from the Internet and display it on your page, as in Figure 6–1. The National Oceanic & Atmospheric Administration (NOAA) provides hourly weather information for almost every airport in the United States. They provide this information on their site at *www.noaa.gov* in many formats. One weather report format they provide is called METAR. METAR is a French acronym that roughly translates as "Aviation Routine Weather Report." METAR provides useful information like current winds, barometric pressure, cloud cover, etc. This script accesses the files stored on the NOAA's datastore for this information, relative to the airport identifier you provide to the script. If you enter "KJFK" for New York's JFK airport, it provides the current weather in the encoded (shorthand for aviation weather reporting) and decoded (readable by us normal people) formats.

SCRIPT 6-1 metar.php

```
1.  <body bgcolor="#FFFFFF" text="#000000">
2.  <h2>METAR Weather Retrieval</h2>
3.  <p>This page retrieves the latest METAR information for
    the requested station.
4.  <p>METAR stations are generally located at all major
    airports and many smaller ones. Station identifiers are
    generally the letter "K" followed by the airport
    identifier. For example, the station identifier for Logan
    International at Boston, MA is "KBOS".
5.  <p>The information is retrieved directly from the NOAA
    Weather Database (see <i>http://weather.noaa.gov/weather/
    metar.shtml</i>).
6.  <p>Various METAR-related information can be found at <a
    href="http://205.156.54.206/oso/oso1/oso12/
    metar.htm">http://205.156.54.206/oso/oso1/oso12/
    metar.htm</a>.
7.  <p><strong>Enter the Station Identifier below:</strong>
8.  <p>
9.  <form action=metar.php mehod=get>
10. <p>METAR Station ID: <input type="text"
    name="metar_station" size="4" maxlength="4">
11. <input type="submit" name="submit" value="Submit">
12. </form>
13. <hr noshade>
14. <?
15. function connect_error($metar_station) {
16.     ?>
17.     <p><span class=navy>Sorry, either that station
    identifier, <strong><? echo strtoupper($metar_station)
    ?></strong>, is not valid, or the connection to the NOAA
    servers is broken.</span>
18.     <?
19.     die();
20. }
21. if(isset($metar_station)) {
22.   $file1 = "ftp://weather.noaa.gov/data/observations/
    metar/decoded/" . strtoupper($metar_station) . ".TXT";
23.   $file2 = "ftp://weather.noaa.gov/data/observations/
    metar/stations/" . strtoupper($metar_station) . ".TXT";
24.   if(!$fd1 = @fopen($file1, "rb")) {
25.     connect_error($metar_station);
26.   } else {
27.     $decoded = fread($fd1, 9999999);
```

```
28.      printf("<h3>METAR Decoded Observation for <span
    class=navy>%s</span></h3><pre>%s</pre>",
    strtoupper($metar_station), htmlentities($decoded));
29.      fclose($fd1);
30.    }
31.    if(!$fd2 = @fopen($file2, "rb")) {
32.      connect_error($metar_station);
33.    } else {
34.      $encoded = fread($fd2, 9999999);
35.      printf("<h3>METAR Encoded Observation for <span
    class=navy>%s</span></h3><pre>%s</pre>",
    strtoupper($metar_station), htmlentities($encoded));
36.      fclose($fd2);
37.    }
38.  }
39.  ?>
40.  </body>
41.  </html>
```

Script 6–1 metar.php Line-by-Line Explanation

LINE	DESCRIPTION
1–7	Provide some basic HTML for the beginning of the page, with a style sheet and some instructions on how to use the script.
9–13	Provide a form asking for the airport station identifier.
14	Begin the PHP part of the page.
15–20	Define a function, connect_error(), to print out an error message in the event that the connection to the NOAA server is not working or an invalid station identifier was entered by the user. This function takes one argument, $metar_station, which is the station identifier entered by the user into the form.
21	If the $metar_station variable is set, then we know that the user has submitted the form, and can continue to the next line. If $metar_station has not been set, then do nothing.
22	Assign the decoded METAR file from the NOAA server to the $file1 variable. The files reside on the server with the format METAR_STATION.TXT—for example, "KBOS.TXT" for Logan airport in Boston, MA. The strtoupper() function makes the user's text all uppercase regardless of what case it was when the user entered it.

Script 6–1 metar.php Line-by-Line Explanation (Continued)

LINE	DESCRIPTION
23	The same as above, only this time open the encoded version of the data and assign it to the $file2 variable.
24–25	Attempt to open the file on the NOAA server. If the file cannot be opened, then throw an error to the connect_error() function to notify the user.
26	If there were no errors opening the file, then execute lines 27–30.
27	Read in the entire contents of the file (we are assuming it is less than 9,999,999 bytes) and assign it to the $decoded variable.
28	Print out the data to the page. We use htmlentities() to translate any data that may be recognized as HTML code into the HTML code for that data.
29	Close the file using the fclose() function.
30	Close out the if statement started on line 26.
31–32	Attempt to open the other file on the NOAA server. If the file cannot be opened, then throw an error to the connect_error() function to notify the user.
33	If there were no errors opening the file, then execute lines 34–37.
34	Read in the entire contents of the file (we are assuming it is less than 9,999,999 bytes) and assign it to the $decoded variable.
35	Print out the data to the page. We use htmlentities() to translate any data that may be recognized as HTML code into the HTML code for that data.
36	Close the file using the fclose() function.
37	Close out the if statement started on line 33.
38	Close out the if statement started on line 31.
39–41	End the PHP and HTML for the script.

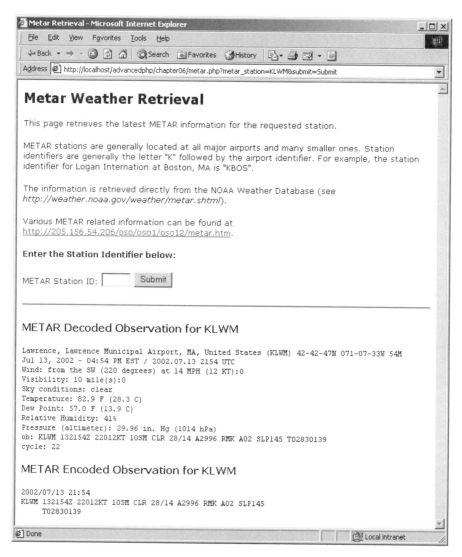

FIGURE 6–1 metar.php

Data Mining

Many Web pages provide a lot of useful information. Sometimes the information you need is surrounded by a lot of other information that you don't need or want. Using PHP, it is possible to read a page on the Web and extract the information you need.

When extracting information from other sites, it is important to remember that any data on another site is most likely copyrighted. Do not use other people's data for your own purposes without express permission from the owner of that data.

This next example details how to retrieve a stock quote from the Reuters News Service Web page. This is merely an example and should not be used on your own site unless you have expressly written consent from Reuters to use their data.

HTML is a rather poor language to specify the type of data contained on a page. It works well for formatting data, but when it comes to being able to find the data you need, you sometimes have to get a little creative.

Before you can extract the data you require, you must look at the data in its "natural" state. In the example below, the data is fetched from the Reuters page at *www.reuters.com/quote.jhtml* after you search for a quote. Looking at the HTML for the page, you will notice that the quote prices are one line below the "Bid" and "Ask" lines, which are unique to the page. Therefore, you can extract the prices by searching for the unique text.

This script uses another method of reading a file, called the file() function:

```
$file = "/home/me/myfile.txt";
$filearray = file($file);
```

The file() function opens the file, reads the file contents into an array with each line in the file corresponding to an array element, and then closes the file. file() takes one argument, the name of the file you wish to open, including the path if applicable.

Once again, remember to respect copyright notices when using scripts that mine Web pages for data! The result of this script can be seen in Figure 6–2.

SCRIPT 6–2 stockquote.php

```
1. <html>
2. <head><title>Stock Quote Mining</title></head>
3. <body>
4. <form action="stockquote.php">
5. <p>Enter Symbol For Quote: <input type="text" name="symbol">
6. <br><input type="submit" name="submit" value="Fetch Quote">
7. </form>
```

SCRIPT 6–2 stockquote.php (Continued)

```
8.   <hr noshade>
9.   <?
10.  if(isset($symbol)) {
11.      $file = "http://www.reuters.com/quote.jhtml?ticker=";
12.      $contents = file($file . $symbol);
13.      $size = sizeof($contents);
14.      echo "<h3>Quote for $symbol:</h3>";
15.      for($i = 0; $i < $size; $i++) {
16.          $data = strip_tags($contents[$i]);
17.          if(trim($data) == "Ask") {
18.              $quote = strip_tags($contents[$i + 1]);
19.              echo "<P>Ask: $quote";
20.          }
21.          if(trim($data) == "Bid") {
22.              $quote = strip_tags($contents[$i + 1]);
23.              echo "<P>Bid: $quote";
24.          }
25.      }
26.  }
27.  ?>
28.  </body>
29.  </html>
```

Script 6–2 stockquote.php Line-by-Line Explanation

LINE	DESCRIPTION
1–8	Print out the beginning HTML for the page, as well as a form asking for the symbol of the stock for which the user wishes to retrieve a quote.
9	Begin the PHP for the page.
10	Check to see if the $symbol variable has been set. If it has, then execute lines 11–26.
11	Assign the $file variable to the page that has stock quote information.
12	Assign the data opened from the file() function to the $contents variable. The file() function's argument ($file . $symbol) is the URL appended with the stock quote symbol entered by the user. For example, if the user entered "CSCO" (the symbol for Cisco Systems), then the argument is "http://www.reuters.com/quote.jhtml?ticker=CSCO".
13	Get the size of the $contents array. This is used below to loop through each record in the array.
14	Print out a heading.

Script 6–2 stockquote.php Line-by-Line Explanation (Continued)

LINE	DESCRIPTION
15–25	Use a for loop to loop through each record in the array.
16	Strip out the HTML tags from the record retrieved from the array and assign this value to the $data variable.
17	If, after trimming whitespace from $data, the resulting value is "Ask", then we know, after analyzing the page we wish to mine, that the value we are looking for is on the next line. Execute lines 18–20.
18	Get the "Ask" quote from the next line in the array ($contents[$i +1]) and assign it to the quote variable.
19	Echo the "Ask" quote to the page.
20	Close out the if statement started on line 17.
21	If, after trimming whitespace from $data, the resulting value is "Bid", then we know, after analyzing the page we wish to mine, that the value we are looking for is on the next line. Execute lines 22–24.
22	Get the "Bid" quote from the next line in the array ($contents[$i +1]) and assign it to the quote variable.
23	Echo the "Bid" quote to the page.
24	Close out the if statement started on line 21.
25	Close out the for loop started on line 15
26	Close out the if statement started on line 10.
27–29	End the PHP and HTML for the page.

FIGURE 6–2 stockquote.php

Parsing Large Files

The method above works well for relatively simple files, but what if you need to parse a large file with a basic structure that has a few subtle variations? One method is to use the ereg() function[1] to seek out patterns of data.

This next script parses a large text file and places its contents into a database. The file is a list of 789 multiple-choice questions that appear on the FAA's private-pilot written exam.[2]

The document follows a basic structure, in that it has numbered questions followed by three possible answers. Some of the questions reference a figure, while other questions reference multiple figures. The goal of the script is to parse the text file and place each of the questions into a MySQL database, along with the corresponding choices for the answers. If there is a figure, or figures, that is referenced by the question, then the script also places it in the database.

The document is available on the Internet at *av-info.faa.gov/ data/airmanknowledge/par.txt*. The document is very large, and the structure of some questions is slightly different, especially when referenced figures are mentioned.

The script takes the questions and places all of the information in a database, so that it is easier to manage the data and port it into a format usable by other applications.

This script makes use of another regular expression function called preg_split(). preg_split() is able to break up a string into an array, similar to the commonly used explode() function. Instead of breaking up the string based on a character, it breaks up the string based on a regular expression match.

Look at the file at *av-info.faa.gov/data/airmanknowledge/par.txt* to become familiar with the general struture of the data before reading over the script descriptions. Things will seem much more clear.

The script is comprised of three files:

---

1. See Chapter 4 for details on the ereg() function.
2. The questions are not under copyright and are freely available.

- parsefile.sql—The SQL statements required to create and set up the database.
- parsefile.php—The PHP script that parses the text file and places the data into a database.
- displaydata.php—The PHP script that reads the data from the database and displays it to the user. This script is just an example of what you can do with the data once it has been placed in the database.

SCRIPT 6–3 parsefile.sql

```
1.   //mysqladmin create faa
2.
3.   grant ALL on faa.* to php@localhost identified by
     "password";
4.
5.   create table questions(
6.     id INT NOT NULL,
7.     code varchar(8),
8.     question TEXT,
9.     primary key(id));
10.
11.  create table answers(
12.    question INT NOT NULL,
13.    letter CHAR(1),
14.    answer TEXT);
15.
16.  create table figures(
17.    question INT NOT NULL,
18.    figure VARCHAR(3),
19.    additional VARCHAR(24));
20.
21.  create table info(
22.    id INT NOT NULL,
23.    version VARCHAR(8),
24.    date VARCHAR(10),
25.    bank VARCHAR(16));
```

Script 6–3 parsefile.sql Line-by-Line Explanation

LINE	DESCRIPTION
1	Use the mysqladmin command line program to create a database called "faa".
3	Grant the required privileges so that a user can access the database using the username "php" and the password "password".
5–9	Create a table to hold the text of the questions.
11–14	Create a table to hold the answers. There are three answers for each question.
16–19	Create a table to hold any figure references contained in a question.
21–25	Create a table to hold the version and date information for the question bank.

SCRIPT 6–4 parsefile.php

```
1. <?
2. function connect() {
3.     if(!mysql_connect("localhost","php","password")) {
4.         die("<h1>Could Not Connect To MySQL Server</h1>");
5.     } elseif(!mysql_select_db("faa")) {
6.         die("<h1>Could Not Access DB</h1>");
7.     }
8.     return 1;
9. }
10.
11. function parse($data) {
12.     global $question_num;
13.     //IF REFERRING TO A FIGURE, account for inconsistent way
    the FAA labels these
14.     if(ereg("(\(Refer to figure )([0-9]+)(\.\)|(\))\.))",
    $data, $regs)) {
15.         $data2 = preg_split("/(\(Refer to figure )([0-
    9]+)(\.\)|(\))\.))/", $data);
16.         sql_query("insert into figures
    values('$question_num','" . $regs[2] . "', NULL)");
17.         return trim($data2[1]);
18.     //IF REFERRING TO MULTIPLE FIGURES, account for
    inconsistent way FAA labels these
19.     } elseif (ereg("(\(Refer to figures |\(Refer to figure
    )([0-9]+|[0-9]+) (, and |and figure )([0-9]+)(\.)(\))",
    $data, $regs)) {
20.         $data2 = preg_split("/(\(Refer to figures |\(Refer to
    figure )([0-9]+|[0-9]+) (, and |and figure )([0-
    9]+)(\.)(\))/", $data);
```

```
21.    sql_query("insert into figures
    values('$question_num','" . $regs[2] . "', NULL)");
22.    sql_query("insert into figures
    values('$question_num','" . $regs[4] . "', NULL)");
23.    return trim($data2[1]);
24.    //IF REFERRING TO A FIGURE WITH AREA(S), account for
    inconsistent way FAA labels these
25.    } elseif(ereg("(\(Refer to figure )([0-9]+)(, | )([a-zA-
    Z]+)( [ a-zA-Z0-9]+)(\.)(\))", $data, $regs)) {
26.    $data2 = preg_split("/(\(Refer to figure )([0-9]+)(, |
    )([a-zA-Z]+)( [ a-zA-Z0-9]+)(\.)(\))/", $data);
27.    sql_query("insert into figures
    values('$question_num','" . $regs[2] . "', 'area " .
    $regs[5] . "')");
28.    return trim($data2[1]);
29.    //FUNKY SEMICOLON AND MULTIPLE FIGURES AREAS SCREWING
    EVERYTHING UP...
30.    } elseif(ereg("(\(Refer to figure )([0-9]+)(, | )([a-zA-
    Z]+)( [ a-zA-Z0-9]+)(; and figure )([0-9]+)(\.)(\))",
    $data, $regs)) {
31.    $data2 = preg_split("/(\(Refer to figure )([0-9]+)(, |
    )([a-zA-Z]+)( [ a-zA-Z0-9]+)(; and figure )([0-
    9]+)(\.)(\))/", $data);
32.    sql_query("insert into figures
    values('$question_num','" . $regs[2] . "', 'area " .
    $regs[5] . "')");
33.    sql_query("insert into figures
    values('$question_num','" . $regs[7] . "', NULL)");
34.    return trim($data2[1]);
35.    //EVERYTHING ELSE
36.    } else {
37.    return $data;;
38.    }
39. }
40.
41. function sql_query($query){
42.    if(!mysql_query($query)) {
43.      die("<h1>Error with QUERY: $query</h1>");
44.    }
45.    //echo "<P>$query";
46. }
47.
48. /***** MAIN *****/
49. //$file = "http://av-info.faa.gov/data/airmanknowledge/
    par.txt";
```

```
50.  $file = "par.txt";
51.  $contents = file($file);
52.  $size = sizeof($contents);
53.  $questions = "not started";
54.
55.  $answer_let = "A";
56.  $question = "";
57.
58.  connect();
59.  mysql_query("delete from questions");
60.  mysql_query("delete from answers");
61.  mysql_query("delete from figures");
62.  mysql_query("delete from info");
63.  insert into info values ('1',NULL,NULL,NULL);
64.  for($i = 0; $i < $size; $i++) {
65.    if(trim($contents[$i]) != ""){
66.      $data = $contents[$i];
67.      if(ereg("^Version", $data)) {
68.        $versioninfo = explode(":", $data);
69.        $version = trim($versioninfo[1]);
70.        sql_query("update info set version = '$version'
    where id = '1'");
71.      } elseif(ereg("[0-9]+/[0-9]+/[0-9]+", $data)) {
72.        $date = trim($data);
73.        sql_query("update info set date = '$date' where id =
    '1'");
74.      } elseif(ereg("^Bank", $data)) {
75.        $bankinfo = explode(":", $data);
76.        $bank = trim($bankinfo[1]);
77.        sql_query("update info set bank = '$bank' where id =
    '1'");
78.      } elseif(ereg("^[0-9]+\.", $data)) {
79.        if($questions == "started") {
80.          sql_query("update questions set question = '" .
    addslashes($question) . "' where id = '$question_num'");
81.          $question = "";
82.        }
83.        $questions = "started";
84.        $data2 = preg_split("/\s+/", $data);
85.        $question_num = rtrim($data2[0], ".");
86.        $code = $data2[1];
87.        sql_query("insert into questions
    values('$question_num', '$code', NULL)");
88.      }elseif(ereg("(^A\.)|(^B\.)|(^C\.)", $data)) {
```

```
89.        $answer = preg_split("/(^A\.)|(^B\.)|(^C\.)/",
   $data);
90.        sql_query("insert into answers values
   ('$question_num','$answer_let','" . addslashes($answer[1])
   . "')");
91.        $answer_let++;
92.        if($answer_let == "D"){
93.          $answer_let = "A";
94.        }
95.      } else {
96.        if($questions == "started") {
97.          $question .= parse($data);
98.        }
99.      }
100.   }
101. }
102. echo "Operation Completed with No Errors";
103. ?>
```

Script 6–4 parsefile.php Line-by-Line Explanation

LINE	DESCRIPTION
2–9	Define a function, connect(), that is used to establish the connection to the database. Replace the mysql_connect variables with those for your MySQL server.
11–39	Define a function, parse(), that parses the data to extract figure references. Since we may want to hyperlink the figure references to actual figures, we need to parse the data using the ereg() function to look for these figure references in the text. This function takes one argument, $data, which is data that has been read by the main program and established as question data.
12	Allow the $question_num variable to be read by this function.
13	Provide a comment explaining the case that is to follow.
14	If $data matches the ereg() expression, then execute lines 15–17. If not, go on to line 19. This line tries to match the data that has a reference to a figure. Since the text is inconsistent in how it labels figures, we need to use a regular expression match that takes into account several variances found in the text. The regular expression matches against the following (where # is any range of numerals): • (Refer to figure #.) • (Refer to figure #) • (Refer to figure #).

Script 6–4 parsefile.php Line-by-Line Explanation (Continued)

LINE	DESCRIPTION
	Notice also that we use the $regs argument to the ereg() function. The $regs argument, when used with ereg(), causes ereg() to return any matches that occur in the parentheses of the ereg search as items in the $regs array. For example, if the text was "(Refer to Figure 8). How many licks does it take to get to the center…", then ereg() would return the following:
	• $regs[0] = "(Refer to figure 8.) How many licks does it take…" //the complete match • $regs[1] = "(Refer to figure " • $regs[2] = "8" • $regs[3] = ".)"
	Nothing else is returned, because we did not specify anything else within parentheses in the ereg() expression.
15	Since the ereg() function matched on line 14, this line separates the figure reference from the actual question. The preg_split() function, as noted earlier, works like explode(). In this case, it takes the match above and "explodes" it so that $data is broken into two parts. The first part is the figure reference, and the second part is the actual question. If we follow the example of $data being "(Refer to figure 8.) How many licks does it take…", then this line would create an array with two items:
	• $data2[0] = "(Refer to figure 8.)" • $data2[1] = "How many licks does it take…"
16	Place the figure reference into the database using the $question_num variable as a pseudo-foreign key.
17	Return the actual questions, *sans* the figure reference, back to the main program. Since file() breaks the text file into an array based on each line, it is possible that the question spans more than one line, and that a line is only a fragment of the question. The main program concatenates the question parts from each line into a full question and later places the full question into the database.
18	Provide a comment explaining the case that is to follow.
19	This case is much the same as the previous, only it tries to match against questions that have multiple figure references, for example:
	• (Refer to figures # and #) • (Refer to figure # and figure #) • (Refer to figures #, and #)
	Since the text has, at most, two figures per question, we need to extract both of the figure numbers to place in the database. Again we use the $regs argument to ereg(), and by carefully grouping the regular expression with

Script 6–4 parsefile.php Line-by-Line Explanation (Continued)

LINE	DESCRIPTION
	parentheses, we know that the figure number will be found in the second and fourth groupings, $regs[2] and $regs[4].
20	As before, we need to split the text to remove the figure reference from the actual question, using the same regular expression as in the previous line for the split.
21–22	Place the multiple figure references in the database.
23	Return the actual question portion of the data back to the main program for further processing.
24	Provide a comment explaining the case that is to follow.
25	If you looked at the text file, you may have noticed that some questions with figure references also have a specific area of the figure that was to be referenced. This ereg() function takes these area references into account.
26	Split the text to extract the actual question portion.
27	Place the figure reference into the database, along with the area reference to the figure.
28	Return the question to the main program.
29	Provide a colorful comment explaining the case that is to follow.
30	Finally, we take into account multiple figures that include areas, with an odd semicolon or comma thrown in for good measure. This ereg() function matches against text such as the following: • (Refer to figure #, area A; and figure #) • (Refer to figure # area #, and figure #) • (Refer to figure # area A, and #)
31	Once again, split the text to extract the actual question.
32–33	Place the figure/area references into the database.
34	Return the actual question to the main program.
35	Provide a comment explaining the case that is to follow.
36–38	If there is no figure reference, then we assume that the remaining data is just lines of the question and return it to the main program to be appended to the other parts of the question that have already been sent.
39	End the function declaration.

Script 6–4 parsefile.php Line-by-Line Explanation (Continued)

LINE	DESCRIPTION
41–46	Define a function, sql_query(), that attempts to send the query to the database. If there is an error, the script is killed. There is an echo line that is commented out. Uncomment this line if you'd like the query statements to be printed to the browser.
48	Begin the main program.
49–50	Define the $file variable that will be used to open the file. Each of these lines does the same thing. If you copied the file to your local machine, then uncomment line 50 and comment line 49. If you have a fast connection to the Internet, do the opposite.
51	Use the file() function to read the contents of $file into an array.
52	Determine how many lines are in the file by seeing how many records are in the array.
53	Define a variable, $questions, and assign it the value "not started". This is done because there is some extraneous information at the beginning of the file that must be parsed over before we can start parsing the questions themselves.
55	Define a variable, $answer_let, and assign it the value of "A". This is used to track the letter of the current answer (A, B, or C).
56	Define a variable, $question, and give it a blank value. This will be used to hold and append the question fragments as they are read from the file.
58	Establish a connection to the database using the connect() function.
59–62	Execute queries to delete the contents of the database. Since the database is only designed to hold one version of questions at a time, you must ensure that there is no existing data in the database.
63	Insert a "default" row into the info table as a placeholder.
64–102	Loop through each line in the text file and parse it.
65	If the line is not blank, then continue. Otherwise, go to line 101.
66	Assign the value of the current line ($contents[$i]) to the $data variable to save some typing.
67–70	If the line starts with "Version", then explode the line on the ":" character, trim any whitespace, and place the version number of the test bank into the database by sending the SQL to the sql_query() function.
71–73	If the line contains a date format—for example, "6/11/2002"—then trim the whitespace around the text and place it into the database.
74–77	If the line starts with "Bank", then explode the line on the ":" character, trim any whitespace, and place the bank information in the database.

Script 6–4 parsefile.php Line-by-Line Explanation (Continued)

LINE	DESCRIPTION
78	If the line begins with a number immediately followed by a period, then we know, from studying the text, that it is a question number. Continue through line 87.
79–82	If the $question variable has been set to started, then we know we have some question data already assembled. Place that question in the database and clear the text from our $question variable, since we will be placing a new question in that variable.
83	Set the $questions variable to started (it may already be set that way, but if this is the first question encountered, it has not been).
84	Split the current line up along any whitespace. The initial line for a question looks like this: "1. A01 PVT" This breaks the line into three array elements and assigns it to the $data2 variable.
85	Get the question number from the $data2 array, trim off the trailing period, and assign it to the $question_num variable.
86	Get the question code from the $data2 variable and assign it to the $code variable.
87	Insert the question number and code into the database. We leave the actual question part out at this time and only place a NULL into the database in its place. A little later, we'll put the complete question in, since it spans multiple lines.
88	If the line begins with an "A.", "B.", or "C.", then we know that this is one of the multiple choice answers to the question. Continue to line 95.
89	Split the answer letter from the actual answer by using the preg_split() function.
90	Insert the answer into the database using the question number as a foreign key. Use the $answer_let variable as the answer letter.
91	Increment the $answer_let variable, since we know the next answer letter is going to be one more than the current.
92–94	If the $answer_let variable is "D", then set it back to "A", since we know each question only has three possible answers, "A", "B", or "C".
95–99	If none of the above has matched, then we know we have an actual question, since it is not preceded by any of the above matches. Send this part of the text to be parsed by the parse() function.
100	End the if statement started on line 65.
101	End the for loop started on line 64.

Script 6–4 parsefile.php Line-by-Line Explanation (Continued)

LINE	DESCRIPTION
102	If we've made it this far without the script dying, then we know that no errors have occurred. Print out a message telling yourself so!
103	End the PHP for the script. Now run displaydata.php to see the result of your labor.

This next script, shown in Figure 6–3, merely displays what we have put in the database. It's just a quick example to show you how thoroughly parsefile.php parsed the large text document.

SCRIPT 6–5 displaydata.php

```
1.    <html>
2.    <head><title>Display Parsed File From Database</title>
3.    <style type=text/css>
4.    h1, h2, h3, p, td, a {font-family: verdana, arial,
      helvetica, sans-serif;}
5.    .navy {color: navy; }
6.    </style>
7.    </head>
8.    <body>
9.    <?
10.
11.   function connect() {
12.     if(!mysql_connect("localhost","php","password")) {
13.        die("<h1>Could not connect to MySQL Server</h1>");
14.     } elseif(!mysql_select_db("faa")) {
15.        die("<h1>Could Not Access DB</h1>");
16.     }
17.     return 1;
18.   }
19.
20.   function display($sql) {
21.     $color = "#FFFFFF";
22.     connect();
23.     $result = mysql_query($sql);
24.     while($row = mysql_fetch_array($result)) {
25.        $question_num = $row['id'];
26.        echo "<tr bgcolor=\"$color\"><td class=navy>" .
      $question_num . "</td><td><pre>" .
      stripslashes($row['question'] . "</pre>");
27.        $sql2 = "select * from figures where question =
      '$question_num' order by figure";
```

SCRIPT 6–5 displaydata.php (Continued)

```
28.        $result2 = mysql_query($sql2);
29.        if(mysql_num_rows($result2) > 0) {
30.          while($row2 = mysql_fetch_array($result2)) {
31.            echo "<br>See Figure: " . $row2['figure'] . " "
      . $row2['additional'];
32.          }
33.        }
34.        echo "</td></tr>";
35.        $sql3 = "select * from answers where question =
      '$question_num' order by letter";
36.        $result3 = mysql_query($sql3);
37.        while($row3 = mysql_fetch_array($result3)) {
38.          echo "<tr bgcolor=\"$color\"><td colspan=2>";
39.          echo $row3['letter'] . ". " .
      stripslashes($row3['answer']);
40.          echo "</td></tr>";
41.        }
42.        if($color == "#FFFFFF") {
43.          $color = "#FFFF80";
44.        } else {
45.          $color= "#FFFFFF";
46.        }
47.        echo "</td></tr>";
48.        flush();
49.      }
50.    }
51.    ?>
52.    <table border=1 cellspacing=0 cellpadding=5>
53.    <?
54.    if(!isset($next)) {
55.      $sql = "select * from questions limit 0, 200";
56.      $next = 0;
57.    } else {
58.      $sql = "select * from questions order by id limit
      $next, 200";
59.    }
60.    display($sql);
61.    $next += 200;
62.    ?>
63.    </table>
64.    <p><a href="displaydata.php?next=<?=$next?>">Next 200
      Questions</a>
65.    </body>
66.    </html>
```

Script 6–5 displaydata.php Line-by-Line Explanation

LINE	DESCRIPTION
1–9	Print out the beginning HTML for the script, including some style sheet formatting.
11–18	Define a function, connect(), to connect to the database.
20–50	Define a function, display(), that displays the data in the database. The display() function takes one argument, $sql, which is the initial SQL statement used to display a set number of questions.
21	Initialize the $color variable. This is used to alternate colors for each of the questions to make the page more readable.
22	Connect to the database using the connect() function.
23	Generate an SQL result using the $sql variable that was passed to the function.
24–34	Display the question and any figure references associated with the question.
35–41	Display the answers to the associated question.
42–46	Change the $color variable so that it is the opposite of the current color.
47	Close out the row.
48	Flush content to the browser so a timeout does not occur.
49	End the while loop started on line 24.
50	End the function declaration.
51	Get out of PHP mode for a moment.
52	Print out the beginning of a table.
53	Get back into PHP mode.
54–56	If the $next variable has not been set, then create an SQL statement to display the first 200 questions in the test bank and set $next to ")" to initialize it.
57–59	If the $next variable has been set, then we know the user has pushed the "Next..." link at the bottom of the page. Create an SQL statement to show the next 200 questions, depending on what questions they have already seen.
60	Execute the display() function using the generated SQL from the previous lines.
61	Increment the $next variable.
62	Get out of PHP mode again.
63	Close the table.
64	Print a link to display the next 200 questions in the bank.
65–66	Close out the HTML for the page.

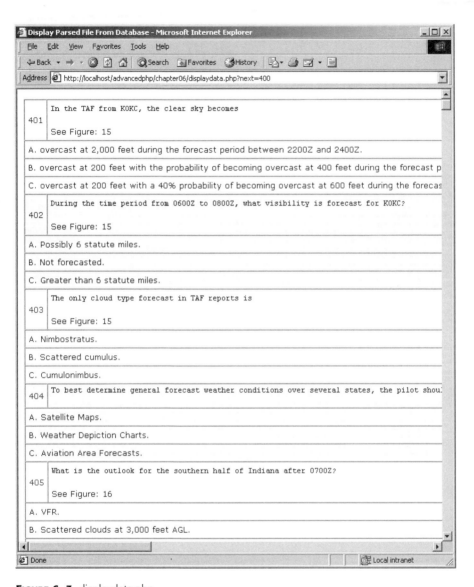

FIGURE 6–3 displaydata.php

7

PHP Authentication Schemes

User Authentication Overview

If you've ever built a Web site that requires user registration, then you have some idea of what is required to restrict access so that you can be sure the user who is registered is the same user who is currently accessing the site. In almost all cases, you must require the user to enter some sort of login and password to gain access to the site.

The current trend in site registration seems to be to require the users to enter their email as part of the registration process, and then subsequently send the users' password to them using that email address. This provides a number of benefits. First, you have the user's email and you know it is at least semivalid, since the user cannot gain access to the site without first submitting an email address and being sent a password. If users forget their passwords, you can easily send it to them (or a hint, if you require one) using some simple code. Additionally, you are able to send updates to users about site features, special events, etc., and you know the updates are going to valid addresses. On a side note, if you do send email to users, you should always ask their permission first in an open "opt-in" method. Additionally, you should provide an automated way for users to unsubscribe by clicking a link in the email you do send. Spam is a problem; let's not contribute to this ever-worsening problem.

Another advantage of requiring an email address is the ability to use it as the user's login. Email addresses must be unique, and only the valid holder of the email is able to receive any passwords that you send. This solves the problem of unique logins for every user. You do not have to write error-checking into your code that suggests alternative login names should one already be taken.

These authentication methods are for casual sites. They should not be used to protect sensitive information, such as social security numbers, credit card numbers, or anything that you wouldn't leave sitting on the street corner. There are ways to get around these methods, be it from hacking, IP spoofing, or good old brute force. However, these methods do work well for community sites where basic authentication is required and there is little to gain from spending hours upon hours in cracking attempts. A malicous hacker has lots to gain when credit cards are on the line, but when the reward is only a user's list of favorite links, there is little incentive to spend the effort required to crack a system. Simply put, don't assume that your information is safe by placing it solely behind a PHP authentication solution.

This chapter goes in depth into some of the above scenarios, as well as some additional ones, such as restricting logins to one domain or even a range of IP addresses.

Generating Passwords

The md5() and crypt() functions encrypt passwords, but they cannot be unencrypted. These are one-way algorithms. You can verify that the users' password matches the password they were initially given by comparing the md5() or crypt() output of the password they use to subsequently enter the site. The two encrypted versions of the same string match (assuming that the same "salt" is used to create the password using the crypt() function).

This is good, because you never store a user's actual password. If your password file falls into the wrong hands, there is little that anybody can do with it. It is very hard to unencrypt a password encrypted by md5() or crypt(). Since you don't store the user's actual password, malicious hackers who may get their hands on your password file can't take that password and easily use it to attempt to break into other sites that your user may visit, since, unfortunately, most people don't use a different password for every site they visit.

Later scripts in this chapter assume that you have already created some sort of file containing usernames and passwords. The general convention for storing passwords in text files is to put one username/password combination on each line, and to separate the user and password with a colon. For example:

```
user1:sih2hDu1acVcA
user2:aSP2C8UUWnxjA
```

The first script in this chapter creates an md5() encrypted password and a crypt() encrypted password for any string you enter. As shown in Figure 7–1, you can use this script to easily generate encrypted passwords and display them on the screen so that you can copy and paste them into a text file. The crypt() encrypted password generated from the script is the same as encrypting a password using Apache's htpasswd program.

SCRIPT 7–1 generating_passwords.php

```
1.  <html>
2.  <head>
3.  <title>Password Creator</title>
```

```
4.   </head>
5.   <body>
6.   <form action=generate_passwords.php method=post>
7.   <h3>Enter a password to create MD5 and Crypt based
     passwords.</h3>
8.   Password: <input type="text" name="password">
9.   <input type="submit" name="create" value="Create
     Passwords!">
10.  </form>
11.  <?
12   if(isset($password)) {
13.     ?>
14.     <h3>The passwords for the string "<?=$password?>"
        are:</h3>
15.     <ul>
16.     <li><b>MD5:</b> <?=md5($password)?>
17.     <li><b>Crypt:</b> <?=crypt($password)?>
18.     </ul>
19.     <?
20.  }
21.  ?>
22   </body>
23.  </html>
```

Script 7–1 generating_passwords.php Line-by-Line Explanation

LINE	DESCRIPTION
1–10	Create an HTML form with one text input field, named "password," and a submit button.
11	Start parsing the page as PHP.
12	Check to see if the $password variable has been set. If it has, continue to line 13; if not, continue on line 20.
13–19	Stop parsing the page as PHP. Print out the values of the password after it has been encrypted by the md5() and crypt() functions. Start parsing the page as PHP again.
20	End the if statement started on line 12.
21	Stop parsing the page as PHP.
23	Print out the closing HTML for the page.

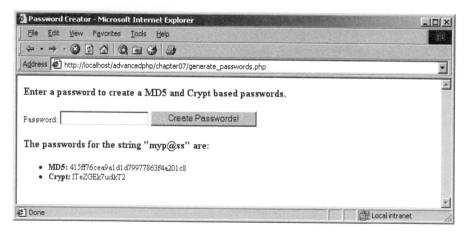

FIGURE 7–1 generating_passwords.php

Authenticating Users Against Text Files

Not all sites contain a database back-end to store data, and some sites probably will never require them. Still, you may want to limit access to certain parts of the site or even the entire site. One way to do this is to authenticate against a text file stored someplace on the server, preferably out of the Web server directory so that there is no way it can be accessed by someone with a Web browser.

This method only requires the standard file functions, as well as the MD5 encryption function.

This script serves a dual purpose. It allows you to add users to a password file, as well as test authentication. This way, you can create a blank text file and easily fill it with some username/password combinations so that you can test the functionality of the script.

This script is not meant to be used in its entirety to check passwords on a site. You would need to remove the functions that allow you to add users before you placed the script in your own site.

SCRIPT 7–2 file_authentication.php

```
1.   <?
2.   $password_file = "C:/apache/passwords/pass.txt";
3.
4.   function check_pass($login, $password) {
5.      global $password_file;
6.      if(!$fh = fopen($password_file, "r")) {die("<P>Could
     Not Open Password File");}
7.      $match = 0;
8.      $password = md5($password);
9.      while(!feof($fh)) {
10.        $line = fgets($fh, 4096);
11.        $user_pass = explode(":", $line);
12.        if($user_pass[0] == $login) {
13.           if(rtrim($user_pass[1]) == $password) {
14.              $match = 1;
15.              break;
16.           }
17.        }
18.     }
19.     if($match) {
20.        return 1;
21.     } else {
22.        return 0;
23.     }
24.     fclose($fh);
25.  }
26.
27.  function print_login_form($login) {
28.     ?>
29.     <p>Please Log In:
30.     <form action=file_authentication.php method=post>
31.     <p>Login: <input type="text" name="login"
     value="<?=$login?>">
32.     <br>Password: <input type="password" name="password">
33.     <br><input type="submit" name="checkpass" value="Login!">
34.     </form>
35.     <?
36.  }
37.
38.  function print_add_form() {
39.     ?>
40.     <p>Add New User:
41.     <form action=file_authentication.php method=post>
42.     <p>Login: <input type="text" name="adduser">
43.     <br>Password: <input type="password" name="addpass">
```

```
44.    <br><input type="submit" name="add" value="Add User!">
45.    </form>
46.    <?
47.  }
48.
49.  function add_user($adduser, $addpass) {
50.    global $password_file;
51.    if(!$fh = fopen($password_file, "a+")) { die("<P>Could
Not Open Password File"); }
52.    rewind($fh);
53.    while(!feof($fh)) {
54.      $line = fgets($fh, 4096);
55.      $user_pass = explode(":", $line);
56.      if($user_pass[0] == $adduser) {
57.        echo "<h2>Duplicate Login. Invalid!</h2>";
58.        return 0;
59.      }
60.    }
61.    $add = $adduser . ":" . md5($addpass) . "\n";
62.    if(!fwrite($fh, $add)) { die("<P>Could Not Write To
Password File"); }
63.    fclose($fh);
64.    echo"<h2>User Added!</h2>";
65.  }
66.  /***** MAIN *****/
67.  if(isset($checkpass)) {
68.      if(check_pass($login, $password)) {
69.        echo "<h2>Login Success!</h2>";
70.      } else {
71.        echo "<h2>Login Failed</h2><p>Bad username or
password. Login and Password are case-sensitive. Try
again:";
72.      print_login_form($login);
73.      }
74.  } elseif(isset($add_form)) {
75.    print_add_form();
76.  } elseif(isset($add)) {
77.    add_user($adduser, $addpass);
78.  } else {
79.    print_login_form("");
80.  }
81.  ?>
82.  <p>You can <a href=file_authentication.php?add_form=1>Add
Users</a> or <a href=file_authentication.php>login</a> an
existing user.
```

Script 7–2 file_authentication.php Line-by-Line Explanation

LINE	DESCRIPTION
2	Define the file that contains the passwords. Note that you should specify the correct path on your machine that points to the password file. On *nix-based systems, you'd obviously omit the "C:\" nonsense in the path.
4	Create a function that checks the user-entered password against the username/password combination stored in the password file.
5	Allow the password file to be read and modified globally by this function.
6	Attempt to open the file and assign it to a file pointer. If the file cannot be opened, then print an error and exit from the script.
7	Initialize a variable to track a username/password match. Initialize it to false (0) to assume the password is incorrect.
8	Since the passwords are stored encrypted, encrypt the user-entered password using the MD5 function.
9–18	Create a while loop that searches through the file until the end of file (EOF) is reached.
10	For each iteration of the loop, get one line from the file and place it in the $line variable.
11	Create an array of the line obtained from the file using the explode function. Since the usernames and passwords are stored in the format: `USER:PASS` and the explode() function breaks up the line on every ":", the script places two items into the $user_pass array: the username at index [0] and the password at index [1].
12	Check if the username from the file, which is stored in $user_pass[0], matches the username entered by the user, $login.
13	If the user-entered username matches the username obtained from the file, then check to see if the password from the file, $user_pass[1], matches the password entered by the user, $password.
14	If the passwords match, then set the $match variable to true (1), since the user-entered username and password match the ones contained in the password file.
15	If the passwords match, then break from the loop.
16	Close out the password-checking if statement.
17	Close out the username-checking if statement.
18	Close out the while loop.

Script 7–2 file_authentication.php Line-by-Line Explanation (Continued)

LINE	DESCRIPTION
19–20	If there was a match, then return true to the calling program or function.
21–23	If there was no match, then return false to the calling program or function.
24	Close the file.
25	End the function declaration.
27	Create a function that prints a login form to the screen. The function takes one argument, called $login, which is used to automatically re-enter the username if there was no match from a previous attempt at logging in.
28	Stop parsing the page as PHP.
29–30	Begin displaying the login form.
31	Print the username field. If this is a subsequent attempt to log in, then automatically enter the username.
32–34	Continue printing the form to the page.
35	Start parsing the page as PHP again.
36	End the function declaration.
38	Create a function that prints a form allowing you to add username/password combinations to the password file.
39–46	Stop parsing the page as PHP and print out a standard HTML form, then continue parsing the page as PHP.
47	End the function declaration.
49	Create a function that adds a username and password combination to the password file. The function takes two arguments: $adduser and $addpass.
50	Allow the password file to be read and modified globally by this function.
51	Attempt to open the file and assign it to a file pointer. If the file cannot be opened, then print an error and exit from the script.
52	Since we opened the file using append mode ("a+") on line 51, rewind the file so that the file pointer is at the beginning of the file. The append mode places the file pointer at the end of the file by default.
53–60	Create a while loop that searches through the file until the end of file (EOF) is reached.
54	For each iteration of the loop, get one line from the file and place it in the $line variable.

Script 7–2 file_authentication.php Line-by-Line Explanation (Continued)

LINE	DESCRIPTION
55	Create an array of the line obtained from the file using the explode function.
56	Check to see if the username stored in $user_pass[0] is the same as the username entered into the Add User form. Usernames should always be unique! This line checks to make sure that a duplicate username is not being entered into the password file.
57	If the usernames match, then you are trying to enter a duplicate username. Print out a message to the users informing them that the username they entered is invalid.
58	Return false to the calling program or function.
61	Since this line has been reached, it means that the username entered was unique (if it was not, then the function would have terminated with the return on line 58). Create a username/password combination by prepending the username to the MD5 encrypted form of the password. A colon is placed in between the two so that the script can parse easily when it checks usernames and passwords. Colons do not occur as output in MD5 encryption, so they are safe characters to use to delimit the two values. (Note that the script doesn't forbid colons in the usernames, which would cause user authentication to always fail if a user placed a colon in a username.)
62	Attempt to write the new username/password combination to the end of the file. You know you are at the end of the file, since the while loop just parsed the entire file. If the write attempt fails, then display an error and kill the script.
63	Close the file.
64	Print a message letting the user know the password was added to the password file.
65	End the function declaration.
66	Begin the main file execution.
67	Check to see if the $checkpass variable has been set. If it is set, this means that the login form was submitted to the script.
68	If the $checkpass variable is set, run the check_pass() function using the user-entered username and password.
69	If the check_pass() function returns true (1), notify the user that authentication succeeded. At this point, you would normally display the content that you were protecting with the user authentication.
70–73	If the check_pass() function returned false, then print a message informing the user of the error.

Script 7–2 file_authentication.php Line-by-Line Explanation (Continued)

LINE	DESCRIPTION
74–75	If the $checkpass variable is not set, but the $add_form variable is set, then print out the form to allow you to add new username/password combinations to the password file.
76–77	If the $checkpass variable is not set and the $add_form variable is not set, but the $add variable is set, then run the add_user function using the values entered into the Add User form.
78–79	If none of the above is true, then print the login form using a null value as the argument so that the login_form function does not generate a warning about use of an uninitialized variable.
81	Stop parsing the page as PHP.
82	Print a line to the browser that provides two links. The first is a link that sets the add_form variable so that the add_form function is called and you can add username/password combinations to the password file. The second link is used to display the login form after you have added a user.

Authenticating Users by IP Address

In some rare instances, you may wish to limit access to a certain page or pages to certain IP addresses. It may be because you have an internal network that has a publicly viewable Web site. You may wish to have certain pages be viewable only by certain machines on the internal network.

Or it may be that you have your own remote Web site, and you wish to restrict access to a certain page or pages so that only you, from a static IP address, can access those pages.

These methods work by determining the IP address of the user trying to view the page and checking it against a set value. If the IP address matches, then the page can be viewed.

Note that this method could be fooled by IP spoofing or other hacks, and should not be used to protect sensitive information, such as credit card numbers, proprietary information, or the like. It is a simple method that can protect pages from the majority of users surfing the net.

When using this script, you should be aware that your computer may have more than one IP address, and that the one your browser is reporting to the script may not be the same one you are attempting to verify against. This is especially true when the browser and Web server reside on the same machine, as you will probably encounter when testing the script.

For example, computers have a default local IP address of 127.0.0.1, otherwise known as "localhost." When I start up the Web server and type in "http://localhost", my browser is telling the script that I am at the IP address of 127.0.0.1. However, the Web browser on my computer is also running on the IP address 192.168.0.1 (an IP address used for an internal network). If I type in the IP address 192.168.0.1, my Web browser reports that I am at 192.168.0.1, but the script only accepts the IP address of 127.0.0.1! If you run into problems, try echoing the value of $REMOTE_ADDR to the screen to see which IP address your browser is reporting to the script.

SCRIPT 7–3 IP_authentication.php

```
1.   <?
2.   $accept = array ("127", "0", "0", "1");
3.   $remote = explode(".", $REMOTE_ADDR);
4.   $match = 1;
5.   for($i = 0; $i < sizeof($accept); $i++) {
6.      if($remote[$i] != $accept[$i]) {
7.         $match = 0;
8.      }
9.   }
10.  if($match) {
11.     echo "<h2>Access Granted!</h2>";
12.  } else {
13.     echo "<h2>Access Forbidden</h2>";
14.  }
15.  ?>
```

Script 7–3 IP_authentication.php Line-by-Line Explanation

LINE	DESCRIPTION
2	Define an array of the acceptable IP address(es) ranges that can view the page. The array must have at least one item. You can restrict by IP subnets by adding more or fewer items to the array. For example: array("192","168","0","1") limits the users who can view the page to the user with the IP address of 192.168.0.1. array("192","168","0") limits the users who can view the page to the users with an IP address in the range of 192.168.0.1 to 192.168.0.255. array("192","168") limits the users who can view the page to the users with an IP address in the range of 192.168.0.1 to 192.168.255.255. array("192") allows anybody with an IP that starts with 192 to view the page. Not very practical, but it would work!
3	Create an array of numbers based on the user's IP address by exploding the $REMOTE_ADDR global variable on the periods in the IP address.
4	Define a variable, $match, and set it to true (1).
5–9	Loop through the acceptable IP address array.
6	Compare the acceptable IP address segment with the IP address segment of the user's browser.
7	If the IP address segments do not match, then set the $match variable to false (0).
8	Close the if statement.
9	Close the for loop.
10–11	If $match is true, then allow access and print a message to the user. This is where you would present your protected content.
12–14	If $match is false (0), then print out a message telling the users that they cannot access the page and exit from the script.
15	Close the if statement started on line 10.

Authenticating Users Using HTTP Authentication

PHP has some built-in support for basic "HTTP Authentication." HTTP authentication is the type of authentication in which a small window pops up in front of the browser prompting you for a username and password. Figure 7–2 and Figure 7–3 show HTTP Authentication windows in Internet Explorer and Mozilla for Linux, respectively. HTTP authentication is server-dependent, the most common example of which is

FIGURE 7-2
HTTP Authentication Login
Window in Internet Explorer

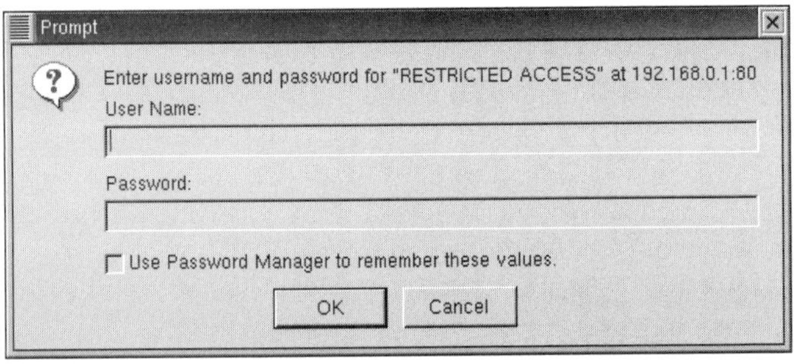

FIGURE 7-3 HTTP Authentication Window in Mozilla on Linux

Apache's HTTP authentication method. The methods described here assume you are using an Apache server.

Typically, the HTTP Authentication method under Apache is defined in .htaccess files.[1] A .htaccess file usually restricts an entire directory. However, PHP provides a way to use Apache based HTTP Authentication without having to define .htaccess files for the same type of authentication. Additionally, you can easily use PHP's HTTP Authentication method on a per page basis.

Using the PHP method, you can also use your own password scheme. Under Apache, you typically placed encrypted passwords in a password file (usually called .htpasswd). Using the PHP method, you can place your passwords in a file, in a

---

1. Complete details are available at *http://httpd.apache.org/docs/howto/ auth.html.*

database, or any other method. You can also use any encryption scheme you want, whereas Apache is restricted to UNIX crypted passwords, their own flavor of MD5 passwords, or plain text.

However, if users forget their passwords, you cannot send it to them, because you only know the encrypted version. You either have to reset the password or provide a hint for the password that may help the users remember what it is they used for the password. More on this later in the chapter.

The next script in this chapter details how to use PHP's method of HTTP Authentication with an Apache server. The script also allows you to use passwords encrypted with the crypt() function (which are portable and can be used with Apache's default HTTP Authentication method) or use the basic PHP md5() function to encrypt passwords. The latter option is useful if you already have several applications that use MD5 encryption for passwords.

SCRIPT 7–4 http_authentication.php

```
1.  <?
2.  function check_pass($login, $password, $mode) {
3.     global $password_file;
4.     if(!$fh = fopen($password_file, "r")) { die("<P>Could
    Not Open Password File"); }
5.     $match = 0;
6.     while(!feof($fh)) {
7.        $line = fgets($fh, 4096);
8.        $from_file = explode(":", $line);
9.        if($from_file[0] == $login) {
10.          if($mode == "crypt"){
11.             $salt = substr($from_file[1],0,2);
12.             $user_pass = crypt($password,$salt);
13.          } elseif ($mode == "md5") {
14.             $user_pass = md5($password);
15.          }
16.          if(rtrim($from_file[1]) == $user_pass) {
17.             $match = 1;
18.             break;
19.          }
20.       }
21.    }
22.    if($match) {
```

SCRIPT 7–4 http_authentication.php (Continued)

```
23.        return 1;
24.    } else {
25.        return 0;
26.    }
27.    fclose($fh);
28. }
29. function authenticate() {
30.    Header("WWW-Authenticate: Basic realm=\"RESTRICTED
    ACCESS\"");
31.    Header("HTTP/1.0 401 Unauthorized");
32.    echo ("<h1>INVALID USERNAME OR PASSWORD. ACCESS
    DENIED<h1>");
33.    exit;
34. }
35. /*** MAIN ***/
36. //select md5 or crypt for $mode. md5 is for md5 encoded
    passwords, crypt is for passwords encoded using apache's
    httpasswd
37. $mode = "md5";
38. $password_file = "C:/apache/passwords/pass.txt";
39. if (!isset($PHP_AUTH_USER)) {
40.    authenticate();
41. } else {
42.    if(check_pass($PHP_AUTH_USER, $PHP_AUTH_PW, $mode)) {
43.        ?>
44.        <h1>ACCEPTED</h1>
45.        <?
46.    } else {
47.    authenticate();
48.    }
49. }
50. ?>
```

Script 7–4 http_authentication.php Line-by-Line Explanation

LINE	DESCRIPTION
2	Define a function called check_pass() that takes three arguments: • $login—the user-entered username. • $password—the user-entered password. • $mode—the encryption mode used in the password file, "md5" or "crypt."
3	Allow $password_file to be used globally by this function.

Script 7–4 http_authentication.php Line-by-Line Explanation (Continued)

LINE	DESCRIPTION
4	Attempt to open the file in read mode and assign a file handle to it. If the file cannot be opened, then print an error and kill the script.
5	Define the variable $match and set it to false (0).
6–21	Create a for loop that loops through the file until the EOF is reached.
7	Read in one line from the file.
8	Explode the contents of the line into an array called $from_file. This should create an array with two items. The first is the username, and the second is the password.
9	If the first element in the array (the username) matches the user-entered username ($login), continue to line 10. Otherwise, go back to line 6 and loop again.
10	Check to see if the $mode variable that was passed to this function is "crypt." If it is, continue to line 11. Otherwise, go to line 13.
11	Define the salt required by the crypt() function. This script can be used with Apache htpasswd generated passwords, so it has to use Apache's method of using crypt()s, which is to use the first two characters of the encrypted password as the salt. This line uses the substr() function to pull out the first two characters from the password obtained from the file and place the value in the $salt variable.
12	Encrypt the user-entered password with the crypt() function using the salt obtained from the previous line. Continue to line 16.
13	Check to see if the $mode variable that was passed to this function is "md5". If it is, continue to line 14. **Note:** The function assumes that $mode is either "crypt" or "md5". If it is neither, then the script loops through the entire file without checking anything and returns no matches, which in turn means that authentication fails. It may be useful to print an error message that $mode was not set to either of the required values, but that won't help a user who is trying to access your site. For debugging, you may want to optionally add another else statement that states that $mode was neither "crypt" nor "md5".
14	Encrypt the user-entered password with the md5() function. Continue to line 16.
16–17	Trim any whitespace from the password obtained from the file and compare it to the encrypted version of the user-entered password. If they match, then set the $match variable to true (1).
18	Break out of the loop, since you found a valid match.

Script 7–4 http_authentication.php Line-by-Line Explanation (Continued)

LINE	DESCRIPTION
19	Close the if statement that checks the password.
20	Close the if statement that checks the username.
21	Close the for loop.
22–23	If $match is true (1), then return true.
24–26	If $match is false(0), then return false.
27	Close the file.
28	End the function declaration.
29	Create a function called authenticate() to display the HTTP Authentication login screen to users if they have not been previously authenticated.
30–31	Use the header() function to send authentication headers to a user's browser. Line 30 attempts to obtain the username/password from the user. Line 31 is executed if the users have already submitted their username/password combination and there was no corresponding match in the password file.
32	Print a message to the screen notifying the users that their username/password combination is invalid.
33	Exit from the script.
34	End the function declaration.
35	Begin the main program.
36	Include a comment in the script as to the nature of the $mode variable.
37	Assign the $mode variable the value "md5" (or "crypt" if your passwords are encrypted using the crypt() function).
38	Assign the location of the password file to the $password_file variable.
39	Check to see if the global variable $PHP_AUTH_USER has been set. $PHP_AUTH_USER is a special PHP variable that is used with HTTP Authentication. This is the variable that is obtained when the user logs in using the HTTP Authentication window.
40	If $PHP_AUTH_USER variable has not been set, then execute the authenticate() function.
41–42	If the $PHP_AUTH_USER variable has been set, then execute the check_pass() function using the $PHP_AUTH_USER, $PHP_AUTH_PW, and $mode variables as arguments. The $PHP_AUTH_PW variable is the special PHP global variable obtained from the HTTP Authentication login window.

Script 7–4 http_authentication.php Line-by-Line Explanation (Continued)

LINE	DESCRIPTION
43–45	If the check_pass() function returns true (1), then print out "ACCEPTED" to the screen. You would normally provide your protected content here.
46–48	If the check_pass() function returns false, execute the authenticate() function again. The users have three chances to correctly enter their username and password. After the third failure, the script returns lines 31 and 32.
49	Close the if statement started on line 39.
50	End the script.

Authenticating Users by Database Query

The most common method of authentication for database-backed sites is to use the database. Why bother with clunky text files when you have the speed and ease of an SQL database at your fingertips?

Database-based authentication can use the same features as file-based authentication, such as md5() or crypt() encryption. Usernames and passwords are stored in a table on the database. You can store other information in this table as well, such as email addresses or first and last names, as you saw in the example applications in Chapter 5.

This next script provides a bare-bones approach to using a database to authenticate users. It uses plain-text passwords, but you can easily include encrypted passwords using the techniques from the earlier scripts in this chapter.

SCRIPT 7–5 DB_authenticate.php

```
1.  <?
2.
3.  /* SQL REQUIRED FOR THIS SCRIPT *****
4.  create table users (
5.    id INT NOT NULL,
6.    username VARCHAR(16),
7.    password VARCHAR(8),
8.    primary key(id));
9.  *****/
10.
11. function connect() {
```

```
12.    if(!$db =
    @mssql_pconnect("localhost","mssqluser","password")){
13.        print("<h1>Cannot Connect to the DB!</h1>\n");
14.        return 0;
15.    } else {
16.        mssql_select_db("php", $db);
17.        return 1;
18.    }
19.  }
20.
21.  function check_user($user, $password) {
22.    if(connect()) {
23.        $password = substr($password, 0, 8);
24.        $sql = "select * from users where username = '$user'
    and password = '$password'";
25.        $result = mssql_query($sql);
26.        if (mssql_num_rows($result) == 1) {
27.          setcookie("user",$user);
28.          setcookie("password",$password);
29.          return 1;
30.        } else {
31.          ?>
32.          <h3>Sorry, you are not authorized!</h3>
33.          <?
34.          return 0;
35.        }
36.    }
37.  }
38.
39.  /***** MAIN *****/
40.  if(!isset($user) or !check_user($user, $password)) {
41.    ?>
42.    <h1>You must log in to view this page</h1>
43.    <form action = "DB_authenticate.php" method="post">
44.    <P>Username: <input type="text" name="user"><br>
45.    Password: <input type="password" name="password"
    maxlength="8" size="8"><br>
46.    <input type="submit" name="submit" value="Submit">
47.    </form>
48.    <?
49.  } else {
50.    ?>
51.    <h1>Authorized!</h1>
```

```
52.    <?
53.    }
54.    ?>
```

Script 7–5 DB_authenticate.php Line-by-Line Explanation

LINE	DESCRIPTION
3–9	These lines provide the SQL statement to use to create a database table that works with this script. Once you have created your table, you can add users using standard SQL statements such as:
	`insert into users values (1, 'username','password');`
	Keep in mind that you need a unique ID for each user that you add.
11	Create a function called connect(). This function is used to create a connection to the database.
12	Attempt to connect to the database, in this case an MS SQL database. (You can replace all the MS SQL functions with MySQL functions simply by changing the first "s" in mssql to a "y"—"mysql".)
13	If the script cannot connect to the database, then print an error.
14	Return false (0) to the calling program, because the database connection failed.
16	If the connection attempt was successful, then select the database on the database server that the script will use.
17	Return true (1) to the calling program, because the connection was successful.
18	Close the if statement started on line 12.
19	End the function declaration.
21	Create a function caller check_user() that checks the user-entered username and password against a valid username and password that is stored in a database. The script takes as arguments $user and $password, both entered by a user through a login form.
22	Attempt to connect to the database using the connect function. If the connection succeeds, then continue to line 23. Otherwise, go to line 36, which is the end of the function.
23	Modify the user-entered password so that it matches the format used by the database. In this case, the script just truncates the password to eight characters. You may want to use one of the md5() or crypt() functions here if you stored encrypted passwords in your database.

Script 7–5 DB_authenticate.php Line-by-Line Explanation (Continued)

LINE	DESCRIPTION
24	Generate an SQL statement that attempts to select a row from the "users" table that matches the user-entered username and password.
25	Run the SQL query and assign the result to the $result variable.
26	Check to see if the result from the query has exactly one row, since usernames are supposed to be unique. (You didn't put duplicate usernames in the database, did you?)
27–28	If the result did have exactly one row, meaning that the user-entered username and password match the same username and password in the database, then set two session cookies on users' browsers so that they remain "logged in" the entire time they are using your protected pages.
29	Return true (1), since the authentication was successful.
30–35	If the result did not contain exactly one row, then the user-entered username and password did not match any in the database. Print an error message and return false to the calling program.
36	Close the if statement started on line 22.
37	End the function declaration.
39	Begin the main program.
40–48	Check to see if the $user variable is set or if the user-entered username and password match any in the database via the check_pass() function. If the $user variable has not been set, then we know that the current user has not attempted to log in yet. If the $user variable is set, but the check_user() function returns false, then we know that the user entered an invalid password. In either case, print the login form so that the user may enter a correct username and password.
49–53	If the script gets to this point, it is because the $user variable has been set and check_user() returned a true value. This must be a valid user! Display a note telling users that they are authorized. At this point, you would display your protected content.

8

Error Management

Overview

Bugs are an everyday part of a programmer's life. We all forget a semicolon or an end bracket at one time or another. Sometimes, we spell a variable name wrong and wonder why the value that is supposed to be showing up on the screen keeps coming up blank. Other times you wonder what gremlins are lurking on the database server because the data just isn't going in (or coming out) the way you intended it. How many times have you looked at a piece of code over and over and wondered why in the heck your program isn't working?

Some bugs—the kind bugs, the ones who don't mind being squashed out—will immediately tell you that they are there, by way of the PHP parser. For example, bugs like the ever-present "Parse error"—or even the occasional "Warning: Division by zero"—let you know on which line they occurred. It's easy enough for you to fix them: You just open your script, add a semicolon here, change the spelling of a variable there, and you are on your way.

Users, unfortunately, don't have this luxury. Have you ever spent an hour or so on some online shopping site, carefully picking out some nice gear for yourself, and going through a long and arduous multipage form to provide your address and credit information before finally clicking that glossy submit button, only to have the page display in plain type "Script Error—Database Connection Failed On Line 193" and nothing else? You just gave these people your credit card number and when their script dies all you see is "Script Error…."

Better sites, smarter sites—that is, YOUR site—should not do that. If there is an error, it would be nice to at least inform users that something went a little awry and the administrators have been notified. Maybe even a note that says the order went through (or didn't). Do you want to subject users of your site to ugly error messages that provide them with no information? Of course not.

In addition, errors can display information that could be useful to malicious users who are trying to crack into your site. Errors typically display file paths, database server information, and other information that could compromise the security of your site.

This chapter explains PHP's error and logging functions.

Error Reporting

Types of Errors in PHP

Before we can get into remedying ugly error messages on your site, you need to understand the different types of errors. PHP4 can produce 11 different errors, as defined in Table 8–1 below (note that fatal errors stop the script from executing):

TABLE 8–1 PHP Error Types

NAME	VALUE	DESCRIPTION
E_ERROR	1	Fatal error that occurs at script runtime.
E_WARNING	2	Nonfatal error that occurs at runtime (for example, if the script is unable to connect to MySQL).
E_PARSE	4	Error that occurs at compile time due to invalid syntax.
E_NOTICE	8	Nonfatal "notice." Not exactly an error, but a hint that you may be doing something you don't want to, such as dividing a number by zero.
E_CORE_ERROR	16	Fatal error that occurs when the PHP engine starts. You cannot run any PHP scripts if this error occurs.
E_CORE_WARNING	32	Nonfatal error that occurs when the PHP engine starts. You can still run PHP scripts, but you may have one or more problems depending on the error (for example, the GD library cannot be found).
E_COMPILE_ERROR	64	Fatal error that occurs when the script is compiled.
E_COMPILE_WARNING	128	Nonfatal error that occurs when the script is compiled.
E_USER_ERROR	256	User-generated fatal error. Same as E_ERROR, but never thrown by PHP. You can throw this error with the trigger_error() function. If you are using PHP's default error handler, then using this error causes script execution to stop.
E_USER_WARNING	512	User-generated nonfatal error. Same as E_WARNING, but never thrown by PHP. You can throw this error with the trigger_error() function.
E_USER_NOTICE	1024	User-generated notice. Same as E_NOTICE, but never thrown by PHP. You can throw this error with the trigger_error() function.

TABLE 8–1 PHP Error Types (Continued)

NAME	VALUE	DESCRIPTION
E_ALL	2047	Not really a type of error. Instead, it is all the errors rolled into one. This makes it easy to say that you want to report all of the errors when using the error_reporting() function.

Of all of these errors, the ones you should mainly concern yourself when it comes to reporting and logging are the following:

- E_WARNING
- E_NOTICE
- E_USER_ERROR
- E_USER_WARNING
- E_USER_NOTICE

Other errors that occur usually result in the script not executing. Your reporting and logging function won't even be run, since there is no script execution.

Error Reporting Settings in *php.ini*

SIDE NOTE This information applies to PHP Version 4 and later. These settings do not work with PHP Version 3.

The reason you see those "ugly" errors when you are coding is that PHP by default is set to show all errors (E_ALL), with the exception of PHP-generated notices (E_NOTICE). Open your *php.ini* file and scroll down to the section entitled *"Error handling and logging."* At the end of all those comments, you should see a line like the following:

```
error_reporting = E_ALL & ~E_NOTICE
```

This is the default error reporting setting. It's written using bitwise operators and is translated simply to "For Error Reporting Use Everything And Not E_NOTICE." You could also write it as follows (note that we leave out E_NOTICE):

```
error_reporting = E_ERROR | E_WARNING | E_PARSE |
E_CORE_ERROR | E_CORE_WARNING | E_COMPILE_ERROR |
E_COMPILE_WARNING | E_USER_ERROR | E_USER_WARNING |
E_USER_NOTICE
```

However, since you are a PHP developer, you really should set this line to read as follows when you are developing an application:

```
error_reporting = E_ALL
```

You want to see all the errors that your script is producing. You'd be surprised at how many uninitialized variables you might be using.

error_reporting()

The error_reporting() function allows you to override the default error reporting setting used in *php.ini*:

```
error_reporting(settings);
```

The error_reporting function takes one argument, which can either be a string that lists the names of the error reporting settings that you want to use (separated by bitwise operators), or an integer that is the sum of the values that you want to use. For example:

```
error_reporting(10);
```

is equivalent to:

```
error_reporting("E_WARNING | E_NOTICE");
```

The first version is easier to type, but the second version is more verbose. Additionally, you can subtract values from the E_ALL value (2047) to use "all but" reporting. The example below allows you to display all errors (E_ALL) except for E_NOTICE (2047 - 8):

```
error_reporting(2039);
```

If you do not want to report any errors, then you could simply use:

```
error_reporting(0);
```

This stops PHP from displaying any error messages on the screen that are caused by E_WARNING, E_NOTICE or any of the user-thrown warnings. Remember, any of the other warnings are thrown automatically by PHP because there is something either really wrong with the script (parse errors) or really wrong with the server itself.

You still may run into a problem if there is an error that causes the script to fail to compile (such as with parse errors). In that case, no portions of your script are even executed, and the error_reporting() variable is not run. When this happens, PHP uses its *php.ini* setting for error reporting.

php.ini Setting: display_errors

Additionally, there is another setting that stops error messages from being displayed on the user's browser. This setting, display_errors, can be found in *php.ini*. In the event that you want to be sure that errors are never displayed on the screen, you can change this setting to "0" in your *php.ini* file. You should leave this setting to "1" or "On" while you are developing your application.

You can also change the display_errors setting on a per file basis using the ini_set() function. The ini_set() function allows you to change *php.ini* file settings for the current script. For example, if you had turned off display_errors in your *php.ini* file, then you could turn it on to debug your script by using the following code, which is the *php.ini* equivalent of display_errors = On:

```
ini_set("display_errors",1);
```

Remember, if your script encounters an error that does not allow it to execute, then PHP uses the settings it finds in *php.ini*, regardless of what you have specified in your script.

php.ini Settings for Development and Testing

While developing and testing your scripts, you should use the following settings in your *php.ini* file:

```
error_reporting = E_ALL
display_errors = 1
```

This allows you to display all errors and get all the information that PHP provides about your script. For production sites, you may want to set your *php.ini* file to completely turn off any error display:

```
display_errors = 0
```

This next script demonstrates how warnings and notices are reported with different error reporting settings.

SCRIPT 8–1 error_reporting.php

```
1.   <?
2.   define("EVERYTHING",E_ALL);
3.   define("NO_NOTICE",(E_ALL &~E_NOTICE));
4.   define("NO_NOTICE_OR_WARN",(E_ALL &~(E_NOTICE |
     E_WARNING)));
5.   $error_level =
     array(EVERYTHING,NO_NOTICE,NO_NOTICE_OR_WARN);
6.   for($i = 0; $i < sizeof($error_level); $i++) {
7.     error_reporting($error_level[$i]);
8.     echo "<h3>Error Reporting Set To " . $error_level[$i] .
     "</h3>";
9.     echo $uninitialized;
10.    $connect = mysql_connect();
11.    echo "<hr>";
12.  }
13.  ?>
14.  <?
15.  define("EVERYTHING",E_ALL);
```

Script 8–1 error_reporting.php Line-by-Line Explanation

LINE	DESCRIPTION
2–4	Define some named constants to use in the script. The reason we define these constants is because we want to use some custom error reporting options, as seen in lines 3 and 4.
5	Create an array of the error reporting values defined in the previous lines.
6–12	Create a for loop to loop through the values in the array.
7	Change the error reporting value to the current value in the array. The error_reporting function cannot take a bitwise operation statement as an argument, so we use the values created on lines 3 and 4.
8	Display a short notice describing which error reporting value is being used. The constants we defined in lines 2–4 are actually redefinitions of existing constants, which are in turn defined by PHP as the corresponding values of the error reporting levels. Therefore, the value displayed on the screen is numerical.

Script 8–1 error_reporting.php Line-by-Line Explanation (Continued)

LINE	DESCRIPTION
9	Print the value of an uninitialized variable. This should display a warning (E_USER_NOTICE) if the error reporting is set to display E_USER_NOTICE.
10	Attempt to connect to a MySQL database. This should generate a warning message if the error reporting message is set to display E_USER_WARNING.
12	Close the for loop started on line 6.

Logging Errors

As was stated earlier, you do not want to reveal error information to end users. At the same time, as the administrator of a
site, you still need to know if something has gone amiss with
the script. PHP provides the error_log() function for this purpose. You can turn disable_errors off in your PHP site and still
monitor any problems that occur using error_log().

The error_log() function can take a variable amount of
arguments depending on which of four types of logging that
you choose to use.

```
error_log($message, $message_type, $destination,
$extra_headers);
```

Table 8–2 below explains the four types of error logging
available in PHP.

TABLE 8–2 Types Of Error Logging In PHP

MESSAGE TYPE	DESCRIPTION
0	Depending on the "error_log" setting in *php.ini*, the $message is sent to a system-specific logging mechanism or to a file. By default, error_log is not set in *php.ini*. If it is not set, and you use this type of error logging, then the error message usually appears in Apache's error log file. Example: `error_log("Error!", 0);`

TABLE 8–2 Types Of Error Logging In PHP (Continued)

MESSAGE TYPE	DESCRIPTION
1	$message is sent to the email address specified in the $destination argument of this function. This is the only type that uses the $extra_headers argument. Example: `error_log("Error!",1,"email@example.com","FROM: Website Error Logging <web@example.com>")`
2	$message is sent to the PHP debugging connection. The $destination argument must be used to specify the host name or IP address of the debugging server. Commercial PHP IDEs (Integrated Development Environments), such as PHPIDE from Nusphere and the ZEND IDE, are able to accept messages in this fashion. Example: `error_log("Error!",2,"192.168.0.1:2020");`
3	$message is written to the end of the file specified by $destination. If the $destination file does not exist, PHP attempts to create it. You must have your permissions set correctly so that PHP can write to the directory specified in $destination. You do not have to specify the fill path for $destination. Example: `error_log("Error!",3,"c:/PHP_ERRORS/script_errors.txt");`

This next script provides some working examples of error logging.

SCRIPT 8–2 error_logging.php

```
1.  <?
2.  echo "<p>Sending Error To Apache Error Log.";
3.  error_log("Test Error Message!",0);
4.  echo "<p>Sending Error To Email.";
5.  error_log("Test Error Message!",1,"admin@example.com","FROM: WEB ERROR LOG <error@example.com>");
6.  echo "<p>Sending Error to File.";
7.  error_log("Test Error Message!\r\n",3,"errors.txt");
8.  ?>
```

Script 8–2 error_logging.php Line-by-Line Explanation

LINE	DESCRIPTION
2	Display a message on the screen stating that an error is being sent to the Apache error log.
3	Send an error to the Apache error log.
4	Display a message on the screen stating that an error is being sent to an email address.
5	Send an error to an email address. Replace "admin@example.com" with your email address.
6	Display a message on the screen stating that an error is being sent to a file.
7	Send an error to the file. If the file does not exist, then PHP attempts to create it in the current directory.

Custom Error Handlers

PHP's default error handlers are useful, but they don't do anything more than just tell you that there is an error. Luckily, PHP allows you to use your own custom error handlers so that you can take a specific action, depending on which error has occurred. The function that allows you to use your own error handler is called set_error_handler():

```
set_error_handler($error_handler);
```

set_error_handler() takes one argument, $error_handler, which is the name of the error handling function that you have created.

If you call set_error_handler() with 0, then the error handler is set back to the default PHP error handler.

```
set_error_handler(0);
//error handler is PHP's default error handler
```

set_error_handler() returns the value of the old error handler when it is called. This allows you to easily revert to the old error handler. For example:

```
set_error_handler("foo");
$old_error_handler = set_error_handler("bar");
//$old_error_handler = "foo";
```

```
set_error_handler($old_error_handler);
//error handler is now "foo"
```

You can also easily revert to the prior error handler by calling the restore_error_handler() function, which takes no arguments:

```
set_error_handler("foo");
set_error_handler("bar");
restor_error_handler();
//error_handler = "foo"
```

When an error is triggered, PHP calls the error function specified in set_error_handler() and sends it the following arguments (in the following order):

- The error number—This is the value of the error from Table 8–1.
- The text of the error.
- The name and path of the file in which the error occurred.
- The line on which the error occurred.
- The context at the time of the error—Basically, a large array containing the states of all the variables available to the script when the error occurred.

You can use as many or as few of these arguments as you want, but the arguments must appear in the order above.

> **SIDE NOTE** If PHP encounters errors in your error_handling function, it uses the default or previous error handling method to deal with the error.

This next script provides an example of a custom error handler.

SCRIPT 8–3 error_handler.php

```
1. <?
2. error_reporting(E_ALL);
3. function error_handler($number, $string, $file, $line) {
4.   error_log("Error ($number) on line $line in file $file.
The error was \"$string\"\n", 3, "errors.txt");
5. }
6. ini_set('display_errors',0);
```

```
7.  set_error_handler("error_handler");
8.  $row = mysql_fetch_array($result);
9.  ?>
```

Script 8–3 error_handler.php Line-by-Line Explanation

LINE	DESCRIPTION
2	Set error reporting to report all errors.
3–5	Define a function to handle errors. Accept the error number, error string, file in which the error occurred, and line number of the error as arguments.
4	Log the error to a text file.
5	Close the error_handler() function.
6	Use the ini_set() function to disable the displaying of errors on the screen.
7	Set the error handler to the custom handler defined on line 3.
8	Generate an error by calling a function that we know will not work.

```
    Error (8) on line 8 in file
    c:\apache\htdocs\chapter08\error_handler.php. The error
1.  was "Undefined variable:  result"
2.  Error (2) on line 8 in file
    c:\apache\htdocs\chapter08\error_handler.php. The error
    was "Supplied argument is not a valid MySQL result
    resource"
```

Script 8–4 Output of error_handler.php Line-by-Line Explanation

LINE	DESCRIPTION
1	The log shows that this is a E_WARNING error, because the error type is (8). The rest of the line contains the information sent to the log from the custom error handler.
2	The log shows that this is an E_NOTICE error, because the error type is (2).

Triggering Errors

At times, it is very useful to trigger your own errors, depending on what has occurred in the script. For example, you may want to log failed login attempts to one of your password-protected sites. You may also want to take a different action depending on what error occurred. For example, if a database connection is not working, you may want to have a message sent to an email address, rather than just log the error into a text file.

The trigger_error() function is called as follows:

```
trigger_error($error_message, $error_type);
```

The trigger_error() function takes two arguments:

- $error_message—A string describing the error.
- $error_type—The type of error that you wish to trigger, which can be one of three values:
  - E_USER_ERROR
  - E_USER_WARNING
  - E_USER_NOTICE

Calling trigger_error() with the error type E_USER_ERROR will cause the script to start running at that point.

> **SIDE NOTE** There is another function called user_error(), which is an alias for trigger_error(). Both functions take the same arguments and do the exact thing.

This next function uses trigger_error() and a custom error handler to provide different actions according to the error.

SCRIPT 8–5 trigger_error.php

```php
1.  <?
2.  function error_handler($number, $string, $file, $line) {
3.      $timestamp = date("m-d-Y H:i:s (T)");
4.      switch($string) {
5.      case("INVALID LOGIN"):
6.          global $username;
7.          error_log("Failed login attempt by $username on
    $timestamp\n",3,"failed_logins.txt");
8.          break;
9.      case("DATABASE CONNECT ERROR"):
10.         global $mysqlerr;
11.         $message = "Database Error!\n";
```

```
12.         $message .= "Unable to connect to database at
       $timestamp\n\n";
13.         $message .= "ERROR INFORMATION:\n";
14.         $message .= "FILE:\t$file\n";
15.         $message .= "LINE:\t$line\n";
16.         $message .="MYSQL:\t$mysqlerr\n";
17.         error_log($message,1,"me@example.com", "FROM: PHP
       MONITOR <noreply@example.com>");
18.         failure();
19.         break;
20.       default:
21.         if($number != 8) {
22.             error_log("Error ($number) on line $line in file
       $file. The error was \"" . trim($string) . "\"\n", 3,
       "error_log.txt");
23.         }
24.         break;
25.     }
26. }
27. function failure() {
28.     ?>
29.     <h3>Sorry,</h3>
30.     <p>A problem has occured. The site administators have
       been notified and the problem should be resolved shortly.
31.     <p>Please try again later.
32.     <?
33. }
34. set_error_handler("error_handler");
35. if(!mysql_connect()) {
36.     $mysqlerr = mysql_error();
37.     trigger_error("DATABASE CONNECT ERROR",E_USER_NOTICE);
38. }
39. $username = "bob";
40. trigger_error("INVALID LOGIN",E_USER_NOTICE);
41. $msg = "Something Went Wrong!";
42. trigger_error($msg,E_USER_ERROR);
43. ?>
```

Script 8–5 trigger_error.php Line-by-Line Explanation

LINE	DESCRIPTION
2–26	Define a custom error-handling function called error_handler(). This function takes as arguments: • $number—The numerical value of the error. • $string—The error message. • $file—The path and name of the file in which the error occurred. • $line—The line on which the error occurred.
3	Create the $timestamp variable and assign it the current date and time.
4–25	Create a switch statement to check the $string variable that is sent by PHP when an error is encountered.
5–8	If $switch is equal to "INVALID LOGIN", then log the error to a file and break out of the switch statement. You must make the $username a global variable in line 6 so that it can be used in this function.
9–19	If $switch = "DATABASE CONNECT ERROR", then execute lines 10–19.
10	Make $mysqlerr a global variable, so that its value can be used in this function.
11–16	Create text for an email message and store it in the $message variable. The text contains the relevant information pertaining to this error.
17	Use the error_log() function to send $message to an email address.
18	Execute the failure() function.
19	Break out of the switch statement.
20–24	If none of the above cases are met, then execute lines 21–24.
21–23	If the error value does not equal "8" (an E_NOTICE error), log the error to a text file.
24	Break out of the switch statement.
25	Close the switch statement.
26	End the function declaration.
27–33	Define a function, failure(), to be used when an error occurs that does not allow the script to run as intended.
28–32	Display a message to the user stating that the site is currently down.
33	End the function declaration.
34	Execute the set_error_handler() function, specifying the custom error handler "error_handler" as the argument. This disables PHP's built-in error-handling mechanism and uses error_handler() in its place.

Script 8–5 trigger_error.php Line-by-Line Explanation (Continued)

LINE	DESCRIPTION
35	Attempt to connect to a MySQL database. We assume this will fail, since we do not provide any connection information (host, username, password). If the connection attempt results in an error (it will), execute lines 36–38.
36	Assign the MySQL error message to the $mysqlerr variable. This variable is used in the error_handler() function.
37	Trigger an error using a custom error string, "DATABASE CONNECT ERROR". This string tells the custom error_handler() function to send an email to the administrator reporting that the database connection is not working.
39	Create the variable $username to hold the string "bob". This will be used as a test case to see if the error_handler() function is correctly logging user login errors.
40	Trigger another error with the string "INVALID LOGIN". This error causes the custom error handler to log the invalid login to a file. The log file stores the username of the person who attempted to log in when the login failed.
41	Create a variable to hold an arbitrary message to send to the trigger_error() message in the next line.
42	Trigger another error, using the $msg variable as the string. This error is logged in the error_log.txt file, since the error string ($msg) does not match any of the switch cases in the error_handler() function.

Tracking User Logins

This next script builds on the previous examples to create a small application that tracks the following:

- Valid Logins—The script logs the date, time, username, IP address, and browser for each successful login.
- Invalid Logins—The script logs the username and the date and time the user tried (unsuccessfully) to access the site.
- Failed Database Connection—The script sends an email to the webmaster's email address in the event that the database connection fails.

SIDE NOTE This can create an incredible amount of spam if it is placed on a busy site. Every time a database connection attempt fails, an email is sent to the email address specified in the script. If you get 1000 hits a day and the database connection is down, then expect to find at least 1000 emails in your inbox (depending on how many connection attempts occur per page).

SCRIPT 8-6 login_track.php

```
1. <?
2. /* SQL REQUIRED FOR THIS SCRIPT *****
3.  create table users (
4.    id INT NOT NULL,
5.    username VARCHAR(16),
6.    password VARCHAR(8),
7.    primary key(id));
8. *****/
9.
10. function connect() {
11.   global $dbuser, $dbpw, $dbhost;
12.   if(!$db = @mysql_pconnect($dbhost,$dbuser,$dbpw)) {
13.     global $mysqlerr;
14.     $mysqlerr = mysql_error();
15.     trigger_error("DATABASE CONNECT ERROR",E_USER_NOTICE);
16.     failure();
17.   } else {
18.     mysql_select_db("php", $db);
19.     return 1;
20.   }
21. } //end connect()
22.
23. function check_user($user, $password) {
24.   if(connect()) {
25.     $password = substr($password, 0, 8);
26.     $sql = "select * from users where username = '$user'
    and password = '$password'";
27.     if(!$result = mysql_query($sql)) {
28.       failure();
29.     }
30.     if (mysql_num_rows($result) == 1) {
31.       setcookie("user",$user);
32.       setcookie("password",$password);
33.       trigger_error("VALID LOGIN",E_USER_NOTICE);
34.       return 1;
35.     } else {
36.       trigger_error("INVALID LOGIN",E_USER_NOTICE);
37.       return 0;
38.     }
```

```
39.    }
40. } //end check_user
41.
42. function error_handler($number, $string, $file, $line) {
43.    global $admin_email;
44.    $timestamp = date("m-d-Y H:i:s (T)");
45.    switch($string) {
46.      case("INVALID LOGIN"):
47.        global $user;
48.        error_log("Failed login attempt by $user on
   $timestamp\n",3,"failed_logins.txt");
49.        echo "<h3>Login Failed. Try Again!</h3>";
50.        break;
51.      case("VALID LOGIN");
52.        global $user, $REMOTE_ADDR, $HTTP_USER_AGENT;
53.        error_log("LOGIN: $user on $timestamp from
   $REMOTE_ADDR using
   $HTTP_USER_AGENT\n",3,"valid_logins.txt");
54.        break;
55.      case("DATABASE CONNECT ERROR"):
56.        global $mysqlerr;
57.        $message = "Database Error!\n";
58.        $message .= "Unable to connect to database at
   $timestamp\n\n";
59.        $message .= "ERROR INFORMATION:\n";
60.        $message .= "FILE:\t$file\n";
61.        $message .= "LINE:\t$line\n";
62.        $message .="MYSQL:\t$mysqlerr\n";
63.        error_log($message,1,$admin_email, "FROM: PHP
   MONITOR <noreply@example.com>");
64.        failure();
65.        break;
66.      default:
67.        if($number != 0) {
68.          error_log("Error ($number) on line $line in file
   $file. The error was \"" . trim($string) . "\"\n", 3,
   "error_log.txt");
69.        }
70.        break;
71.    }
72. } //end error_handler
73.
74. function failure() {
75.    ?>
76.    <h3>Sorry,</h3>
```

```
77.   <p>A problem has occured. The site administators have
      been notified and the problem should be resolved shortly.
78.   <p>Please try again later.
79.   <?
80.   die();
81. } // end failure
82.
83.
84. function head() {
85.   ?>
86.   <html>
87.   <head>
88.   <title>Login Tracker</title>
89.   </head>
90.   <body bgcolor="#FFFFFF">
91.   <h1>Login Tracker</h1>
92.   <?
93. } //end head
94.
95. /***** MAIN *****/
96. $admin_email = "email@example.com";
97. $dbuser = "mysqluser";
98. $dbpw = "password";
99. $dbhost = "192.168.0.5";
100. $page = "login_track.php";
101.
102. error_reporting(0);
103. set_error_handler("error_handler");
104.
105. if(!isset($user) or !check_user($user, $password)) {
106.   head();
107.   ?>
108.   <h1>You must log in to view this page</h1>
109.   <form action = "<?=$page?>" method="post">
110.   <P>Username: <input type="text" name="user"><br>
111.   Password: <input type="password" name="password"
      maxlength="8" size="8"><br>
112.   <input type="submit" name="submit" value="Submit">
113.   </form>
114.   <?
115. } else {
116.   head();
117.   ?>
118.   <h1>Authorized!</h1>
119.   <P>Your content here...
```

SCRIPT 8–6 login_track.php (Continued)

```
120.    <?
121. }
122. ?>
123. </body>
124. </html>
```

Script 8–6 login_track.php Line-by-Line Explanation

LINE	DESCRIPTION
2–8	The SQL required for this script.
10–21	Define a function, connect(), that is used to connect to the database.
11	Allow these variables to be used in the function.
12	Attempt to connect to the database (in this case, a MySQL database). If an error occurs, execute lines 13–16. If no error occurs, execute lines 17–20.
13	Assign the variable $mysqlerr to the global scope of the script.
14	Assign the error information to the $mysqlerr variable that is provided from the mysql_error() function.
15	Trigger a user-defined error that gets sent to the error_handler() function.
16	Execute the failure() function.
17–20	Since no error occurred, select the proper database on the MySQL server and return true to the calling function.
21	End the function declaration.
23–40	Define a function, check_user(), that is used to check the user-entered username/password combination against the values stored in the database.
24	Attempt to connect to the database. If the connection fails, the connect function automatically logs the error and kills the script.
25	Truncate the user-entered password so that it is only eight characters long.
26	Define an SQL statement to select all the information from the users' table that has a username and password that matches the user-entered values.
27–29	Send the query to the server and check to make sure the query actually went through. If it did not, then call the failure() function to display the failure notice to the user.

Script 8–6 login_track.php Line-by-Line Explanation (Continued)

LINE	DESCRIPTION
30	If there is one row in the result set, we know that the user entered the correct values. If no rows are returned from the database, then we know that the user's values did not match those in the database. (There shouldn't be more than one result row, because your application that enters the information into the database should be using unique email addresses.)
31–32	Set cookies in users' browsers so that they do not have to enter their username and password anymore, since we know the values are correct.
33	Trigger an error so that the successful login attempt is stored in the log file.
34	Return true to the calling function so that it knows the attempt was successful.
35–38	If the user-entered values do not match those in the database, then log the attempt and return false to the calling function.
39	Close out the if statement started on line 24.
40	End the function declaration.
42	Define the custom error-handling function, including the error number ($number), error string ($string), file in which the error occurred ($file), and line on which the error occurred ($line) as arguments.
43	Assign $admin_email as a global so that it can be used by this function.
44	Create a variable to hold the current date and time.
45–71	Create a switch statement that reads through the possible error strings.
46–50	If the error string is "INVALID LOGIN", grab the value of $user from the global variable space, log the error to the "failed_logins.txt" file, and print an error message to the user, then break out of the switch.
51–54	If the error string is "VALID LOGIN", grab the value of $user, $REMOTE_ADDR (IP address of the user), and $HTTP_USER_AGENT (user's Web browser) from the global variable space, and log the information to the "valid_logins.txt" file, then break out of the switch.
55–65	If the error string is "DATABASE CONNECT ERROR", then execute lines 56–65.
56	Grab the value of $mysqlerr from the global variable space. This variable was assigned a value when the error first occurred.
57–62	Create a lengthy message containing all of the available error information.
63	Send the message to the value of the $admin_email variable.

Script 8–6 login_track.php Line-by-Line Explanation (Continued)

LINE	DESCRIPTION
64	Execute the failure() function, which prints an error message to the screen and kills the script.
65	Break out of the switch statement.
66–70	If the error string is anything other than the above (and the error number was not "0", which is merely a warning), then log the error with the available information to the "error_log.txt" file. Finally, break out of the switch.
71	Close out the switch statement.
72	End the function declaration.
74–81	Define a function, failure(), that, when called, prints an error message to the user and kills the script.
75–79	Print the error message to the user.
80	Kill the script with the die() function.
81	End the function declaration.
84–93	Define a function, head(), that prints out the beginning HTML for the page as well as a heading.
95	Begin the main execution phase of the script.
96–100	Define some variables that are used by the script.
102	Turn off error reporting using the error_reporting() function.
103	Set the error handler to the custom error-handling function defined above.
105	If the $user variable has not been set or the check_user() function failed, execute lines 106–115.
106	Print out the beginning HTML for the page.
107–114	Print out the form so that users can enter their username and password to view the content of the page.
115–121	If the $user variable is set and the check_user() function returned true, then the user is valid and may view the protected content.
122–124	Print out the closing HTML for the page.

9

Using What You Have Learned—A Meeting Tracker Application

- Introduction
- Setting It Up
- The Code

Introduction

This Meeting Manager application was designed to be a simple way to coordinate meetings. You can specify actual meeting room locations, or use the built-in virtual room and conduct the meeting over a conference call or Web meeting service. You can specify the phone number and the Web address right in the meeting.

An administrator sets up the users and rooms via an administration interface. Once that has been done, users can log in and begin scheduling meetings.

Meetings are created by using a step-by-step wizard. The wizard checks the availability of rooms and users, and only allows rooms that have not been scheduled for the current meeting time to be used. Users who are already scheduled for a meeting are listed as "busy," but can still be invited to the meeting.

Once the meeting time, room, and users have been selected, you can then provide an agenda and a conference call number and Web address.

When the meeting is finalized, an email notification is sent to all the participants.

When users log in, they can schedule a new meeting or view their current meetings. Clicking on a meeting name in the meeting list brings up complete details for that meeting.

If a user scheduled a meeting, that user can cancel that meeting. Once a meeting is cancelled, the room that was specified for the meeting is freed and all users receive notification of the cancelled meeting.

Additionally, the meeting is removed from users' schedules.

Simple Administration Interface

The Meeting Manager provides an ultrasimple administration interface, shown in Figure 9–1, that allows the administrator to add a new user or room. Once a user or room is added, it is immediately available to be scheduled for meetings.

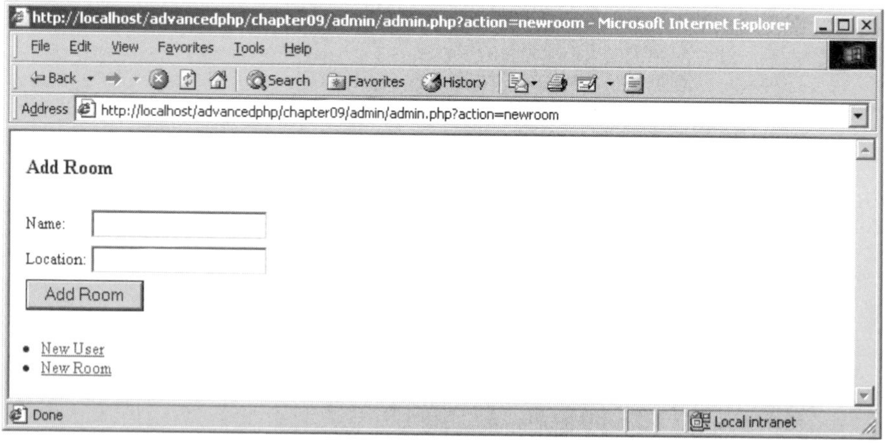

FIGURE 9–1 Administration Interface

Setting It Up

Setting up the Meeting Manager application is easy. Just install the files as specified in the table below and set up your database using the supplied SQL. Remember to change any parameters in the code for the database and paths to match your system.

The general layout of the installation is shown in Table 9–1:

TABLE 9–1 Directory Structure for the Shopping Cart

FOLDER	CONTAINS
Top Level	• meeting.php • meeting_inc.php
admin directory[a]	• admin.php

a. This directory must be password protected!

The Code

This section details the code involved in the script. The descriptions are of a high level, as most of the topics have already been covered. Additional descriptions are provided when new topics are introduced.

meeting.sql

meeting.sql is the SQL code used to create the database for this application.

SCRIPT 9–1 meeting.sql

```
1.   CREATE TABLE users (
2.      id INT NOT NULL,
3.      first VARCHAR(32),
4.      last VARCHAR(32),
5.      phone VARCHAR(16),
6.      email VARCHAR(64),
7.      pass VARCHAR(8),
8.      PRIMARY KEY(id));
9.
10.  CREATE TABLE rooms (
```

SCRIPT 9–1   meeting.sql (Continued)

```
11.     id INT NOT NULL,
12.     name VARCHAR(32),
13.     location VARCHAR(128),
14.     PRIMARY KEY(id));
15.
16.  INSERT INTO rooms VALUES(0,'Virtual Room','Virtual
     Location');
17.
18.  CREATE TABLE meetings (
19.     id INT NOT NULL,
20.     name VARCHAR(64),
21.     startdate DATETIME,
22.     enddate DATETIME,
23.     room INT,
24.     agenda TEXT,
25.     phone VARCHAR(16),
26.     web VARCHAR(128),
27.     originator INT,
28.     PRIMARY KEY(id));
29.
30.  CREATE TABLE meetingusers (
31.     meeting INT,
32.     userid INT);
```

Script 9–1 meeting.sql Line-by-Line Explanation

LINE	DESCRIPTION
1–8	Create the table that holds the user information.
10–14	Create the table that holds the room information.
16	Create a default room to be used in "virtual" meetings that occur over the phone or on the Web.
18–28	Create the table to hold the meeting data. "room" and "originator" are pseudo-foreign keys that link back to the users and rooms tables.
30–32	Create a table to hold the users for each meeting. Each row in the table corresponds to keys for a user and a meeting. One meeting can have several records in this table.

meeting.php

meeting.php is the main script for the application. It contains all of the commonly used functions.

```
1.  <?
2.  function addmeetingwizard($step) {
3.      session_start();
4.      head();
5.      global $fields, $page, $HTTP_POST_VARS, $user;
6.      switch($step) {
7.        case("1"):
8.          if(isset($fields)) { session_unregister("fields"); }
9.          ?>
10.         <form action="<?=$page?>" method="post">
11.         <table border=0>
12.         <tr><td colspan=2><h3>Add New Meeting - Step 1</
    h3></td></tr>
13.         <tr><td>Name: </td><td><input type="text"
    name="name"></td></tr>
14.         <tr><td>Start Date & Time:</td>
15.         <td>
16.         <?createdate("start");?>
17.         </td></tr>
18.         <tr><td>End Date & Time: </td>
19.         <td>
20.         <?createdate("end");?>
21.         <br><i>(YYYY-MM-DD HH:MM)</i></td></tr>
22.         <tr><td colspan=2><input type="submit"
    name="addmeeting" value="Next"></td><tr>
23.         </table>
24.         <input type="hidden" name="step" value="2">
25.         </form>
26.         <?
27.         break;
28.       case("2"):
29.         ?><h2>Step 2 - Select Room</h2><?
30.         session_register("fields");
31.         if($HTTP_POST_VARS['name'] == "") {
32.         ?>
33.         <h2>You must select a name!</h2>
34.         <form action=<?=$page?> method="post">
35.         <input type="hidden" name="step" value="1">
36.         <input type="submit" name="addmeeting"
    value="Back">
37.         </form>
38.         <?
39.         } else {
40.           $dbconn = connect();
41.           $sql = "select id from users where email = '$user'";
```

SCRIPT 9–2 meeting.php (Continued)

```
42.          $result = $dbconn->query($sql);
43.          errortrap($result);
44.          $result->fetchInto($r);
45.          $fields['originator'] = $r['id'];
46.          $fields['name'] = $HTTP_POST_VARS['name'];
47.          $fields['startdate'] =
     $HTTP_POST_VARS['startyears'] . "-" .
     $HTTP_POST_VARS['startmonths'] . "-" .
     $HTTP_POST_VARS['startdays'] . " " .
     $HTTP_POST_VARS['starthours'] .
     $HTTP_POST_VARS['startminutes'];
48.          $fields['enddate'] = $HTTP_POST_VARS['endyears']
     . "-" . $HTTP_POST_VARS['endmonths'] . "-" .
     $HTTP_POST_VARS['enddays'] . " " .
     $HTTP_POST_VARS['endhours'] .
     $HTTP_POST_VARS['endminutes'];
49.          $sql = "select room from meetings where startdate
     <= '" . $fields['enddate'] . "' AND enddate >= '" .
     $fields['startdate'] . "' AND room != '0'";
50.          $result = $dbconn->query($sql);
51.          errortrap($result);
52.          meetingdisplay($fields);
53.          ?>
54.          <p>
55.          <h3>The following rooms are available for your
     meeting time:</h3>
56.          <form action=<?=$page?> method=post>
57.          <input type="hidden" name="step" value="3">
58.          <p>Select One:
59.          <?
60.          $sql = "select * from rooms where id != '";
61.          while($result->fetchInto($row)) {
62.              $sql .= $row['room'] . "' AND id != '";
63.          }
64.          $sql .= "-1'";
65.          $result = $dbconn->query($sql);
66.          errortrap($result);
67.          while($result->fetchInto($row)) {
68.              $sql = "select * from rooms where id = '" .
     $row['id'] . "'";
69.              $resultroom = $dbconn->query($sql);
70.              errortrap($resultroom);
71.              $resultroom->fetchInto($roomrow);
72.              if($roomrow['id'] == '0') {
73.                  ?>
```

```
74.            <br><input type="radio" name="roomchoice"
      value="<?=$roomrow['id']?>" checked> <?=$roomrow['name']?>
      <?=$roomrow['location']?>
75.            <?
76.         } else {
77.            ?>
78.            <br><input type="radio" name="roomchoice"
      value="<?=$roomrow['id']?>"> <?=$roomrow['name']?>
      <?=$roomrow['location']?>
79.            <?
80.         }
81.      }
82.      ?>
83.      <p><input type="submit" name="addmeeting"
      value="Next">
84.      </form>
85.      <?
86.   }
87.   break;
88. case("3"):
89.   ?><h2>Step 3 - Select Attendees</h2><?
90.   $fields['roomchoice'] =
      $HTTP_POST_VARS['roomchoice'];
91.   $busyuser = array();
92.   $openuser = array();
93.   meetingdisplay($fields);
94.   ?>
95.   <p>Select People to Invite (CTRL-Click to choose
      multiple. Be sure to invite yourself!):
96.   <?
97.   //determine from meetings table which people are
      available and which are not
98.   $dbconn = connect();
99.   $sql = "select id from meetings where startdate <=
      '" . $fields['enddate'] . "' AND enddate >= '" .
      $fields['startdate'] . "'";
100.  $result = $dbconn->query($sql);
101.  errortrap($result);
102.  while($result->fetchInto($row)) {
103.     $sql = "select userid from meetingusers where
      meeting = '" . $row['id'] . "' order by userid";
104.     $userresult = $dbconn->query($sql);
105.     errortrap($userresult);
106.     while($userresult->fetchInto($row2)) {
107.        $busyuser[$row2['userid']] = $row2['userid'];
```

```
108.          }
109.        }
110.        $sql = "select id from users";
111.        $result = $dbconn->query($sql);
112.        errortrap($result);
113.        while($result->fetchInto($row)) {
114.          $count = 0;
115.          if(sizeof($busyuser) > 0) {
116.            foreach($busyuser as $buser) {
117.              if($row['id'] == $buser) {
118.                $count++;
119.              }
120.            }
121.          }
122.          if($count == 0) {
123.            $openuser[] = $row['id'];
124.          }
125.        }
126.        ?>
127.        <form action="<?=$page?>" method="post">
128.        <select name="attendees[]" size="8" multiple>
129.        <?
130.        foreach($openuser as $ouser) {
131.          $row = datafromid($dbconn, "users", $ouser);
132.          printf("<option value=%s>%s, %s</option>",
      $row['id'], $row['last'], $row['first']);
133.        }
134.        foreach($busyuser as $buser) {
135.          $row = datafromid($dbconn, "users", $buser);
136.          printf("<option value=%s>%s, %s (busy)</option>",
      $row['id'], $row['last'], $row['first']);
137.        }
138.        ?>
139.        </select>
140.        <input type="hidden" name="step" value="4">
141.        <p><input type="submit" name="addmeeting"
      value="Next">
142.        </form>
143.        <?
144.        break;
145.      case("4"):
146.        ?><h2>Step 4 - Define Agenda and Phone/Web Options</
      h2><?
147.        if(sizeof($fields['attendees']) == 0) {
148.          if($HTTP_POST_VARS['attendees'] != "") {
```

```
149.              $fields['attendees'] =
      $HTTP_POST_VARS['attendees'];
150.          }
151.      }
152.      if(sizeof($fields['attendees']) == 0) {
153.          ?>
154.          <h2>You must select at least one attendee!</h2>
155.          <form action=<?=$page?> method="post">
156.          <input type="hidden" name="step" value="3">
157.          <input type="submit" name="addmeeting"
      value="Back">
158.          </form>
159.          <?
160.      } else {
161.          meetingdisplay($fields);
162.          ?>
163.          <p>Define Phone, Web, and Agenda:
164.          <form action="<?=$page?>" method="post">
165.          Agenda:<br><textarea cols="20" rows="5"
      name="agenda"></textarea>
166.          <br>Web Address: <input type="text" name="web">
167.          <br>Phone Number: <input type="text"
      name="phone">
168.          <input type="hidden" name="step" value="5">
169.          <p><input type="submit" name="addmeeting"
      value="Next">
170.          </form>
171.          <?
172.      }
173.      break;
174.   case("5"):
175.      ?><h2>Step 5 - Confirmation</h2><?
176.      if($HTTP_POST_VARS['agenda'] == "") {
177.          ?>
178.          <h2>You must enter an agenda!</h2>
179.          <form action=<?=$page?> method="post">
180.          <input type="hidden" name="step" value="4">
181.          <input type="submit" name="addmeeting"
      value="Back">
182.          </form>
183.          <?
184.      } else {
185.          $fields['agenda'] = $HTTP_POST_VARS['agenda'];
186.          $fields['web'] = $HTTP_POST_VARS['web'];
187.          $fields['phone'] = $HTTP_POST_VARS['phone'];
```

```
188.            meetingdisplay($fields);
189.            ?>
190.            <h2>Click the button below to schedule your
      metting!</h2>
191.            <form action=<?=$page?> method="post">
192.            <input type="hidden" name="step" value="6">
193.            <input type="submit" name="addmeeting"
      value="Finish!">
194.            </form>
195.            <?
196.          }
197.          break;
198.      case("6"):
199.          ?><h2>Finished!</h2><?
200.          $dbconn = connect();
201.          $id = $dbconn->nextID('meeting_id',true);
202.          errortrap($id);
203.          $sql = "insert into meetings values('$id', '" .
      $fields['name'] . "','" . $fields['startdate'] . "','" .
      $fields['enddate'] . "','" . $fields['roomchoice'] . "','"
      . $fields['agenda'] . "','" . $fields['phone'] . "','" .
      $fields['web'] . "','" . $fields['originator'] . "')";
204.          $result = $dbconn->query($sql);
205.          errortrap($result);
206.          foreach($fields['attendees'] as $attendee) {
207.            $sql = "insert into meetingusers values('$id',
      '$attendee')";
208.            $result = $dbconn->query($sql);
209.            errortrap($result);
210.          }
211.          session_unset();
212.          session_destroy();
213.          notifyusers($id);
214.          choices();
215.          break;
216.      default:
217.          head();
218.          ?>
219.          <h3>There was an error. Please restart from the
      beginning.</h3>
220.          <?
221.          session_unset();
222.          session_destroy();
223.          ?>
224.          <form action=<?=$page?> method="post">
```

```
225.        <input type="hidden" name="step" value="1">
226.        <input type="submit" name="addmeeting"
     value="Restart">
227.        </form>
228.        <?
229.        break;
230.   } //end switch
231. } //end addmeetingwizard
232.
233. function meetingdisplay($fields) {
234.    ?>
235.    <h3>Meeting: <?=$fields['name']?></h3>
236.    <h4>Start: <?=$fields['startdate']?></h4>
237.    <h4>End: <?=$fields['enddate']?></h4>
238.    <?
239.    if(sizeof($fields) > 4) {
240.    ?>
241.    <h4>Room:
242.      <?
243.      $dbconn = connect();
244.      $row = datafromid($dbconn, "rooms",
     $fields['roomchoice']);
245.      printf("%s - %s", $row['name'], $row['location']);
246.      ?>
247.    </h4>
248.    <?
249.    }
250.    if(sizeof($fields) > 5) {
251.      ?>
252.      <h4>Attendees:</h4>
253.      <?
254.      foreach($fields['attendees'] as $attendee) {
255.        $row = datafromid($dbconn, "users", $attendee);
256.        printf("<li>%s, %s - <a href=mailto:%s>%s</a>",
     $row['last'], $row['first'], $row['email'],
     $row['email']);
257.      }
258.    }
259.    if(sizeof($fields) > 6) {
260.      ?>
261.      <h4>Agenda: <?=$fields['agenda']?></h4>
262.      <h4>Web: <?=$fields['web']?></h4>
263.      <h4>Phone: <?=$fields['phone']?></h4>
264.      <?
265.    }
```

```php
266. } //end meetingdisplay
267.
268. function viewschedule($email) {
269.    $dbconn = connect();
270.    $sql1 = "select id from users where email = '$email'";
271.    $result1 = $dbconn->query($sql1);
272.    errortrap($result1);
273.    $result1->fetchInto($row1);
274.    $userid = $row1['id'];
275.    $sql2 = "select meeting from meetingusers where userid =
    '$userid'";
276.    $result2 = $dbconn->query($sql2);
277.    errortrap($result2);
278.    $bgcolor = "#FFFF99";
279.    ?>
280.    <p>You have the following meetings on your schedule:
281.    <p><table border=1 cellspacing=0 cellpadding=4>
282.    <tr bgcolor="<?=$bgcolor?>"><td colspan=3><b>Meeting
    Name</b></td></tr>
283.    <tr bgcolor="<?=$bgcolor?>"><td><b>Start</b></
    td><td><b>End</b></td><td><b>Location</b></td></tr>
284.    <?
285.    $bgcolor ="#FFFFFF";
286.    while($result2->fetchInto($row2)) {
287.        $row3 = datafromid($dbconn, "meetings",
    $row2['meeting']);
288.        $room = datafromid($dbconn, "rooms", $row3['room']);
289.        ?>
290.        <tr bgcolor="<?=$bgcolor?>"><td colspan=2><a
    href=<?=$page?>?action=viewmeetingdetails&id=<?=$row2['mee
    ting']?>><?=$row3['name']?></a></td><td>
291.        <?
292.        $sql = "select originator from meetings where id = '"
    . $row2['meeting'] . "'";
293.        $result = $dbconn->query($sql);
294.        errortrap($result);
295.        $result->fetchinto($r);
296.        if($r['originator'] == $userid) {
297.            ?><a
    href=<?=$page?>?action=deletemeeting&id=<?=$row2['meeting'
    ]?>><b>Cancel</b><?
298.        } else {
299.            echo " ";
300.        }
301.        ?>
```

```
302.     </td></tr>
303.     <tr
    bgcolor="<?=$bgcolor?>"><td><?=$row3['startdate']?></td>
304.     <td><?=$row3['enddate']?></
    td><td><?=$room['name']?><br><?=$room['location']?></td></
    tr>
305.     <?
306.     if($bgcolor == "#FFFFFF") {
307.         $bgcolor = "#FFFF99";
308.     } else {
309.         $bgcolor = "#FFFFFF";
310.     }
311.     }
312.     ?>
313.     </table>
314.     <?
315. } //end viewschedule
316.
317.
318. function view_meeting_details($id) {
319.     $dbconn = connect();
320.     $row = datafromid($dbconn, "meetings", $id);
321.     $row2 = datafromid($dbconn, "users",
    $row['originator']);
322.     $row3 = datafromid($dbconn, "rooms", $row['room']);
323.     $originator = $row2['first'] . " " . $row2['last'];
324.     ?>
325.     <h3>Meeting Details</h3>
326.     <table border=1 cellspacing=0 cellpadding=5>
327.     <tr><td>Meeting Name: <?=$row['name']?></
    td><td>Orginator: <?=$originator?></td></tr>
328.     <tr><td>Start Time: <?=$row['startdate']?></td><td>End
    Time: <?=$row['enddate']?></td></tr>
329.     <tr><td>Room: <?=$row3['name']?></td><td>Location:
    <?=$row3['location']?></td></tr>
330.     <tr><td colspan=2>Invited Guests:
331.     <?
332.     $sql = "select * from meetingusers where meeting =
    '$id'";
333.     $result = $dbconn->query($sql);
334.     errortrap($result);
335.     while($result->fetchinto($r)) {
336.         $users = datafromid($dbconn, "users", $r['userid']);
337.     ?>
338.     <li><?=$users['first']?> <?=$users['last']?>
```

```
339.        <?
340.        }
341.    ?>
342.    </td>
343.    <tr><td colspan=2>Agenda:<br><pre><?=$row['agenda']?></
        pre></td></tr>
344.    <tr><td colspan=2>Website: <?=$row['web']?> </td></tr>
345.    <tr><td colspan=2>Call-in Number: <?=$row['phone']?> </
        td></tr>
346.    </table>
347.    <?
348. }
349.
350. function deletemeeting($id) {
351.    $dbconn = connect();
352.    $row = datafromid($dbconn, "meetings", $id);
353.    $row2 = datafromid($dbconn, "users",
        $row['originator']);
354.    $name = $row['name'];
355.    $start = $row['startdate'];
356.    $end = $row['enddate'];
357.    $originator = $row2['first'] . " " . $row2['last'];
358.    $subject = "Meeting $name Cancelled!";
359.    $msg = "The meeting $name scheduled by $originator has
        been cancelled.\n";
360.    $msg .= "The meeting was to take place from $start to
        $end\n";
361.    $msg .= "If you log in to the Meeting Manager, you will
        see the meeting has been removed from your schedule.\n";
362.    $sql = "select * from meetingusers where meeting =
        '$id'";
363.    $result = $dbconn->query($sql);
364.    errortrap($result);
365.    while($result->fetchinto($r)) {
366.      $r2 = datafromid($dbconn, "users", $r['userid']);
367.      $to = $r2['email'];
368.      if(!mail($to, $subject, $msg, "From: Meeting Tracker
        Admin <noreply@example.com?")) {
369.        echo "<h1>Mail Failed!</h1>";
370.      }
371.      echo "<h3>Meeting Cancelled</h3>";
372.    }
373.    $sql1 = "delete from meetings where id = '$id'";
374.    $result1 = $dbconn->query($sql1);
375.    errortrap($result1);
```

```
376.    $sql2 = "delete from meetingusers where meeting =
        '$id'";
377.    $result2 = $dbconn->query($sql2);
378.    errortrap($result2);
379. }
380.
381. function notifyusers($id) {
382.    $dbconn = connect();
383.    $row = datafromid($dbconn, "meetings", $id);
384.    $row2 = datafromid($dbconn, "users",
        $row['originator']);
385.    $name = $row['name'];
386.    $start = $row['startdate'];
387.    $end = $row['enddate'];
388.    $originator = $row2['first'] . " " . $row2['last'];
389.    $subject = "Meeting $name Scheduled!";
390.    $msg = "A meeting has been scheduled: $name.\n Scheduled
        by $originator.\n";
391.    $msg .= "The meeting will take place from $start to
        $end\n";
392.    $msg .= "If you log in to the Meeting Manager, you will
        see the meeting has been added your schedule.\n";
393.    $sql = "select * from meetingusers where meeting =
        '$id'";
394.    $result = $dbconn->query($sql);
395.    errortrap($result);
396.    while($result->fetchinto($r)) {
397.       $r2 = datafromid($dbconn, "users", $r['userid']);
398.       $to = $r2['email'];
399.       if(!mail($to, $subject, $msg, "From: Meeting Tracker
        Admin <noreply@example.com?")) {
400.          echo "<h1>Mail Failed!</h1>";
401.       }
402.    }
403. }
404.
405. function check_user($user, $password) {
406.    $timestamp = date("m-d-Y H:i:s (T)");
407.    $dbconn = connect();
408.    $password_enc = substr(md5($password), 0, 8);
409.    //echo "<P>USERPASS:" . $user . $password_enc;
410.    $sql = "select * from users where email = '$user' and
        pass = '$password_enc'";
411.    $result = $dbconn->query($sql);
412.    errortrap($result);
```

```
413.    if ($result->numRows() == 1) {
414.       setcookie("user",$user);
415.       setcookie("password",$password);
416.       error_log("Sucessful login by $user on
        $timestamp\n",3,"sucessful_logins.txt");
417.       return 1;
418.    } else {
419.       setcookie("user");
420.       setcookie("password");
421.       ?>
422.       <h3>Sorry, you are not authorized!</h3>
423.       <?
424.       error_log("Failed login attempt by $user on
        $timestamp\n",3,"failed_logins.txt");
425.       return 0;
426.    }
427. }
428.
429. function login() {
430.    global $page;
431.    ?>
432.    <h1>You must log in to view this page</h1>
433.    <form action = "<?=$page?>" method="post">
434.    <P>Email: <input type="text" name="user"><br>
435.    Password: <input type="password" name="password"
        maxlength="8" size="8"><br>
436.    <input type="submit" name="submit" value="Submit">
437.    </form>
438.    <?
439. }
440.
441. function choices() {
442.    ?>
443.    <p>
444.    <li><A href="<?=$page?>?action=viewschedule">View
        Schedule</a>
445.    <li><A href="<?=$page?>?action=addmeeting">Add A
        Meeting</a>
446.    <?
447. }
448.
449. /***** MAIN *****/
450. $page = "meeting.php";
451. require_once("meeting_inc.php");
452. if(!isset($user) or !check_user($user, $password)) {
```

```
453.    login();
454.  } else {
455.    if(isset($addmeeting)) {
456.       addmeetingwizard($HTTP_POST_VARS['step']);
457.    } elseif(isset($action)) {
458.       switch($action) {
459.         case("viewschedule"):
460.            head();
461.            choices();
462.            viewschedule($user);
463.            break;
464.         case("addmeeting"):
465.            addmeetingwizard("1");
466.            break;
467.         case("deletemeeting"):
468.            head();
469.            choices();
470.            deletemeeting($id);
471.            break;
472.         case("viewmeetingdetails"):
473.            head();
474.            choices();
475.            view_meeting_details($id);
476.            break;
477.         default;
478.            break;
479.       } //end switch
480.    } else {
481.       head();
482.       choices();
483.    }
484.  }
485.
486.  ?>
487.  </body>
488.  </html>
```

Figure 9–2 shows an example of the Schedule View.

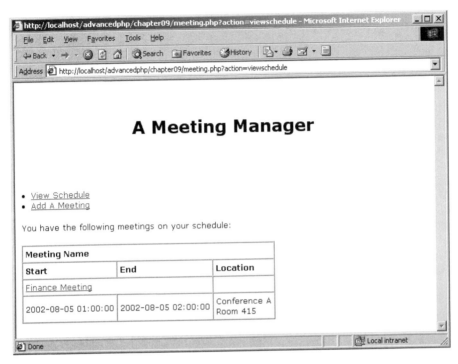

FIGURE 9–2 meeting.pgp—viewing a schedule

Script 9–2 meeting.php Line-by-Line Explanation

LINE	DESCRIPTION
2–231	Define a function, addmeetingwizard(), that guides the user through creating a meeting. This function takes one argument, the current step of the wizard.
3	Start a session to hold variables for the wizard.
4	Print out the beginning of the HTML for the page. We need to do this after the session_start() function, because sessions will not work if you have already printed text to a page.
5	Define some global variables that are used in the script.
6	Create a switch statement. Each case in the switch statement corresponds to a step in the wizard.
7–27	Begin the first step in the wizard. Here we ask the user for the name of the meeting, as well as the time duration on which the meeting occurs. Use a hidden form field to send the users to the next step when they submit this form.

Script 9–2 meeting.php Line-by-Line Explanation (Continued)

LINE	DESCRIPTION
28–87	Begin step two of the wizard. This step first checks to see if the user entered a name for the meeting. If no name is entered, the user is sent back to step one. If the user has entered a name, then the script creates an array called $fields in which to store the values for the meeting. The script also gets the id for the user and enters it into the $fields array as the originator of the meeting. It then adds the name and times of the meeting into the $fields array. The current information that has been entered is displayed on the screen using the meetingdisplay() function. The script then goes on to determine which rooms are available and lists the open rooms, as well as the "virtual" room. Once the user selects a room, the script goes to step three.
88–144	Begin step three of the wizard. Determine which users have already been scheduled for a meeting, and place them in the list with the word "(busy)" next to their name. Once the user has selected the attendees, go on to step four.
145–173	Begin step four of the wizard. Verify that at least one user has been selected as an attendee. If no users have been selected as attendees, then send the user back to step three. If at least one person has been selected as an attendee, then provide a form so that the user can enter the agenda, phone number, and Web site of the meeting.
174–197	Begin step five of the wizard. Verify that the agenda has been filled in. If it has not, then send the user back to step four. If the agenda has been filled in, then provide a button so that the user can finalize the meeting.
198–215	Enter the values from the session $fields array into the database and call the notifyuser() function to send email to all of the invited participants.
216–229	Provide a default case or the switch, in case anything happens to cause the function to skip over the other cases. Print an error message to the user.
230	Close out the switch statement started way back on line 6!
231	End the function declaration for addmeetingwizard().
233–266	Define a function, meetingdisplay(), to display the details of the meeting while the user is going through the meeting creation wizard. Since the $fields array has items added to it during each step, we only show the information that the user has entered.
268–315	Define a function, viewschedule(), that allows the users to view all of their meetings at once within a table. This function also provides a link so that the users may view the full details of the meeting or, if they are the originator, a link to cancel a meeting.

Script 9–2 meeting.php Line-by-Line Explanation (Continued)

LINE	DESCRIPTION
318–348	Define a function, view_meeting_details(), that allows the user to view the full details for a particular meeting.
350–379	Define a function, deletemeeting(), that deletes a meeting from the database and notifies all the participants by email that the meeting has been cancelled.
381–403	Define a function, notifyusers(), that sends out email notifying the users that they have been invited to a new meeting.
405–427	Define a function, check_user(), that verifies a user login. This is similar to the function used in Chapter 7.
429–439	Define a function, login(), that prints a form allowing the user to log in.
441–447	Define a function, choices(), that allows users to view their schedules or schedule new meetings.
449	Begin the main program.
450	Define the $page variable that is used in the functions that have forms.
451	Require the meeting_inc.php script, as it contains some functions used by this script.
452–453	Check to see if the user is logged in. If not, call the login() function so that the user may log in.
454–456	If the user is logged in and the $addmeeting variable is set, then we know the user is in the middle of the meeting creation wizard. Send the user back to the wizard.
457–479	If the user is logged in and the $action variable is set, then we know the user is starting or finishing a particular task. Send the user to the correct function depending on which action is being taken.
480–483	If the user is logged in but not creating a meeting or doing any other tasks, then provide some options to do something with the choices() function.
484	Close out the if statement started on line 452.
486	End the PHP for the page.
487–488	End the HTML for the page.

Figure 9–3 shows an example of the Meeting Detail View.

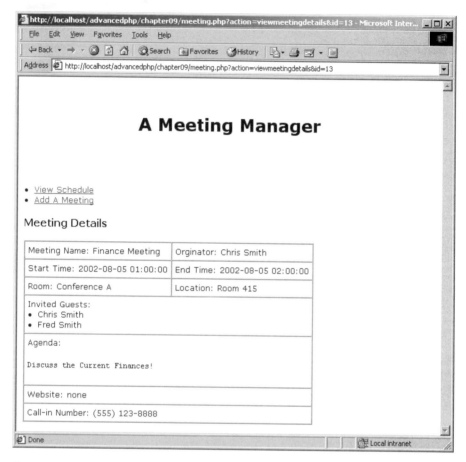

FIGURE 9–3 meeting.php—viewing meeting details

meeting_inc.php

meeting_inc.php contains code used by both meeting.php and admin.php.

SCRIPT 9–3 meeting_inc.php

```
1.   <?
2.
3.   /***** FUNCTIONS *****/
4.   function connect() {
5.     ini_set("include_path", "G:\apache\Apache\php\pear");
6.     require_once("DB.php");
```

```
7.      $type = "mysql";
8.      $username = "php";
9.      $password = "password";
10.     $host = "localhost";
11.     $database = "meeting";
12.     $dsn = $type . "://" . $username . ":" . $password .
        "@" . $host . "/" . $database;
13.     $dbconn = DB::connect($dsn);
14.     errortrap($dbconn);
15.     $dbconn->setFetchMode(DB_FETCHMODE_ASSOC);
16.     return $dbconn;
17. }//end connect
18.
19. function errortrap($result) {
20.     if(DB::isError($result)) {
21.        ?><h3>There was an error!</h3><?
22.        die($result->getMessage());
23.     }
24. } //end errortrap
25.
26. function datafromid($dbconn, $table, $id) {
27.     $sql = "select * from $table where id = '$id'";
28.     $result = $dbconn->query($sql);
29.     errortrap($result);
30.     $result->fetchInto($row);
31.     return $row;
32. } //end datafromid
33.
34. function createdate($type) {
35.     $years = array("2002","2003","2004");
36.     $minutes = array(":00", ":15", ":30", ":45");
37.     $months = array();
38.     $days = array();
39.     $hours = array();
40.     for($i = 1; $i < 13; $i++) {
41.        if($i < 10) {
42.           $months[] = "0" . $i;
43.        } else {
44.           $months[] = $i;
45.        }
46.     }
47.     for($i = 1; $i < 32; $i++) {
48.        if($i < 10) {
49.           $days[] = "0" . $i;
50.        } else {
```

```
51.          $days[] = $i;
52.        }
53.      }
54.      for($i = 1; $i < 25; $i++) {
55.        $hours[] = $i;
56.      }
57.      $fields = array("years", "months", "days", "hours",
     "minutes");
58.      foreach($fields as $field) {
59.        ?>
60.        <select name="<? echo $type . $field ?>">
61.        <?
62.          foreach($$field as $item) {
63.            echo"<option value=$item>$item</option>\n";
64.          }
65.        ?>
66.        </select>
67.        <?
68.        if($field == "days") {
69.          echo " at ";
70.        }
71.      }
72.    } //end createdate
73.
74.    function head() {
75.      ?>
76.      <html>
77.      <head>
78.      <style type=text/css>
79.      h1, h2, h3, p, td, li {font-family: verdana, sans-serif; }
80.      </style>
81.      </head>
82.      <body bgcolor="#FFFFFF">
83.      <div align=center>
84.      <table width="74%" border="0" cellspacing="0"
     cellpadding="0" height="128" bgcolor="#FFFFFF">
85.          <tr>
86.            <td height="134" align="center"><h1>A Meeting
     Manager</h1></td>
87.          </tr>
88.        </table>
89.      </div>
90.      <?
91.    }
92.    ?>
```

Script 9–3 meeting_inc.php Line-by-Line Explanation

LINE	DESCRIPTION
4–17	Define a function, connect(), that establishes a connection to the database. Be sure to change the values so that they match your particular setup.
19–24	Define a function, errortrap(), that traps any PEAR DB errors that might occur.
26–32	Define a function, datafromid(), that selects all of the information from a particular table based on an id. This is used throughout the script and saves a lot of typing.
34–72	Define a function, createdate(), that creates a nice dropdown menu for date formats.
74–91	Define a function, head(), that prints out the beginning of the HTML for any given page.
92	End the PHP for the script.

Figure 9–4 shows an example of the Create Meeting Wizard.

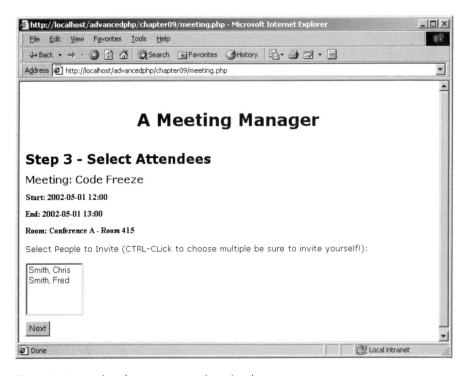

FIGURE 9–4 meeting.php—create meeting wizard

admin.php

admin.php is the administration interface for the application.

SCRIPT 9–4 admin.php

```
1. <?
2. function adduserform() {
3.    global $page;
4.    ?>
5.    <form action="<?=$page?>" method="post">
6.    <table border=0>
7.    <tr><td colspan=2><h3>Add User</h3></td></tr>
8.    <tr><td>First Name: </td><td><input type="text"
   name="first"></td></tr>
9.    <tr><td>Last Name: </td><td><input type="text"
   name="last"></td></tr>
10.   <tr><td>Phone: </td><td><input type="text"
   name="phone"></td></tr>
11.   <tr><td>Email: </td><td><input type="text"
   name="email"></td></tr>
12.   <tr><td>Password:</td><td><input type="text"
   name="password" size="8" maxlength="8"></td></tr>
13.   <tr><td colspan=2><input type="submit" name="adduser"
   value="Add User"></td></tr>
14.   </table>
15.   </form>
16.   <?
17. } //end adduserform
18.
19. function adduser($HTTP_POST_VARS) {
20.   if(($HTTP_POST_VARS['first'] or $HTTP_POST_VARS['last']
   or $HTTP_POST_VARS['email'] or
   $HTTP_POST_VARS['password']) == "") {
21.     return 0;
22.   } else {
23.     $dbconn = connect();
24.     $id = $dbconn->nextID('user_id',true);
25.     if(DB::isError($id)) {
26.       die($id->getMessage());
27.     }
28.     $password = md5($HTTP_POST_VARS['password']);
29.     $sql = "INSERT INTO users VALUES('$id', '" .
   $HTTP_POST_VARS['first'] . "','" . $HTTP_POST_VARS['last']
   . "','" .
```

```
30.           $HTTP_POST_VARS['phone'] . "','" .
    $HTTP_POST_VARS['email'] . "', '$password')";
31.      $result = $dbconn->query($sql);
32.      errortrap($result);
33.      return 1;
34.    }
35. } //end adduser
36.
37. function addroomform() {
38.    global $page;
39.    ?>
40.    <form action="<?=$page?>" method="post">
41.    <table border=0>
42.    <tr><td colspan=2><h3>Add Room</h3></td></tr>
43.    <tr><td>Name: </td><td><input type="text" name="name"></
    td></tr>
44.    <tr><td>Location: </td><td><input type="text"
    name="location"></td></tr>
45.    <tr><td colspan=2><input type="submit" name="addroom"
    value="Add Room"></td></tr>
46.    </table>
47.    </form>
48.    <?
49. } //end addroomform
50.
51.
52. function addroom($HTTP_POST_VARS) {
53.    $dbconn = connect();
54.    $id = $dbconn->nextID('room_id',true);
55.    errortrap($id);
56.    $sql = "INSERT INTO rooms VALUES('$id', '" .
    $HTTP_POST_VARS['name'] . "','" .
    $HTTP_POST_VARS['location'] . "')";
57.    $result = $dbconn->query($sql);
58.    errortrap($result);
59.    return 1;
60. } //end addroom
61.
62. function admin_choices() {
63.    ?>
64.    <li><a href="<?=$page?>?action=newuser">New User</a>
65.    <li><a href="<?=$page?>?action=newroom">New Room</a>
66.    <?
67. }
68.
```

```
69. /***** MAIN *****/
70.
71. $page = "admin.php";
72. require_once("../meeting_inc.php");
73.
74. if(isset($addroom)) {
75.   if(addroom($HTTP_POST_VARS)) {
76.     echo "<h3>Room Added!</h3>";
77.   }
78. }
79. if(isset($adduser)) {
80.   if(adduser($HTTP_POST_VARS)) {
81.     echo "<h3>User Added!</h3>";
82.   } else {
83.     ?>
84.     <h2>You must enter First and Last Name, Email, and a
    Password!</h2>
85.     <h3>Please Try Again</h3>
86.     <?
87.     adduserform();
88.   }
89. }
90.
91. if(isset($action)) {
92.   switch($action) {
93.     case("newuser"):
94.       adduserform();
95.       break;
96.     case("newroom"):
97.       addroomform();
98.       break;
99.     default:
100.       echo "Bad Action";
101.   }
102. }
103.
104. admin_choices();
105. ?>
106. </body>
107. </html>
```

Script 9–4 admin.php Line-by-Line Explanation

LINE	DESCRIPTION
2–17	Define a function, adduserform(), that prints out the form so the administrator can add a new user to the database.
19–35	Define a function, adduser(), that processes the data entered into the form above and adds a user to the database.
37–49	Define a function, addroomform(), that prints out a form so the administrator can add a new room to the database.
52–60	Define a function, addroom(), that processes the data entered from the form above and adds the room to the database.
62–67	Define a function, admin_choices(), that presents the administrator with the option of adding a new user or room to the database.
69	Begin the main program.
71	Define the $page variable that is used in the above function to submit forms.
72	Require the meeting_inc.php script so that this script can use its functions.
74–78	If the $addroom variable is set, then we know the administrator has submitted the form to add a room. Call the addroom() function to add the room.
79–89	If the $adduser variable is set, then we know the administrator has submitted the form to add a user. Verify that the First Name, Last Name, Email, and Password fields have been filled out, then call the addroom() function to add the room.
91–102	If the $action variable is set, then we know that the administrator has clicked on one of the links from the admin_choices() function. Take the required action depending on which link was clicked.
104	Execute the admin_choices() function so that the administrator can add rooms or users.
105	End the PHP for the script.
106–107	End the HTML for the page.

PHP and XML

Overview

X ML (eXtensible Markup Language) is finally in the mainstream and showing the benefits that the faithful have been spouting since XML's inception. A quick look at XML support in Apache and the Java language should be enough to affirm that XML is here to stay.

PHP has built-in support for XML in the form of an extension. Unlike other extensions, XML is compiled in by default so you should not require any additional configuration to get XML to work. The PHP XML extension uses James Clark's expat library, complete details of which can be found at *www.jclark.com/xml/*.

A quick look, as in Figure 10–1, at a PHP page containing the phpinfo() function should confirm that XML is enabled in your build of PHP.

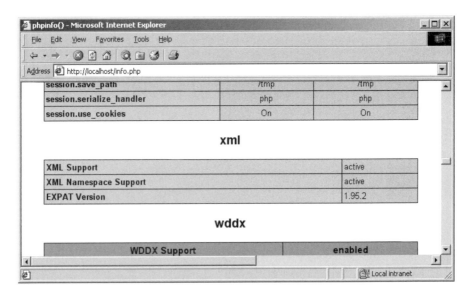

FIGURE 10–1 Confirming XML Is Enabled Using phpinfo()

PHP's XML extension allows you to parse an XML file. You can read through an XML file following its nodes and branches and perform operations on the data contained within.

PHP's XML extension does not validate XML files. That is, it cannot compare an XML file to a DTD (Document Type Definition) and verify that the file is valid according to the DTD. Having said that, you must make sure that the XML you send to PHP is either valid or well-formed.

Creating an XML Parser

Before you can use PHP's XML extension to read XML files, you must create a parser. Since XML documents are extensible, there is no way for PHP to know what elements you are searching for in the XML. Therefore, you must tell PHP how it should parse the document. You tell PHP how to parse the document by defining a new XML parser instance and then defining element handlers and character handlers. An element handler is simply a function that runs when an element is encountered in the XML. You need to define two element handlers, one handler for when an element is encountered by PHP and another handler for when the PHP parser leaves the current element. Additionally, you must specify a handler for the character data that exists between elements. If you are a little rusty on your XML-speak, here is a short example of an XML document:

```
<?xml version="1.0"?>
<document>
    <title>XML Is Easy</title>
    <body>Demystifying XML. Read about it here.</
body>
  </document>
```

Looks simple enough, right? That's because it is. Since you are already familiar with HTML, the basics of XML should be readily apparent. Elements are enclosed by "<" and ">". Start and end elements are differentiated by the presence or absence of the "/" symbol. Think of a first-level heading tag: <h1>A Heading</h1>. The first <h1> tag starts the element, and the second </h1> tag closes the element. The characters in between are the character data. Now this is a hugely simplified example, but if you are unfamiliar with XML, then it should shed some light on what we are about to do as we create a parser.

Defining the XML Parser

You define an XML Parser by using the xml_parser_create() function:

```
$parser = xml_parser_create(ENCODING);
```

You assign xml_parser_create() to a variable, which is passed to the other functions required for parsing XML pages. Additionally, you can optionally assign the type of encoding that the parser should use. Encoding is the character encoding in the XML document. You can choose one of three encoding types:

- ISO-8859-1 (default)
- US-ASCII
- UTF-8

Once you have defined a new parser instance, you can then create your handlers to do the actual work of reading through an XML file.

Defining the Element Handlers

Element handlers are defined using the xml_set_element_handler()
function:

```
xml_set_element_handler(XML_PARSER, START_FUNCTION,
END_FUNCTION);
```

xml_set_handler takes three arguments:
- XML_PARSER—The variable that you created when you
  called the xml_create_parser() function.
- START_FUNCTION—The name of the function to call
  when the parser encounters a start element.
- END_FUNCTION—The name of the function to call
  when the parser encounters an end element.

Defining Character Handlers

Character handlers are defined using the set_character_handler()
function:

```
xml_set_character_handler(XML_PARSER,
CHARACTER_FUNCTION);
```

xml_set_character_handler() takes two arguments:
- XML_PARSER—The variable that you created when you
  called the xml_create_parser() function.
- CHARACTER_FUNCTION—The name of the function
  to call when character data is encountered.

Starting the Parser

The final piece to the puzzle is the function that starts the
whole process, xml_parse():

```
xml_parse(XML_PARSER, XML);
```

xml_parse() takes two arguments:
- XML_PARSER—The variable that you created when you
  called the xml_create_parser() function.
- XML—The XML that is to be parsed.

Cleaning Up

After you have finished parsing the document, you should free the memory holding the parser by calling the xml_parser_free() function:

```
xml_parser_free(XML_PARSER);
```

xml_parser_free() takes one argument, XML_PARSER, which is the variable that you created when you called the xml_create_parser() function.

Let's look at an example to solidify the principles we've just discussed. The following example uses all of the functions just discussed. It opens a simple XML file, aptly named simple.xml, and parses the XML within. Figure 10–2 displays the output. Here is simple.xml, which you'll need to create and place in the same directory as the xml1.php example:

SCRIPT 10–1 simple.xml

```
1.  <?xml version="1.0"?>
2.  <document>
3.  <title>XML Exposed</title>
4.  <body>Demystifying XML. Read about it here.</body>
5.  </document>
```

SCRIPT 10–2 xml1.php

```
1.  <?
2.  function startElement($xml_parser, $name, $attributes) {
3.     print("<p><i>Encountered Start Element For:</i>$name\n");
4.  }
5.
6.  function endElement($xml_parser, $name) {
7.     print("<p><i>Encountered End Element For:</i>$name\n");
8.  }
9.
10. function characterData($xml_parser, $data) {
11.    if($data != "\n") {
12.       print("<p><i>Encountered Character Data:</i>$data\n");
13.    }
14. }
15.
16. function load_data($file) {
```

```
17.    $fh = fopen($file, "r") or die ("<P>COULD NOT OPEN
       FILE!");
18.    $data = fread($fh, filesize($file));
19.    return $data;
20.  }
21.  /***** MAIN *****/
22.  $file = "simple.xml";
23.  $xml_parser = xml_parser_create();
24.  xml_set_element_handler($xml_parser, "startElement",
       "endElement");
25.  xml_set_character_data_handler($xml_parser,
       "characterData");
26.  xml_parse($xml_parser, load_data($file)) or die
       ("<P>ERROR PARSING XML!");
27.  xml_parser_free($xml_parser);
28.  ?>
```

Script 10–2 xml1.php Line-by-Line Explanation

LINE	DESCRIPTION
2	Create a function called startElement() to handle any start elements that the script encounters as it parses the XML. The function takes the following as its arguments (required by PHP):
	• $xml_parser
	• $name
	• $attributes
3	Print a message to the screen when a start element is encountered.
4	End the function declaration.
6	Create a function called endElement() to handle any end elements that the script encounters as it parses the XML. The function takes the following as its arguments (required by PHP):
	• $xml_parser
	• $name
7	Print a message to the screen when an end element is encountered.
8	End the function declaration.
10	Create a function called characterData() to handle the data found between elements as the script parses the XML. The function takes the following as arguments (required by PHP):
	• $xml_parser
	• $data

Script 10–2 xml1.php Line-by-Line Explanation (Continued)

LINE	DESCRIPTION
11–13	If there is actual character data between the elements (not just a newline character), print a message to the screen when character data is encountered.
14	End the function declaration.
16	Create a function called load_data() to read the data from an XML file into the script so that it may be parsed. The function takes one argument, $file, which is the name (with an optional path) of the XML file that you want to parse.
17	Attempt to assign a file handle to the file. If unsuccessful, kill the script and print out an error message.
18	If the file opening was successful, read in the entire file into the $data variable. Note that this is wildly inefficient for large files.
19	Return the $data variable to the calling program.
20	End the function declaration.
21	Begin the main program.
22	Assign a file name to the $file variable. Note that you can use a full path to the file, such as: • Windows: `$file = "C:\winnt\xml\myxmlfile.xml";` • Linux: `$file = "/home/me/xml/myxmlfile.xml";`
23	Create a variable called $xml_parser and assign it as a PHP xml parser using the xml_parser_create() function.
24	Define the custom start and end element handler functions that you created above using the xml_set_element_handler() function. Whenever PHP encounters a start or end element, it will use the respective function.
25	Define the custom data handler function that you created above using the xml_set_character_data_handler() function. Whenever PHP encounters character data, it will use the characterData() function.
26	Begin parsing the XML with the xml_parse function. The xml_parse() function requires the name of the XML parser ($xml_parser) and the XML data that you want to parse. In this case, we provide the XML data by using the custom load_data($file) function. If the xml_parse() function fails, then kill the script and display an error message.
27	After the xml_parse() function has completed parsing the XML, free the memory associated with the parser by using the xml_parser_free() function.

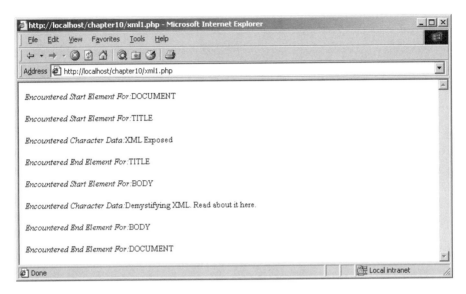

Figure 10–2 xml1.php

Parsing and Transforming XML Documents

The example above works well for parsing ultrasimple documents, but it doesn't take into account nested elements or attributes.

In the real world, XML documents are highly structured and precisely defined. A great deal of effort goes into designing XML information products. One reason for the amount of effort that is required is the extensible nature of XML. XML gives you a set of rules that allows you to create these complex structured documents. Those rules, however, provide for an almost infinite amount of possibilities for defining a document's structure. Keep that in mind when creating a PHP XML parsing application. Each application that you create will only work with one particular document structure. The extra effort spent designing the document structure pays off when you code applications that will parse that data.

Having said that, this next example tackles a couple of problems you will find in coding parsers for your own XML documents. These problems include multiple instances of the same element (usually differentiated by attributes or content) and attributes: two things you are sure to find in "real" XML documents. The complexity of the example document, bebop.xml, is fairly basic, but as you will see, the complexity of coding a PHP parser to read more complex documents doesn't necessarily increase; it is really just doing a lot more of the same thing over and over. The basic function of the element and character handlers does not change. You just need to add additional cases to encompass the additional variations that your document requires.

This next example shows how a more complex document can be parsed and how to present the resulting data. The XML file is the beginning of series synopsis for the popular anime title, *Cowboy Bebop*. Although it is far from complete as far as the series information goes, the XML structure allows for adding data to make the document more comprehensive. The output appears in Figure 10–3.

The first part of the script, bebop.xml, is the actual XML file that is read into the parser.

SCRIPT 10–3 bebop.xml

```
 1.  <?xml version="1.0"?>
 2.  <series title="Cowboy Bebop" genre="Anime"
     subgenre="Science Fiction">
 3.     <dvd number="1">
 4.        <episode number="1">
 5.           <title>Asteroid Blues</title>
 6.           <synopsis>Jet and Spike track down a drug
     dealer.</synopsis>
 7.           <characters>
 8.              <character>Jet</character>
 9.              <character>Spike</character>
10.           </characters>
11.        </episode>
12.        <episode number="2">
13.           <title>Stray Dog Strut</title>
14.           <synopsis>Ein Joins the crew.</synopsis>
15.           <characters>
16.              <character>Jet</character>
17.              <character>Spike</character>
18.              <character>Ein</character>
19.           </characters>
20.        </episode>
```

```
21.        <episode number="3">
22.          <title>Honkey Tonk Woman</title>
23.          <synopsis>Introduction of Faye Valentine.</
      synopsis>
24.          <characters>
25.            <character>Jet</character>
26.            <character>Spike</character>
27.            <character>Ein</character>
28.            <character>Faye</character>
29.          </characters>
30.        </episode>
31.        <episode number="4">
32.          <title>Gateway Shuffle</title>
33.          <synopsis>Having fun at the casino.</synopsis>
34.        </episode>
35.        <episode number="5">
36.          <title>Ballad Of Fallen Angels</title>
37.          <synopsis>Spike's past comes back to haunt him.</
      synopsis>
38.        </episode>
39.      </dvd>
40.      <dvd number="2">
41.        <episode number="6">
42.          <title>Sympathy For The Devil</title>
43.          <synopsis>The mystery of the boy Wen.</synopsis>
44.        </episode>
45.        <episode number="7">
46.          <title>Heavy Metal Queen</title>
47.          <synopsis>Truckers in space.</synopsis>
48.        </episode>
49.        <episode number="8">
50.          <title>Waltz for Venus</title>
51.          <synopsis>Welcome to Venus.</synopsis>
52.        </episode>
53.        <episode number="9">
54.          <title>Jamming With Edward</title>
55.          <synopsis>Edward joins the crew.</synopsis>
56.          <characters>
57.            <character>Jet</character>
58.            <character>Spike</character>
59.            <character>Ein</character>
60.            <character>Faye</character>
61.            <character>Edward</character>
62.          </characters>
63.        </episode>
```

SCRIPT 10–3 bebop.xml (Continued)

```
64.      <episode number="10">
65.        <title>Ganymede Elegy</title>
66.        <synopsis>Homecoming for Jet.</synopsis>
67.      </episode>
68.    </dvd>
69.  </series>
```

SCRIPT 10–4 xml_series.php

```
1.  <html>
2.  <head>
3.  <title>XML - DVD SERIES PARSER</title>
4.  <style type=text/css>
5.  h1, h2, h3 {font-family: verdana, helvetica, sans-serif;}
6.  p, blockquote {font-family: verdana, helvetica, sans-
    serif; font-size: 10pt}
7.  .navy {color: navy; }
8.  .characters {font-size: 8pt; color: red}
9.  </style>
10. </head>
11. <body>
12. <?
13. function startElement($xml_parser, $name, $attributes) {
14.     global $TagsOpen, $counter;
15.     switch($name) {
16.       case($name = "SERIES"):
17.         $TagsOpen["SERIES"] = 1;
18.         ?>
19.         <h1>DVD Series</h1>
20.         <h2>Title: <span
    class=navy><?=$attributes["TITLE"]?></span>
21.         <br>Genre: <span
    class=navy><?=$attributes["GENRE"]?></span>
22.         <br>Subgenre: <span
    class=navy><?=$attributes["SUBGENRE"]?></span></h2>
23.         <?
24.         break;
25.       case($name = "DVD"):
26.         $TagsOpen["DVD"] = 1;
27.         ?>
28.         <h3>DVD <span
    class=navy><?=$attributes["NUMBER"]?></span>
29.         <?
30.         break;
31.       case($name = "EPISODE"):
```

```
32.          $TagsOpen["EPISODE"] = 1;
33.          ?>
34.          <p><span class=navy>Episode:
     <?=$attributes["NUMBER"]?>
35.          <?
36.          break;
37.     case($name = "TITLE");
38.          $TagsOpen["TITLE"] = 1;
39.          break;
40.     case($name = "SYNOPSIS"):
41.          $TagsOpen["SYNOPSIS"] = 1;
42.          break;
43.     case($name = "CHARACTERS"):
44.          $TagsOpen["CHARACTERS"] = 1;
45.          ?>
46.          <blockquote>Characters:<span class=characters>
47.          <?
48.          break;
49.     case($name = "CHARACTER"):
50.          $TagsOpen["CHARACTER"] = 1;
51.          $counter++;
52.          break;
53.     }
54. }
55.
56. function endElement($parser, $name) {
57.     global $TagsOpen, $counter;
58.     switch($name) {
59.       case($name = "SERIES"):
60.          $TagsOpen["SERIES"] = 0;
61.          break;
62.       case($name = "DVD"):
63.          $TagsOpen["DVD"] = 0;
64.          break;
65.       case($name = "EPISODE"):
66.          $TagsOpen["EPISODE"] = 0;
67.          break;
68.       case($name = "TITLE");
69.          $TagsOpen["TITLE"] = 0;
70.          ?>
71.          </span>
72.          <?
73.          break;
74.       case($name = "SYNOPSIS"):
75.          $TagsOpen["SYNOPSIS"] = 0;
```

```
76.          break;
77.      case($name = "CHARACTERS"):
78.          $TagsOpen["CHARACTERS"] = 0;
79.          ?>
80.          </span></blockquote>
81.          <?
82.          $counter = 0;
83.          break;
84.      case($name = "CHARACTER"):
85.          $TagsOpen["CHARACTER"] = 0;
86.          break;
87.  }
88. }
89.
90. function characterData($parser, $data) {
91.    global $TagsOpen, $counter;
92.    switch($TagsOpen) {
93.      case($TagsOpen["CHARACTER"] == 1):
94.          if($counter == 1) {
95.             echo " $data";
96.          } else {
97.             echo ", $data";
98.          }
99.          break;
100.      case($TagsOpen["SYNOPSIS"] == 1):
101.          echo "<br>$data\n";
102.          break;
103.      case($TagsOpen["TITLE"] == 1):
104.          echo " - \"$data\"";
105.  }
106. }
107.
108. function load_data($file) {
109.    $fh = fopen($file, "r") or die ("<P>COULD NOT OPEN
     FILE!");
110.    $data = fread($fh, filesize($file));
111.    return $data;
112. }
113.
114. $TagsOpen = array(
115.        "SERIES" => 0,
116.        "DVD" => 0,
117.        "EPISODE" => 0,
118.        "TITLE" => 0,
119.        "SYNOPSIS" => 0,
```

```
120.          "CHARACTERS" => 0,
121.          "CHARACTER" => 0
122.          );
123.
124. $counter = 0;
125.
126. $file = "bebop.xml";
127. $xml_parser = xml_parser_create();
128. xml_parser_set_option($xml_parser,
     XML_OPTION_CASE_FOLDING, true);
129. xml_set_element_handler($xml_parser, "startElement",
     "endElement");
130. xml_set_character_data_handler($xml_parser,
     "characterData");
131. xml_parse($xml_parser, load_data($file)) or die ("<P>ERROR
     PARSING XML!");
132. xml_parser_free($xml_parser);
133. ?>
134. </body>
135. </html>
```

Script 10–4 xml_series.php Line-by-Line Explanation

LINE	DESCRIPTION
1–11	Display the beginning part of the HTML page for the script, including some basic styles to format the output.
12	Begin parsing the page as PHP.
13–54	Create a function called startElement() to handle any start elements that the script encounters as it parses the XML. The function takes the following as its arguments (required by PHP): • $xml_parser • $name • $attributes
14	Allow the variables $TagsOpen and $counter to be accessed and modified by this function. $TagsOpen is an array that tracks which tags are open or closed. $counter is an integer that is used for formatting purposes when displaying character data.
15–53	Create a switch statement to evaluate the value of the start element name.
16–24	Add a case to the switch statement to check if the $name variable equals "SERIES".

Script 10–4 xml_series.php Line-by-Line Explanation (Continued)

LINE	DESCRIPTION
17	Set the $TagsOpen["SERIES"] flag to true (1), since the SERIES tag is open.
18–23	Print out some information to the screen, including the attributes of the SERIES tag, which include the title, genre, and subgenre of the series.
24	Break out of the switch statement, since we are done evaluating the $name variable.
25–30	Add a case to the switch statement to check if the $name variable equals "DVD".
26	Set the $TagsOpen["DVD"] flag to true (1), since the DVD tag is open.
27–29	Print out some information to the screen regarding the DVD tag, including its attributes.
30	Break out of the switch statement, since we are done evaluating the $name variable.
31	Add a case to the switch statement to check if the $name variable equals "EPISODE".
32	Set the $TagsOpen["EPISODE"] flag to true (1), since the EPISODE tag is open.
33–35	Print out some information to the screen regarding the EPISODE tag, including its attributes.
36	Break out of the switch statement, since we are done evaluating the $name variable.
37	Add a case to the switch statement to check if the $name variable equals "TITLE".
38	Set the $TagsOpen["TITLE"] flag to true (1), since the TITLE tag is open. We don't need to print anything for TITLE, because there are no attributes associated with this tag.
39	Break out of the switch statement, since we are done evaluating the $name variable.
40	Add a case to the switch statement to check if the $name variable equals "SYNOPSIS".
41	Set the $TagsOpen["SYNOPSIS"] flag to true (1), since the SYNOPSIS tag is open. We don't need to print anything for SYNOPSIS because there are no attributes associated with this tag.
42	Break out of the switch statement, since we are done evaluating the $name variable.

Script 10–4 xml_series.php Line-by-Line Explanation (Continued)

LINE	DESCRIPTION
43	Add a case to the switch statement to check if the $name variable equals "CHARACTERS".
44	Set the $TagsOpen["CHARACTERS"] flag to true (1), since the CHARACTERS tag is open.
45–47	Print out some formatting that will be used when we print out the individual character names.
48	Break out of the switch statement, since we are done evaluating the $name variable.
49	Add a case to the switch statement to check if the $name variable equals "CHARACTER".
50	Set the $TagsOpen["CHARACTER"] flag to true (1), since the CHARACTER tag is open. We don't need to print anything for CHARACTER, because there are no attributes associated with this tag.
51	Increment the $counter variable, as it is used to help format the output when the individual character names are displayed.
52	Break out of the switch statement, since we are done evaluating the $name variable.
53	Close the switch statement.
54	End the function declaration.
56	Create a function called endElement() to handle any end elements that the script encounters as it parses the XML. The function takes the following as its arguments (required by PHP): • $xml_parser • $name
57	Allow the variables $TagsOpen and $counter to be accessed and modified by this function. $TagsOpen is an array that tracks which tags are open or closed. $counter is an integer that is used for formatting purposes when displaying character data.
58	Create a switch statement to evaluate the value of the start element name.
59	Add a case to the switch statement to check if the $name variable equals "SERIES".
60	Set the $TagsOpen["SERIES"] flag to false (0), since the SERIES tag has been closed.

Script 10–4 xml_series.php Line-by-Line Explanation (Continued)

LINE	DESCRIPTION
61	Break out of the switch statement, since we are done evaluating the $name variable.
62	Add a case to the switch statement to check if the $name variable equals "DVD".
63	Set the $TagsOpen["DVD"] flag to false (0), since the DVD tag has been closed.
64	Break out of the switch statement, since we are done evaluating the $name variable.
65	Add a case to the switch statement to check if the $name variable equals "EPISODE".
66	Set the $TagsOpen["EPISODE"] flag to false (0), since the EPISODE tag has been closed.
67	Break out of the switch statement, since we are done evaluating the $name variable.
68	Add a case to the switch statement to check if the $name variable equals "TITLE".
69	Set the $TagsOpen["TITLE"] flag to false (0), since the TITLE tag has been closed.
70–72	Print out the closing span, which was started when the parser found an open TITLE tag.
73	Break out of the switch statement, since we are done evaluating the $name variable.
74	Add a case to the switch statement to check if the $name variable equals "SYNOPSIS".
75	Set the $TagsOpen["SYNOPSIS"] flag to false (0), since the SYNOPSIS tag has been closed.
76	Break out of the switch statement, since we are done evaluating the $name variable.
77	Add a case to the switch statement to check if the $name variable equals "CHARACTERS".
78	Set the $TagsOpen["CHARACTERS"] flag to false (0), since the CHARACTERS tag has been closed.
79–81	Close out the blockquote and span tags that were started when the parser encountered an open CHARACTERS tag.

Script 10–4 xml_series.php Line-by-Line Explanation (Continued)

LINE	DESCRIPTION
82	Set the $counter variable to "0". The characterData() function will use this to help display the names of the characters.
83	Break out of the switch statement, since we are done evaluating the $name variable.
84	Add a case to the switch statement to check if the $name variable equals "CHARACTER".
85	Set the $TagsOpen["CHARACTER"] flag to false (0), since the CHARACTER tag has been closed.
86	Break out of the switch statement, since we are done evaluating the $name variable.
87	Close the switch statement.
88	End the function declaration.
90	Create a function called characterData() to handle any character data that the script encounters as it parses the XML. The function takes the following as its arguments (required by PHP): • $xml_parser • $data
91	Allow the variables $TagsOpen and $counter to be accessed and modified by this function. $TagsOpen is an array that tracks which tags are open or closed. $counter is an integer that is used for formatting purposes when displaying character data.
92	Create a switch statement to evaluate the value of the $TagsOpen array. By examing this array, the function can determine at which point in the XML file PHP is parsing and display the data in the proper format.
93	Add a case to the switch statement to check if the CHARACTER element tags are open. We check them to see if the CHARACTER element is open before we check if any other tags are open, since the CHARACTER element is the most deeply nested element in our XML file.
94–98	Check the value of the $counter variable. If the counter variable is set to 1, then it means that this is the first character encountered in the current node of the XML. If it is the first character, then just print the character name. If it is not the first character, then print a comma and the character name. This allows you to display the entries separated by a comma.
99	Break out of the switch statement, since we are done evaluating the $TagsOpen variable.

Script 10–4 xml_series.php Line-by-Line Explanation (Continued)

LINE	DESCRIPTION
100	Add a case to the switch statement to check if the SYNOPSIS element tags are open. We check to see if the SYNOPSIS element is open next, because it is one node up from the deepest node.
101	If the SYNOPSIS tags are open, then print the data that exists inside SYNOPSIS tags.
102	Break out of the switch statement, since we are done evaluating the $TagsOpen variable.
103	Add a case to the switch statement to check if the TITLE element tags are open. We check them to see if the TITLE element is open next, because it is one node up from SYNOPSIS.
104	If the TITLE tags are open, then print the data that exists inside TITLE tags.
105	Break out of the switch statement, since we are done evaluating the $TagsOpen variable.
106	Close the switch statement. **Note:** We do not have to check any of the other elements because none of those elements contain any actual character data in between their open and close tags. They contain only other elements, so there is no need to use this function to check for data in those elements.
107	End the function declaration.
108	Create a function called load_data() to read the data from an XML file into the script so that it may be parsed. The function takes one argument, $file, which is the name (with an optional path) of the XML file that you want to parse.
109	Attempt to assign a file handle to the file. If unsuccessful, kill the script and print out an error message.
110	If the file opening was successful, read the entire file into the $data variable. Note that this is wildly inefficient for large files.
111	Return the $data variable to the calling program.
112	End the function declaration.
114–122	Define and initialize the $TagsOpen array. You need to define an array element for each element that needs to be tracked. The array item's key is the name of the element, and the value is either 1 or 0 (true or false). Set all the values to false (0) in the beginning, since no tags are supposed to be open before you even start parsing the file.
124	Initialize the $counter variable to "0".

Script 10–4 xml_series.php Line-by-Line Explanation (Continued)

LINE	DESCRIPTION
126	Assign a file name to the $file variable. Note that you can use a full path to the file such as: • Windows: `$file = "C:\winnt\xml\myxmlfile.xml";` • Linux: `$file = "/home/me/xml/myxmlfile.xml";`
127	Define a parser option using the xml_set_parser_option() function. This function changes options as to how the parser operates. It requires three arguments: • The XML parser that you created using the xml_parser_create function. • The option you want to set. • The value of the option you are setting. In this case, we are setting the option "XML_OPTION_CASE_FOLDING" to true, which changes the case of element names to uppercase when the parser reads the XML file. This way, we do not have to worry if there is mixed case in the element names in the XML file. When checking to see if a particular element is encountered, you only need to check for the uppercase version of the element name.
128	Create a variable called $xml_parser and assign it as a PHP xml parser using the xml_parser_create() function.
129	Define the custom start and end element handler functions that you created above using the xml_set_element_handler() function. Whenever PHP encounters a start or end element, it will use the respective function.
130	Define the custom data handler function that you created above using the respective function. Whenever PHP encounters character data, it will use the characterData() function.
131	Begin parsing the XML with the xml_parse function. The xml_parse() function requires the name of the XML parser ($xml_parser) and the XML data that you want to parse. In this case, we provide the XML data by using the custom load_data($file) function. If the xml_parse() function fails, then kill the script and display an error message.
132	After the xml_parse() function has completed parsing the XML, free the memory associated with the parser by using the xml_parser_free() function.
133–135	Stop parsing the page as PHP and close out the HTML for the page.

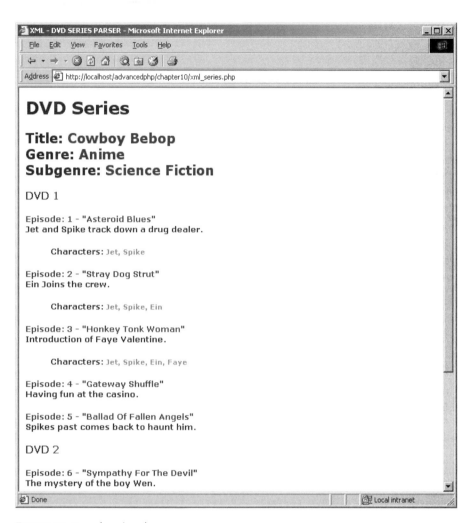

FIGURE 10–3 xml_series.php

Dumping Database Contents into an XML File

Although it doesn't require the PHP XML functions, dumping data from a database into an XML file using PHP is a great way to get some structured XML that you can use in other XML-enabled applications.

The nature of database data lends itself nicely to use in XML applications. You have already created a database structure for the data by specifying the table structures. Using PHP, you can easily extract those tables into an XML file, which can be stored in a text file or displayed in a browser window.

This next script extracts the contents of a database table containing address book entries and displays that information in the browser. If you have a browser such as Internet Explorer, then you can view the XML natively, as in Figure 10–4. Otherwise, you can view the browser source to see the XML.

SCRIPT 10–5 xml_dump.php

```
1.  <?
2.  /* SQL Table Required For This Script
3.  create table xmladdressbook (
4.      id INT NOT NULL,
5.      first VARCHAR(32),
6.      last VARCHAR(32),
7.      phone VARCHAR(12),
8.      email VARCHAR(64),
9.      address VARCHAR(64),
10.     city VARCHAR(32),
11.     state VARCHAR(2),
12.     zip VARCHAR(5),
13.     type VARCHAR(16)
14.     primary key(id));
15.
16.     insert into xmladdressbook values (1,
    'Neil','Armstrong','555-555-1234','neil@example.com','1
    Moon Road','Lunar City','LN', '99999', 'Friend');
17.     insert into xmladdressbook values (2,
    'Buzz','Aldrin','555-555-1235','buzz@example.com','2
    Moon Road','Lunar City','LN', '99999', 'Business');
18.  */
19.
20.  function connect() {
21.      if(!$db =
    @mssql_pconnect("localhost","mssqluser","password")) {
22.         print("<h1>Cannot Connect to the DB!</h1>\n");
23.         return 0;
24.      } else {
25.         mssql_select_db("php", $db);
26.         return 1;
27.      }
28.  }
29.
```

SCRIPT 10–5 xml_dump.php (Continued)

```
30.  if(connect()) {
31.      print('<?xml version="1.0"?>');
32.      ?><addressbook><?
33.      $sql = "select * from xmladdressbook order by last,
     first";
34.      $result = mssql_query($sql);
35.      while($row = mssql_fetch_array($result)) {
36.          ?>
37.          <contact type="<?=$row["type"]?>">
38.              <name>
39.                  <last_name><?=$row["last"]?></last_name>
40.                  <first_name><?=$row["first"]?></first_name>
41.              </name>
42.              <details>
43.                  <phone><?=$row["phone"]?></phone>
44.                  <email><?=$row["email"]?></email>
45.                  <address><?=$row["address"]?></address>
46.                  <city><?=$row["city"]?></city>
47.                  <state><?=$row["state"]?></state>
48.                  <zip><?=$row["zip"]?></zip>
49.              </details>
50.          </contact>
51.          <?
52.      }
53.      ?></addressbook><?
54.  }
55.  ?>
```

Script 10–5 xml_dump.php Line-by-Line Explanation

LINE	DESCRIPTION
2–14	Use these lines to create the table in your SQL database.
16	Create an entry in the database.
17	Create an additional entry in the database.
20–28	Create a function called connect(). This function is used to create a connection to the database.
21	Attempt to connect to the database, in this case, an MS SQL database. (You can replace all the MS SQL functions with MySQL functions simply by changing the first "s" in mssql to a "y"—"mysql").
22	If the script cannot connect to the database, then print an error.

Script 10–5 xml_dump.php Line-by-Line Explanation (Continued)

LINE	DESCRIPTION
23	Return false (0) to the calling program, because the database connection failed.
24–25	If the connection attempt was successful, then select the database on the database server that the script will use.
26	Return true (1) to the calling program, because the connection was successful.
27	Close the if statement started on line 12.
28	End the function declaration.
30	If the connect() function returns true, then continue on to the next line.
31	Print out the XML required to begin an XML page. You need to use the print statement to enclose the native <? and ?> XML processing instructions so that they are not interpreted to be PHP tags.
32	Print the top level XML tag to the screen. Since this is an address book, the top level tag is <addressbook>.
33	Generate an SQL statement to select all of the contents of the table and order the results by last name, then first name.
34	Execute the SQL query and place the result in the $result variable.
35–52	Loop through the result set with a while loop.
36–51	Stop processing the page as PHP. Since we are printing out a lot of data, it's easier to just have the server send out plain XML instead of processing each line as a print statement. Print out each of the results returned in the current row as part of a "contact" element. The subelements found within "contact" contain the details of the address book entry.
52	Close the while loop.
53	Close out the XML by printing out a close tag for the root element <addressbook>.
54	Close the if statement started on line 30.
55	End the script.

FIGURE 10–4 xml_dump.php shown in Internet Explorer

Generating Dynamic Graphics with PHP

Overview

PHP is able to dynamically generate and modify images. To use this advanced functionality in PHP, you need to include some additional libraries that are not included by default when you install PHP.

The GD Library

PHP provides the ability to create and manipulate images through support of the GD library. The GD home page is located at *www.boutell.com/gd/* and lists the definition of GD as:

"An ANSI C library for the dynamic creation of images. GD creates PNG and JPEG images, among other formats. GD does not create GIF images."

Previously, GD was widely used for creating GIF images, but Unisys Corp., the company which owns the patent for the LZW compression algorithm used in GIF images, recently started enforcing their patent rights, and GIF creation was subsequently dropped from the list of GD features.

However, GD can still be used to create JPEG and PNG graphics, both of which are supported by most of the popular Web browsers. In addition, GD supports creation of WBMP images, which are used for small mobile wireless devices.

Basically, GD should cover your bases nicely for your scripted graphic creation needs. Note that GD is not a paint program. It can be used to manipulate existing images by adding text to them or to create new images out of two or more existing images.

GD is most useful in creating button images, as well as embedding captions in existing images.

Enabling GD Support

GD support is not enabled by default. You must enable the extension if you are using Windows, or compile-in/link the extension if you are using Linux.

Enabling GD for Windows

Enabling GD support for Windows is very easy, since the DLL file for GD has been pre-compiled and included in the basic PHP Windows installation. Open your *php.ini* file in a text editor and search for the line that says:

```
extension_dir =  ./
```

This line should point to the place where your PHP extensions reside. If you copied the extensions to the same directory as the *php.ini* file, then you do not need to modify the line. If you did not move the PHP extensions to the same directory as the *php.ini* file, then you need to edit the line to point to the correct directory, for example:

```
extension_dir = C:\Apache\php\extensions
```

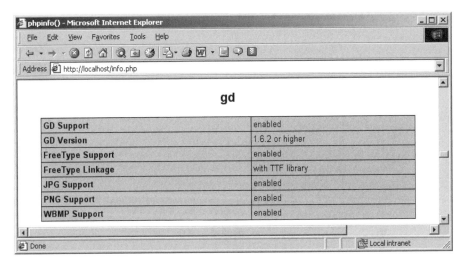

FIGURE 11–1 phpinfo() results with GD enabled for Windows

Next, find the section in the *php.ini* file that says:

```
;Windows Extensions
```

This line will be followed by many lines of Windows .dll extensions for PHP. To enable GD support, uncomment the line (delete the semicolon at the beginning of the line) that contains the GD library DLL:

```
extension=php_gd.dll
```

After you have uncommented the line, save the file and restart the Apache Web server.

You can verify the GD has been correctly installed by using the phpinfo(); as seen in Figure 11–1.

Enabling GD for Linux

If you compiled PHP using Apache's APXS functionality (`com-pile --with-apxs=/path/to/apache/bin/apxs`), then adding functionality to the PHP module is a breeze.

Before recompiling PHP, I first suggest that you delete the config.cache file and clean up files left over from the previous compile. This can be done as follows:

```
cd /path/to/php/source
rm config.cache
make clean
```

After you issue the make clean command, you will notice quite a few files being deleted. Don't worry about it. The make program is just cleaning up files it won't need when you recompile. If you don't run the make clean command, then you may start running into some problems. If you have been compiling PHP with no problems and suddenly it won't compile right even though you haven't changed anything, it's a good bet that the make clean command will solve your problem.

Once you've cleaned up the mess from the previous compile, you can get started with the new compile.

To compile PHP with GD support enabled:

```
./compile --with-apxs=/usr/local/apache/bin/apxs \
--with-gd \
--with-gd-native-ttf \
--with-ttf
```

After the configure runs, issue the command:

```
make
```

Assuming no errors occur, you can then issue the command:

```
make install
```

The final command copies the libphp4.so library file to /path/to/apache/libexec/.

Restart Apache to load the new library:

```
/path/to/apache/bin/apachectl restart
```

You can verify the GD has been correctly installed by using the phpinfo() function.

Generating Graphics with GD

Once you have configured PHP to use the GD library, you can start creating some graphics.

The Lines and Text

The base function to use when creating images using the GD library is the ImageCreate() function.

```
$length = 300;
$width = 100;
$image = ImageCreate($length, $width);
```

Once you have created an image, you need to add some color to it using the ImageColorAllocate() function. ImageColorAllaocate() takes as its arguments the image you are creating and an RGB color value:

```
$blue = ImageColorAllocate($image, 0, 0, 255);
```

So now you have created a box and given it a color. Now all that is left is to display the image in a browser. To do that, you need two more lines of code:

```
Header("Content-type: image/png");
ImagePNG($image);
```

The first line tells the browser to expect a PNG image, and the second line is the function that outputs the image that you have created to the browser. Before you go typing that all in, though, let's add some text.

Now that you have your created your base image, you can add some shapes onto it. The most basic "shape" you can add to your image is a line. A line is created by connecting two endpoints on your image. Lines are created with the ImageLine() function:

```
ImageLine($image, $x1, $y1, $x2, $y2, $color);
```

The points which you specify in the ImageLine() function are x,y vertices, almost like those used in plotting points in mathematics, except that the grid used here is a little different. The grid used to place shapes in GD starts at the x,y point 0,0 in the top left corner. The x coordinate moves to the right, as in a normal math graph. The y coordinate however, moves down, instead of upward as it does in a math graph, so the point (10,20) is 10 pixels to the right of the upper left corner of the image and 20 pixels down.

GD also supports some basic string functions that allow you to print text onto the image. You can only use one basic font and there are only five sizes, listed in Table 11–1, but it works well for graphs and charts where flashy fonts are not required. To add text to your image:

```
IMageString($image, $fontSize, $x1, $y1, $string,
$color);
```

TABLE 11–1 Font Sizes That Can Be Used for GD String Functions

FONT SIZE	FONT	SIZE
1	gdFontTiny	8 × 5 pixels
2	gdFontSmall	13 × 6 pixels
3	gdFontMediumBold	13 × 7 pixels
4	gdFontLarge	15 × 8 pixels
5	gdFontGiant	15 × 9 pixels

The next script creates a simple graph, shown in Figure 11–2, using the ImageLine() and ImageString() functions to illustrate how the graph works and the appearance of the text sizes:

SCRIPT 11–1 gd_grid.php

```
1.  <?
2.  $height = 301;
3.  $width = 301;
4.  $image = ImageCreate($width, $height);
5.  $white = ImageColorAllocate($image, 255, 255, 255);
6.  $blue = ImageColorAllocate($image, 0, 0, 255);
7.  $red = ImageColorAllocate($image, 255, 0, 0);
8.  for($i = 0; $i < $height; $i = $i + 20) {
9.    ImageLine($image, $i, 0, $i, $height, $blue);
10.   ImageLine($image, 0, $i, $width, $i, $blue);
11.   ImageString ($image, 1, $i+2, 0, $i, $red);
12.   ImageString ($image, 1, 2, $i, $i, $red);
13. }
14. ImageString ($image, 1, 82, 22, "Size 1 Font", $red);
15. ImageString ($image, 2, 82, 62, "Size 2 Font", $red);
16. ImageString ($image, 3, 82, 102, "Size 3 Font", $red);
17. ImageString ($image, 4, 82, 142,"Size 4 Font", $red);
18. ImageString ($image, 5, 82, 182, "Size 5 Font", $red);
```

```
19.  header ("Content-type: image/png");
20.  ImagePng($image);
21.  ImageDestroy($image);
22.  ?>
```

Script 11–1 gd_grid.php Line-by-Line Explanation

LINE	DESCRIPTION
2	Define a height of 301 pixels for the image (the extra pixel is so that the final line on the outside of the grid is visible).
3	Define a width of 301 pixels for the image.
4	Create the base image using the ImageCreate() function, specifying the height and width defined earlier.
5	Define the $white variable using the ImageColorAllocate() function. The arguments allow the color white (RGB value 255,255,255) to be used by $image. It is also used as the background color for $image, since it is the first color allocated to $image.
6	Define the color blue and allow it to be used by $image.
7	Define the color red and allow it to be used by $image.
8–13	Create a for loop to loop through and draw a line every 20 pixels starting at the coordinate 0,0 (upper left corner of image).
9	While in the for loop, create a line inside $image from point $i, 0 (0,0 20,0 40,0, etc.) to point $i, $height (0, 301 20,301 40,301, etc.). Each iteration of the loop draws a vertical line from the top of the image to the bottom of the image spaced at 20 pixels from left to right.
10	While in the for loop, create a line inside $image from point 0, $i (0,0 0,20 0,40, etc.) to point $width, $i (301,0 301,20 301,40, etc.). Each iteration of the loop draws a horizontal line from the left of the image to the right of the image spaced at 20 pixels from top to bottom.
11	While in the for loop, create a small label to display the current pixel of the current vertical line using the ImageString() function. Remember, ImageString($image, $fontsize, $x, $y, $text, $color);
12	While in the for loop, create a small label to display the current pixel of the current horizontal line ImageString() function.
13	End the for loop.
14–18	Create some text at various points on the screen to display the various font types.

Script 11–1 gd_grid.php Line-by-Line Explanation (Continued)

LINE	DESCRIPTION
19	Send the image headers to the user's browser.
20	Display the image, $image, that you have created.
21	Destroy the image from the server memory, since it has already been sent to the browser.

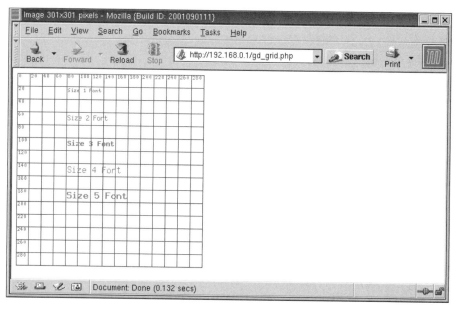

FIGURE 11–2 gd_grid.php

Adding TrueType Font to Your Images

You can add better-looking text to your images using TrueType fonts. The function that accomplishes this is ImageTTFText().

```
ImageTTFText($image, $size, $angle, $xcoord, $ycoord,
$color, $font, $text);
```

The arguments for ImageTTFText() are:

- $image—The image handler for the image in which you are placing this font.
- $size—The size of the text, in points.

- $angle—The angle in number of degrees that the text slants. Note that this isn't the slant of the characters themselves, such as when using italic font, but the slant of the "line" on which the text is written.
- $xcoord—The x coordinate in the image of the bottom left of the first character in $text.
- $ycoord—The y coordinate in the image of the bottom left of the first character in $text.
- $color—The color of the text. This must be a color that has been previously allocated to the $image.
- $font—The location of the TrueType Font file (.ttf).
- $text—The text that you want to print out in the image.

Script 11–2, gd_text.php, provides an example of a simple GD image with some text, shown in Figure 11–3.

SCRIPT 11–2 gd_text.php

```
1.  <?
2.  $height = 150;
3.  $width= 300;
4.  $image = ImageCreate($width, $height);
5.  $blue = ImageColorAllocate($image,0,0,255);
6.  $white = ImageColorAllocate($image,255,255,255);
7.  $font = "arial.ttf";
8.  $text = "Advanced\n\rPHP";
9.  ImageTTFText($image, 50, 0, 10, 55, $white, $font, $text);
10. Header("Content-type: image/png");
11. ImagePNG($image);
12. ImageDestroy($image);
13. ?>
```

Script 11–2 gd_text.php Line-by-Line Explanation

LINE	DESCRIPTION
2	Define a height of 300 pixels for the image.
3	Define a width of 150 pixels for the image.
4	Create the base image using the ImageCreate() function, specifying the height and width defined earlier.
5	Define the $blue variable using the ImageColorAllocate() function. The arguments allow the color blue (RGB value 0,0,255) to be used by $image. It is also used as the background color for $image, since it is the first color allocated to $image.

Script 11–2 gd_text.php Line-by-Line Explanation (Continued)

Line	Description
6	Define the color white and allow it to be used by $image.
7	Assign a font file to the variable $font. You need to place this font file in the same directory from which this script is executed. In Windows, you can typically find TrueType font files in C:\Windows\Fonts or C:\WINNT\fonts. You can use any TrueType font file; just make sure the file name of the TrueType font that you copy into the same directory as this script is defined here.
8	Assign a simple text string to the $text variable. You can use the syntax "\n\r" for newlines and returns. Some *nix sytems do not require the "\r".
9	Add text to $image using the ImageTTFText() function.
10	Send the image headers to the user's browser.
11	Display the image, $image, that you have created.
12	Destroy the image from the server memory, since it has already been sent to the browser.

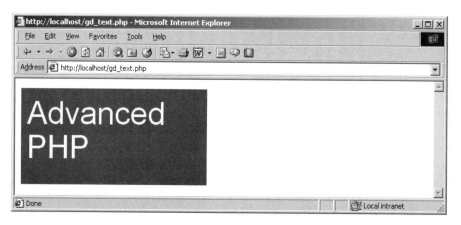

Figure 11–3 gd_text.php

Adding Text to Base Images

GD is also useful in that you can import an existing image to work with as the base of a new image. For example, you can take a blank image of a button, and then superimpose text onto it. This way, you can create multiple buttons from only one base image file.

To create a button, you need to use two new GD functions. These functions are ImageCreateFromPNG() and ImageTTFBbox().

ImageCreateFromPNG() is a very simple function that just creates a new image from the existing PNG file:

```
$image = ImageCreateFromPNG("blank_blue_bttn.png");
```

You would then manipulate $image just as you would if you had created it from ImageCreate.

You can get the length and width of the $image you create using the ImageCreateFromPNG() function by using the ImageSX($image) and ImageSY($image) functions, respectively; SX and SY mean Size of the X axis (the width) and Size of the Y axis (the height) of the image.

The ImageTTFBbox() function is a fairly complicated function that returns the corner coordinates of a bounding box around your text. You provide the size, angle, font, and text string of the text and the function returns the corner coordinates in an array. This array allows you to calculate how much space your text uses. Usage of the script is:

```
$textbox = ImageTTFBbox($size, $angle, $font, $text);
```

Table 11–2 lists the coordinates for each of the elements in the array returned from the ImageTTFBbox() function. Additionally, Figure 11–4 provides a graphical representation of the array elements in the bounding box.

TABLE 11–2 Coordinates Returned from ImageTTFbox()

ARRAY POSITION	BOUNDING BOX COORDINATE
0	X coordinate of the lower left hand corner
1	Y coordinate of the lower left hand corner
2	X coordinate of the lower right hand corner
3	Y coordinate of the lower right hand corner
4	X coordinate of the upper right hand corner
5	Y coordinate of the upper right hand corner
6	X coordinate of the upper left hand corner
7	Y coordinate of the upper left hand corner

6,7   **4,5**

0,1   **2,3**

FIGURE 11–4 Array Elements for the coordinates in a bounding box

This next script demonstrates how to take a blank button and add text to make many different buttons. See Figure 11–5 for an example of the output.

SCRIPT 11–3 gd_button.php

```
1.   <?
2.   $image = ImageCreateFromPNG("blank_blue_bttn.png");
3.   $white = ImageColorAllocate($image,255,255,255);
4.   $font = "arial.ttf";
5.   if(!isset($text)) { $text = "BUTTON"; }
6.   $size = "20";
7.   $angle="0";
8.   $textbox = ImageTTFBbox($size, $angle, $font, $text);
9.   $textbox_width = abs($textbox[2] - $textbox[0]);
10.  $textbox_height = abs($textbox[7] - $textbox[1]);
11.  $image_width = ImageSX($image);
12.  $image_height = ImageSY($image);
13.  $x = ($image_width - $textbox_width) / 2;
14.  $y = ($image_height - $textbox_height) / 2 + $textbox_height;
15.  ImageTTFText($image, $size, $angle, $x, $y, $white,
     $font, $text);
16.  Header("Content-type: image/png");
17.  ImagePNG($image);
18.  ImageDestroy($image);
19.  ?>
```

Script 11–3 gd_button.php Line-by-Line Explanation

LINE	DESCRIPTION
2	Create a new image using the ImageCreateFromPNG() function, specifying "blank_blue_bbtn.png" as the base image.

Script 11–3 gd_button.php Line-by-Line Explanation (Continued)

LINE	DESCRIPTION
3	Define the $white variable using the ImageColorAllocate() function. The arguments allow the color white (RGB value 255,255,255) to be used by $image.
4	Assign a font file to the variable $font. You need to place this font file in the same directory from which this script is executed. In Windows, you can typically find TrueType font files in C:\Windows\Fonts or C:\WINNT\fonts. You can use any TrueType font file; just make sure the file name of the TrueType font that you copy into the same directory as this script is defined here.
5	Check to see if the $text variable is set. If it is not, then assign the string "BUTTON" to $text. The reason for this will be apparent in the next script.
6	Assign a font size to the $size variable.
7	Assign an angle to the font using the $angle variable. This argument is required for the ImageTTFbox variable. You assign it to be "0", since you want the text to be horizontal across the page, with no angle.
8	Create the text box by assigning the value of the function ImageTTFbox() to the variable $textbox.
9	Determine the width of the text box by getting the absolute value of the text box's lower right-hand x coordinate subtracted from the text box's lower left-hand x coordinate. You use the abs() function, since you want to have a positive number, even though the resulting number may be negative. The abs() value of a number removes the negative sign.
10	Determine the height of the text box by getting the absolute value of the text box's upper left-hand y coordinate subtracted from the text box's lower left-hand y coordinate.
11	Determine the width of the entire image by using the ImageSX() function.
12	Determine the height of the entire image by using the ImageSY() function.
13	Determine where to place the x value of the text in relation to the base image by subtracting the width of the text box from the width of the base image and dividing by 2. If your base image was 10 pixels wide, and your text box was 8 pixels wide, then your resulting x position for the text would be at 1. This leaves one pixel on either side of the text box for the base image to overlap. This, of course, does not work very well if your text box is larger than your base image.
14	Determine where to place the y value of the text in relation to the base image by subtracting the text box height from the base image height and dividing by 2. Then add the height of the text box. As above, if your base image was 10 pixels high and your text box was 8 pixels high, this would give you a value of 1 for the y coordinate. However, since you specify the lower left-hand corner (and not the upper left-hand corner as you might assume), you need to also add the height of the text box, giving you a value of 9.

Script 11–3 gd_button.php Line-by-Line Explanation (Continued)

LINE	DESCRIPTION
15	Add the text to the base image using the ImageTTFText() function. You use the x,y values that you have just determined to properly space the text in relation to the base image.
16	Send the image headers to the user's browser.
17	Display the image, $image, that you have created.
18	Destroy the image from the server memory, since it has already been sent to the browser.

You can easily reuse this script, as shown in Figure 11–6, by adding a parameter to the URL—for example, http://localhost/gd_text.php?text=HOME.

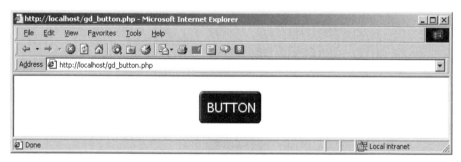

FIGURE 11–5 gd_button.php

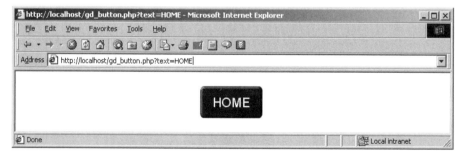

FIGURE 11–6 gd_text.php?text=HOME

You can also call several buttons on one page using the HTML <img> tags and referencing the same script using different values for "text", as in the following short script. See Figure 11–7 for example output.

SCRIPT 11–4 buttons.html

```
1.   <html>
2.   <head>
3.     <title>Buttons!</title>
4.   </head>
5.   <body>
6.   <img src="gd_button.php?text=HOME"><br>
7.   <img src="gd_button.php?text=GAMES"><br>
8.   <img src="gd_button.php?text=NEWS"><br>
9.   <img src="gd_button.php?text=LINKS">
10.  </body>
11.  </html>
```

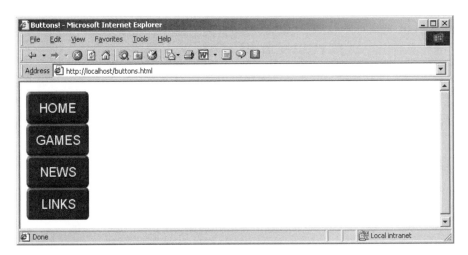

FIGURE 11–7 buttons.html

Creating Rectangles with GD

In addition to text and lines, you can also easily use GD to create rectangles, either filled with a color or unfilled (use ImageeRectangle() with the same arguments to create an unfilled rectangle):

```
ImageFilledRectangle($image, $x1coord, $y1coord,
$x2coord, $y2coord, $color);
```

The arguments to ImageRectangle() and ImageFilledRectangle() are:

- $image—The image handler for the image in which you are placing this rectangle.
- $x1coord—The x coordinate of the upper left corner of the rectangle.
- $y1coord—The y coordinate of the upper left corner of the rectangle.
- $x2coord—The x coordinate of the lower right corner of the rectangle.
- $y2coord—The y coordinate of the lower right corner of the rectangle.
- $color—The color of the rectangle. This must be a color that has been previously allocated to the $image.

Rectangles are plotted from upper left to lower right. Remember that the coordinate 0,0 starts at the upper right corner of the image, not in the lower right corner as is normally done when plotting in mathematics.

This next script uses lines, text, and rectangles to create a dynamic bar graph. You can plug various numeric values into the graph and specify a size and labels for the image. The graph automatically changes scale depending on the numeric values you enter. Figure 11–8 illustrates the graph-entry screen.

SCRIPT 11–5 gd_graph.php

```
1.  <?
2.  if(!isset($render)) {
3.          ?>
4.          <form action=gd_chart.php method=post>
5.          <br>Values (enter numbers seperated by a comma):
6.          <br><textarea cols="40" rows="4"
    name="values_in">50,100,150,20,75,23,55,200,135,63,103,1
    63</textarea>
7.          <br>Labels (enter labels seperated by a comma):
8.          <br><textarea cols="40" rows="4"
    name="labels_in">Jan,Feb,Mar,Apr,May,Jun,Jul,Aug,Sep,Oct
    ,Nov,Dec</textarea>
9.          <br>Image Height: <input type="text" name="height"
    value="500">
```

```
10.         <br>Image Width: <input type="text" name="width"
   value="500">
11.         <br>Vertical Scale Label: <input type="text"
   name="vlabel" value="Widget Production in Thousands">
12.         <br>Horizontal Scale Label: <input type="text"
   name="hlabel" value="Month">
13.         <br><input type="submit" name="render"
   value="Render Chart">
14.         </form>
15.         <?
16. } else {
17. $values = explode(",", $values_in);
18. $labels = explode(",", $labels_in);
19. $xoffset = $width / 10;
20. $yoffset = $height / 10;
21. /* Determine Font Sizes */
22. if (($width > 400) and ($height > 400)) {
23.         $sm_font = 2;
24.         $md_font = 3;
25.         $lg_font = 4;
26. } else {
27.         $sm_font = 1;
28.         $md_font = 2;
29.         $lg_font = 2;
30. }
31. /* Create Base Image */
32. $image = ImageCreate($width, $height);
33. /* Allocate Colors */
34. $white = ImageColorAllocate($image, 235, 235, 235);
35. $blue = ImageColorAllocate($image, 0, 0, 255);
36. $red = ImageColorAllocate($image, 255, 0, 0);
37. /* Find Largest Item In Values Array */
38. $greatest = 0;
39. for($i = 0; $i < sizeof($values); $i++) {
40.         $values[$i] = trim($values[$i]);
41.         if($values[$i] > $greatest)
42.                 $greatest = $values[$i];
43. }
44. /* Determine Scale And Spacing */
45. $scale = ($height / $greatest) * .8;
46. $h_spacing = floor(($width - $xoffset) / sizeof($values))
   / 2;
47. $barwidth = $h_spacing;
48. /* Draw Bars, Labels, and Values*/
49. $x = $xoffset + 5;
```

```
50.   for($i = 0; $i < sizeof($values); $i++) {
51.          $y = $height - ($values[$i] * $scale);
52.          ImageFilledRectangle($image, $x, $y - $yoffset, $x
      + $barwidth, $height - $yoffset, $red);
53.          ImageString ($image, $sm_font, $x, $y-$yoffset-12,
      $values[$i], $blue);
54.          $labels[$i] = trim($labels[$i]);
55.          ImageString ($image, $md_font, $x, $height -
      $yoffset + 2, $labels[$i], $blue);
56.          $x+=($h_spacing * 2);
57.   }
58.   /* Determine Ticks */
59.   $ticks_every = "1";
60.   for($i = 1; $i < (round(log10($greatest))); $i++) {
61.          $ticks_every .= "0";
62.   }
63.   /* Draw Ticks And Numbers */
64.   for($i = 0; $i < $height - $yoffset; $i+=
      $ticks_every*$scale) {
65.          $y = ($height - $yoffset) - $i;
66.          ImageLine($image, $xoffset / 2, $y, $xoffset, $y,
      $blue);
67.          ImageLine($image, $xoffset + 5, $y, $width +
      $xoffset, $y, $white);
68.          ImageString ($image, $sm_font, $xoffset / 2, $y,
      $i / $scale , $blue);
69.   }
70.   /* Draw Left and Bottom Edge of Graph */
71.   ImageLine($image, 0 + $xoffset, 0, $xoffset, $height -
      $yoffset, $blue);
72.   ImageLine($image, 0 + $xoffset, $height - $yoffset,
      $width + $xoffset, $height - $yoffset, $blue);
73.   /* Draw Axis Labels */
74.   ImageString ($image, $lg_font, $width / 2, $height -
      ($yoffset / 2), $hlabel, $blue);
75.   ImageStringUp ($image, $lg_font, 1, $height - $height /
      3, $vlabel, $blue);
76.   /* Display Image */
77.   header ("Content-type: image/png");
78.   ImagePNG($image);
79.   ImageDestroy($image);
80.   }
81.   ?>
```

Script 11–5 gd_graph.php Line-by-Line Explanation

LINE	DESCRIPTION
2	Check to see if the $render variable is set. If it is not, then execute lines 3–15, else execute from line 16 to the end of the script.
3–15	Print out a standard HTML form asking for some values for the script. You can specify: • The numerical values for the bar graph, separated by a comma. • The corresponding labels for those bars, separated by a comma. You should have one label for each value you input in the form above. • The width and height of the chart. • The labels for the scales. The script enters some values as a default for testing.
17	Take the values entered from the form and turn them into an array using the explode() function and assigning the array to the $values variable.
18	Take the labels entered from the form and turn them into an array using the explode() function and assigning the array to the $labels variable.
19	Determine the offset for the x-axis, which is 1/10th the total width of the chart. This offset allows for room for some text on the left side of the chart. 1/10th is an arbitrary number that works well for charts that are 300 pixels wide or larger.
20	Determine the offset for the y-axis, which is 1/10th the total height of the chart. This offset allows for room for some text on the bottom of the chart.
22–30	Determine the appropriate font sizes for the chart. The chart uses three sizes: small, medium, and large. If the chart is smaller than 400 × 400, then use smaller fonts. Otherwise, use larger fonts.
32	Create the base image using the width and height obtained from the form.
34–36	Allocate three colors to the image: white, blue, and red. The white here (RBG: 235,235,235) is actually a little grey so that the chart stands out better from the page.
38	Initialize the variable $greatest with 0.
39–43	Use a for loop to loop through the $values array and find the highest value. Once we know the largest number that has to be plotted, we can determine the scale of the chart. Note that, on line 40, the script trims any whitespace from the numerical value. This is to avoid errors if users separate their values when they enter them into the form with spaces in addition to commas.
45	Determine the scale of the chart by taking 80 percent of the largest value divided by the height. This creates a scale that allows the largest bar on the graph to occupy 80 percent of the height.

Script 11–5 gd_graph.php Line-by-Line Explanation (Continued)

LINE	DESCRIPTION
46	Determine the horizontal spacing for the individual bars in the chart by rounding off the width minus the width offset (which gives us the total amount of space available to the bars), then dividing it by the number of values that need to be charted, and finally dividing that number by two, since we want to create an equal space-bar ratio.
47	Determine the width of the bar. Here we set it to the same as the spacing, but you may find you need to alter it a bit for your specific chart. If you do alter it, take into account that the above line allocates half of the space to spacing. You may need to alter that line as well.
49	Initialize the variable $x to be five pixels more than the offset. This allows you to start the first bar five pixels away from the edge that you allocated as space for text.
50–57	Create a for loop that loops through $values array and draws the bars on the bar graph.
51	Determine the base y coordinate of the bar. This is a bit tricky, because the script automatically scales the presentation of the bars depending on the size of the greatest value. To determine the base y coordinate, you need to subtract the height from the size of the value multiplied by the scale. If the value was 10, then it would automatically be scaled down to 8. You then subtract the y offset (for the extra space at the bottom for text) and the overall height of the image (because the GD library uses the top left corner of the image as the 0,0 point instead of the lower left corner). The script is calculating how far the bar should start from the TOP of the image, rather than how long the bar should actually be (which would, of course, be easier, but the GD library doesn't seem to want to let you do it that way).
52	Create the bar using the ImageFilledRectangle() function. The first two coordinate arguments ($x, and $y) plot the top left corner of the rectangle. The second two coordinate arguments ($x + $barwidth, and $height – $yoffset) plot the bottom right of the rectangle.
53	Write the numerical value of the bar above the bar using the ImageString() function. The y coordinate is listed as $y – 12 so that the value is written 12 pixels above the bar itself. Remember that the script calculates how far from the top of the image the text should be written, not how far from the top of the bar.
54	Use the trim() function to trim any whitespace from around the label.
55	Write the label of the current bar at the bottom of the bar. Notice that the y coordinate is $height – $yoffset + 2. That puts the label two pixels BELOW the top of the whitespace along the bottom of the image.

Script 11–5 gd_graph.php Line-by-Line Explanation (Continued)

LINE	DESCRIPTION
56	Increment the value of the next x coordinate so that it allows room for ample space between the bars. You'll have to modify this line in addition to lines 46 and 47 if you want to muck about with the spacing. Note that in most cases the way it is coded here should work fine.
57	Close the for loop.
59	Initialize the variable $ticks_every.
60–62	Create a for loop to determine the scale of the tick marks that occur on the bars. The tick marks are actually lines that are the same color as the background of the image. They are drawn over the bars to make the bars look like equally segmented blocks. Since it's conceivable that you could have values that are in the tens or in the thousands, you would not automatically want to have a tick mark every 10 units. This for loop is a cheap way to determine how many "ticks" should be spaced in between tick lines. It takes the greatest value and computes the log10 of that value. Each time it does so and the value is less than $i, it adds a "0" to the $ticks_every function. Basically, if the greatest value is 1 to 316, then there is a line every 10 ticks (not necessarily pixels, because you need to take into account scaling). From 316 to 3162, it uses tick marks every 100 ticks, etc. It's not an exact science, but it gives pretty good results.
64–69	Create a for loop that draws "tick" marks on the bars, as well as numbers along the y axis of the graph, spaced according to the interval defined in $ticks_every.
65	Calculate the y coordinate for the tick mark.
66	Draw a short line to the left of the offset. This short blue line is used as a divider between the numerical scale that is displayed along the y axis of the chart.
67	Draw a long line across the image to divide the bars into equal easily-readable segments.
68	Display the "tick" number to the left of the y axis for the chart.
69	Close the for loop.
71	Draw the blue x-axis line across the bottom of the image (between the bars and their labels).
72	Draw the blue y-axis line along the right side of the image (between the unit numbers and the bars).
74	Display the label for x-axis. In the default case, this is "Month."

Script 11–5 gd_graph.php Line-by-Line Explanation (Continued)

LINE	DESCRIPTION
75	Display the label for the y-axis. In the default case, this is "Widget Production in Thousands."
77	Send the image headers to the user's browser.
78	Display the image, $image, that you have created.
79	Destroy the image from the server memory, since it has already been sent to the browser.
80	Close the if statement started on line 2.

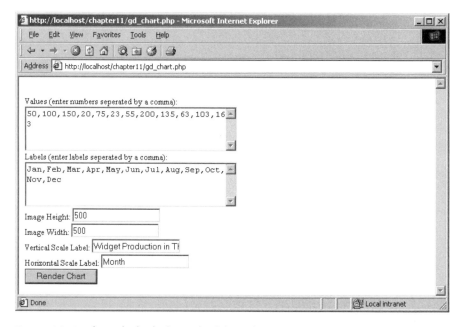

FIGURE 11–8 gd_graph.php before submitting values

Figure 11–9 shows example output for the script.

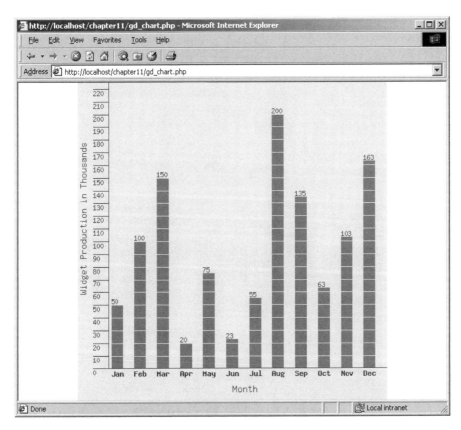

FIGURE 11–9 gd_graph.php after submitting values

PHPGTK

- Introduction to PHPGTK
- Installing PHPGTK
- Creating Basic GTK Objects
- Putting It All Together
- A Simple PHPGTK Application

Introduction to PHPGTK

PHPGTK is an extension to PHP that allows you to create graphical user interface (GUI) applications. Instead of running in a browser, your PHP application runs in its own application window. These applications are client-side only. They do not reside on the Web server. The files instead reside on the user's hard drive. For users to use the PHPGTK application, they must have the proper version of PHP (with the GTK+ extension) installed on their system.

GTK+ was originally designed for the open-source image editing program called the GIMP (GNU Image Manipulation Program). GTK stands for the GIMP Tool Kit. Later, the Gnome team decided to use GTK+ to create their desktop environment for Linux. GTK+ has been ported to Windows, Linux, and BeOS, and thus makes for a good cross-platform GUI library.

PHPGTK uses GTK+ to draw the "widgets" required in any GUI application. Widgets are things like scroll bars, text input fields, and buttons, among other things. When you start almost any Windows application, such as a Web browser, you are looking at a collection of widgets.

Widgets need to be contained in some type of framework to be useful and logical. You can't just have a bunch of buttons and text fields scattered randomly about the screen. To solve this problem, we use a special kind of widget called a container. A container is another structure that organizes the widgets however you think it best for your application. For example, the menu bar at the top of most applications is a container.

Widgets have many different properties that control how they look and act. Each type of widget has its own unique set of properties, in addition to properties that are common to other widgets.

Widgets send signals to your program when they are activated. An example of widget activation is when a user clicks on a button. Once a widget sends a signal, you generally respond to that signal with a callback. A callback is basically just a function. Some signals end up in callbacks that are automatically handled by GTK (default handlers). Other signals end up executing one of your functions (user-defined handlers). The user-defined functions are written in PHP.

As of the writing of this document, the current version of PHPGTK was 0.5.1, released on April 26, 2002. While still in its early stages, PHPGTK 0.5.1 is a vast improvement over the original 0.1 release.

PHPGTK is very complex. It takes basically two complete languages and puts them together. This lone chapter cannot hope to explain in detail the many methods and classes that are available, but I wish to provide a general overview of PHPGTK insofar as this space allows. Check the PHPGTK Web site at *http://gtk.php.net* for a wealth of information!

Installing PHPGTK

Before you can start using PHPGTK, you need to download the appropriate files. The PHPGTK team has set up a nice Web site at *http://gtk.php.net*. The PHPGTK Web site has downloads and documentation for the GTK extension.

Before You Install

PHPGTK still has not reached the 1.0 version, and as such I wouldn't recommend that you use this version of PHP on your production Web server. In fact, there really isn't a reason that you'd want to install PHPGTK on your production Web server. It is a client-side application!

PHPGTK is a developers' toy at the moment, and anything is subject to change, at least before PHPGTK reaches version 1.0. Have some fun with it, try it out, but don't base your company's next big product on PHPGTK 0.5.0.

Installing on Windows

Installing PHPGTK on a Windows machine is fairly straightforward and similar to installing the normal version of PHP. Download the Windows binary file from the PHPGTK Web site at *http://gtk.php.net*.

Unzip the file using a zip utility such as WinZip. Extract the files to your C: drive.

The following folders are created when you unzip the file:

- php4—Contains the PHP executable, as well as some GTK library files.
- test—Contains some sample *.php files that use the GTK widget set.

If you are using Windows 98 or Windows ME, then you will notice that folders called "winnt" and "winnt/system32" have been created. You should copy the contents of those folders into your C:\windows directory. Note that you may have to set your system files to be viewable so that you can see the necessary DLL files to copy them over to C:\windows.

Additionally, you should see a new *php.ini* file. Copy this to your C:\Windows or C:\WINNT directory. Be sure to first back up your existing *php.ini* file.

To test out the installation, type the following from a command prompt:

```
c:\php4\php.exe -q c:\test\gtk.php
```

See Figure 12–1 for a screen shot of the gtk.php file in action.

Installing on Linux

Installing PHPGTK on Linux is easier than installing the normal PHP; you don't have to worry about compiling with Apache. You can compile GTK functionality into an existing standalone version of PHP, but for our purposes we'll start from scratch and make a brand new PHP executable that has GTK functionality built in. Before you begin:

1. Download the source file for PHP from the download page at *www.php.net*.
2. Download the source file PHPGTK from the download page of *http://gtk.php.net*.

Once you have the necessary file, unzip and untar the regular PHP source file:

```
tar -zxvf php-4.x.x.tar.gz
```

This creates a new directory named php-4.x.x, where the "x" denotes the exact version number of PHP that you downloaded.

Compile PHP using the minimum options. We just want to create a standalone executable. If you want to add additional functionality, you can recompile later. For now, you just want to make sure you can create a working version of PHPGTK. Change directory into your newly created PHP source directory. Compile by typing:

```
./configure
```

That's all there is to it. This automatically creates an executable that has built-in MySQL support as well.

Once you have the php binary file, you must copy it to /usr/local/bin. The PHPGTK installation will be looking for it in that location. You need to be root to do this.

```
cp php /usr/local/bin
```

Now, it's time to build the GTK extension onto your PHP executable. Go back to where you downloaded the PHPGTK source file and extract it:

```
tar -zxvf php-gtk-0.5.0.tar.gz
```

This creates a new directory named php-gtk-0.5.0. Change directory into that directory and compile the source file. You will need to be root to perform the final step, make install. To compile PHPGTK, type the following (a lot of text will print to the screen after you type each command):

1. `./compile`
2. `make`
3. `make install`

You can test your installation by going into the test directory and running a few of the scripts. X-Windows will need to be running!

```
cd test
php -q gtk.php
```

A window should pop up showing various GTK widget buttons. Click the different widgets to get a brief idea of what they do.

Figure 12–1 shows the gtk.php file as it appears in Linux (using the Gnome desktop) on the left and in Windows 2000 on the right.

You can also try running the other *.php files in the test directory. Use the -q flag to suppress printing HTTP header information to the screen (the php "quiet" option).

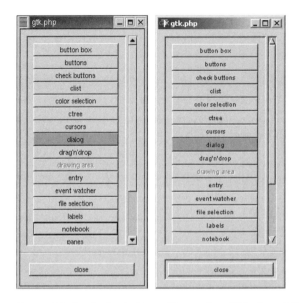

FIGURE 12–1 gtk.php in Linux (Gnome) and Windows 2000

Creating Basic GTK Objects

The GTK+ extension is an object oriented programming (OOP) extension to PHP. You need to use OOP syntax and structures to use the GTK+ library. If you haven't already done so, you may want to go all the way back to Chapter 1 and review the material about OOP in PHP.

Creating Your First PHPGTK Window

Before you can create any PHPGTK applications, you must tell PHP which GTK library you want to use. Since GTK runs on Windows and many flavors of UNIX, that leaves us with two types of libraries. Windows uses dynamic link libraries, also called DLLs. Most *nix based operating systems use .so libraries. Since you want your application to be able to be used on both types of operating systems without modification, you must provide a dynamic method of loading the libraries. The standard method of doing this is:

```
if (!class_exists('gtk')) {
if (strtoupper(substr(PHP_OS, 0, 3)) == 'WIN')
        dl('php_gtk.dll');
else
        dl('php_gtk.so');
}
```

> **SIDE NOTE** If you intend for your script to run on platforms other than Linux or Windows (if support for these other platforms is added in later versions of PHPGTK), then you must ensure that the proper PHPGTK library is loaded using the same manner as above.

The core part of any PHPGTK application is the main window. Each application you create should have a main window that acts as a container into which you place your other widgets.

The basic window class in PHPGTK is GtkWindow(). You create a new window object like this:

```
$window = &new GtkWindow();
```

Now that you have a window, you must provide for a way to destroy that window. In most operating systems, a user can destroy a window by clicking the "X" in the upper right corner of the window (some Linux desktops provide a different control).

When you click the "X" in a PHPGTK application, two signals are sent to the application. These signals are delete_event and destroy. For now we'll just concentrate on the destroy signal.

Signals are generally user input, and callbacks are functions that you create to do something in response to the user input. However, you need to connect the signal to the callback. To do this, you use the connect() method. To connect the destroy signal to our destroy callback:

```
$window->connect('destroy','destroy');
```

The first argument is the name of the signal that is sent by PHPGTK. The second argument is the name of the function (callback) that you want to call in response to the signal. To keep things simple, we'll name the function (callback) 'destroy'.

```
function destroy() {
Gtk::main_quit();
}
```

The Gtk::main_quit(); is the PHPGTK function that kills the application.

Now we have created a window and provided a means for the user to get rid of the window. But we still can't run the application. PHPGTK requires two more things to be done. First, we need to show the window. You show a window by calling the show_all() method:

```
$window->show_all();
```

Finally, you need to start the event sequence (polling events?) by calling the special PHPGTK function main():

```
Gtk::main();
```

> **SIDE NOTE** You must begin your scripts with the full "<?php" tag when using PHPGTK. Using the shorthand "<?" may cause PHPGTK to just echo the entire script to the screen instead of creating a GTK window.

When we put it all together, you get Script 12–1, basic_window.php.

SCRIPT 12–1 basic_window.php

```
1.  <?php
2.    if (!class_exists('gtk')) {
3.    if (strtoupper(substr(PHP_OS, 0, 3)) == 'WIN')
4.      dl('php_gtk.dll');
5.    else
6.      dl('php_gtk.so');
7.  }
8.  function destroy(){
9.    Gtk::main_quit();
10. }
11. $window = &new GtkWindow();
12. $window->connect('destroy', 'destroy');
13. $window->show_all();
14. Gtk::main();
15. ?>
```

Run the script from the command line (remember, you need to add the full path to the PHP executable if it is not in the current directory):

```
php -q basic_window.php
```

The result should look similar to Figure 12–2. You can close the window by clicking the "X" in the upper right corner.

Script 12–1 basic_window.php Line-by-Line Explanation

LINE	DESCRIPTION
2	If the GTK class has not been defined, then execute lines 3–7. If the GTK class has been defined, then the script needs to do nothing.
3	Check the first three characters of the PHP_OS environment variable.
4	If it is WIN, then the system is running Windows. Load the PHPGTK library for Windows.
5–7	If the PHP_OS environment variable is not WIN, then assume that PHP is running on a Linux system and load the Linux PHPGTK library.
8–10	Define a function, destroy(), that stops the script when called.
9	Execute the Gtk::main_quit() method to stop the script and close the GTK window.
10	End the function declaration.
11	Create a new window object called $window.
12	Connect the destroy method of the window to the destroy() function that you defined earlier. The destroy method is called when the user clicks the "X" on the top right of the window.
13	Issue the show_all() function call to the $window object so that everything within the object is displayed.
14	Call the Gtk::main() method to run the script.

FIGURE 12–2
basic_window.php

Adding a GTK Button

The simplest and most basic example in all of programming is the Hello World example. The goal of the example, if you didn't know, is to get the program to print out the words "Hello, World!" We are going to enhance our Hello World program slightly. Instead of merely printing out "Hello World," let's add that text to a button. When the button is clicked, we'll close our application. Try out this example, then look at the brief line-by-line explanation for details. Figure 12–3 shows the output of the script in Linux and in Windows.

SCRIPT 12–2 hello.php

```php
1.  <?php
2.  if (!class_exists('gtk')) {
3.     if (strtoupper(substr(PHP_OS, 0, 3)) == 'WIN')
4.        dl('php_gtk.dll');
5.     else
6.        dl('php_gtk.so');
7.  }
8.  function destroy() {
9.     Gtk::main_quit();
10. }
11. function hello(){
12.    global $window;
13.    print "Hello World!\n";
14.    $window->destroy();
15. }
16. $window = &new GtkWindow();
17. $window->connect('destroy', 'destroy');
18. $button = &new GtkButton('Hello World!');
19. $button->connect('clicked', 'hello');
20. $window->add($button);
21. $window->show_all();
22. Gtk::main();
23. ?>
```

Script 12–2 hello.php Line-by-Line Explanation

LINE	DESCRIPTION
2	If the GTK class has not been defined, then execute lines 3–7. If the GTK class has been defined, then the script needs to do nothing.
3	Check the first three characters of the PHP_OS environment variable.
4	If it is WIN, then the system is running Windows. Load the PHPGTK library for Windows.
5–7	If the PHP_OS environment variable is not WIN, then assume that PHP is running on a Linux system and load the Linux PHPGTK library.
8–10	Define a function, destroy(), that stops the script when called.
9	Execute the Gtk::main_quit() method to stop the script and close the GTK window.
10	End the function declaration.
11–14	Define a function, hello(), that prints the text "Hello World!"
12	Allow the $window object to be accessed by this function.
13	Print the text "Hello World!" to STDOUT (the same command line from which you executed the script).
14	Use the destroy() method on the $window object to close the window.
15	End the function declaration.
16	Create a new window object called $window.
17	Connect the 'destroy' method of the window to the destroy() function that you defined earlier. The 'destroy' method is called when the user clicks the "X" on the top right of the window.
18	Create a new button object called $button.
19	Connect the 'clicked' method of the button to the hello() function.
20	Add the button to the window using the add() method.
21	Issue the show_all() function call to the $window object so that everything within the object is displayed.
22	Call the Gtk::main() method to run the script.

FIGURE 12–3
hello.php in Linux (Gnome) and Windows

Modifying Basic Widget Appearance

The syntax for creating buttons and windows looks very similar. That is because they are both classes of a GTK widget. Each object (buttons, windows, etc.) has certain methods available to them—for example, the connect() method.

If you run the hello.php script, you will notice that the window size is pretty small—in fact, it is only as big as the button inside it. That's because PHP shrinks the window to the smallest size possible when creating it. We can modify the default appearance of the GtkWindow widget by using some methods. For example, if you wanted to set a default size for the window, you could use the set_default_size($width, $height)method:

```
$window->set_default_size(200,200);
```

This would create a window that is 200 pixels by 200 pixels. You can also set a window title:

```
$window->set_title("My PHPGTK APP");
```

Figure 12–4 shows a window modified by the set_default _size() and set_title() methods.

There are many methods available that can affect the appearance and behavior of GTK widgets. See the documentation on *http://gtk.php.net* for details on these methods.

Text Entry

A desktop application wouldn't be too useful if you couldn't insert data into it. GTK provides a text entry widget that allows you to input a line of text to your application. To create a text entry field:

```
$text1 = &new GtkEntry();
```

A text entry field isn't really useful unless you have some way to label it. That's where the GtkLabel comes in handy:

```
$label1 = &new GtkLabel("A Text Entry Field:");
```

Now that we have our new text entry field and a label, we need to put it into our window. There's a slight problem, though. You just can't add() multiple widgets into the top-level

FIGURE 12–4 Window modified with property methods (Linux and Windows)

window. Instead, you place a box into the window, and add your subobjects into that box.

hbox and vbox

There are two types of boxes that you can use to hold your widgets in place within the main window. They are the hbox (horizontal) and the vbox (vertical). As their names imply, the hbox allows you to place objects into it so that the objects are aligned horizontally, and the vbox allows you to place objects into it so that the objects are aligned vertically. Since we want to align our text entry field and label horizontally (like normal applications do), we'll create an hbox and add it to our window, then pack the label and text entry field into the box:

```
$box = &new GtkHBox();
$window->add($box);
```

The hbox and vbox widgets are special containers into which you can add multiple widgets. To add them, you need to pack the widgets into the box:

```
$box->pack_start($label1, false, false, 0);
$box->pack_start($text1, false, false, 0);
```

pack_start

The pack_start method allows you to add the widgets into the box. If you are packing widgets into vbox, then pack_start adds the widgets from the top of the box. Each time you pack another widget into the box, the preceding widget is moved down and the newly added widget is at the top of the vbox. If you are packing widgets into an hbox, then pack_start adds the widgets into the box from the left. Each time you pack a new widget into the box, it is placed to the right of the preceding widget.

The pack_start() method takes four arguments:

- The object you are packing.
- Whether or not to expand the object if the box is resized (true or false).
- Whether or not the object should fill the space which is available to it (true or false).
- The amount of padding to use around the object (an integer).

The default arguments used, if none are specified, are true, true, 0. These mean to expand and fill and use no padding.

Let's look at a script the uses the label and text entry field. See Script 12–3, text_entry.php, below. See Figure 12–5 for the example output.

SCRIPT 12–3 text_entry.php

```php
1.  <?php
2.    if (!class_exists('gtk')) {
3.      if (strtoupper(substr(PHP_OS, 0, 3)) == 'WIN')
4.        dl('php_gtk.dll');
5.      else
6.        dl('php_gtk.so');
7.    }
8.  function destroy(){
9.    Gtk::main_quit();
10.  }
11.  $window = &new GtkWindow();
12.  $window->connect('destroy', 'destroy');
13.  $text1 = &new GtkEntry();
14.  $label1 = &new GtkLabel("A Text Entry Field");
15.  $box = &new GtkHBox();
16.  $window->add($box);
17.  $box->pack_start($label1, false, false, 0);
18.  $box->pack_start($text1, false, false, 0);
19.  $window->show_all();
20.  Gtk::main();
21.  ?>
```

Script 12–3 text_entry.php Line-by-Line Explanation

LINE	DESCRIPTION
2	If the GTK class has not been defined, then execute lines 3–7. If the GTK class has been defined, then the script needs to do nothing.
3	Check the first three characters of the PHP_OS environment variable.
4	If it is WIN, then the system is running Windows. Load the PHPGTK library for Windows.
5–7	If the PHP_OS environment variable is not WIN, then assume that PHP is running on a Linux system and load the Linux PHPGTK library.
8–10	Define a function, destroy(), that stops the script when called.
9	Execute the Gtk::main_quit() method to stop the script and close the GTK window.
10	End the function declaration.
11	Create a new window object called $window.
12	Connect the 'destroy' method of the window to the destroy() function that you defined earlier. The 'destroy' method is called when the user clicks the "X" on the top right of the window.
13	Create a new text-entry object called $text1.
14	Create a new label object called $label1 containing the text "A Text Entry Field".
15	Create a new horizontal box object called $box.
16	Add the box to the window using the add() method.
17	Pack the label object into the box.
18	Pack the text-entry object into the box.
19	Issue the show_all() function call to the $window object so that everything within the object is displayed.
20	Call the Gtk::main() method to run the script.

FIGURE 12–5
text_entry.php

Putting It All Together

So now you know how to make a label, a button (with a label in it), and a text entry field. With these three tools, you can begin to build an application!

First, we need to know how to get the text the user enters in the text entry widget. The GtkTextEntry widget has a method that meets our needs:

```
$input = $text1->get_text();
```

You can assign the user-entered data using the get_text() method on the $text1 object to a variable (for example $input), then do whatever you want with that text. The following script puts it all together and provides a short example of a function to handle the user-entered text. See Figure 12–6 for example output.

SCRIPT 12–4 text_submit.php

```php
1.   <?php
2.     if (!class_exists('gtk')) {
3.     if (strtoupper(substr(PHP_OS, 0, 3)) == 'WIN')
4.       dl('php_gtk.dll');
5.     else
6.       dl('php_gtk.so');
7.   }
8.   function destroy(){
9.     Gtk::main_quit();
10.  }
11.  function submit(){
12.    global $text1;
13.    $input = $text1->get_text();
14.    echo $input . "\n";
15.    $text1->set_text('');
16.  }
17.  $window = &new GtkWindow();
18.  $window->connect('destroy', 'destroy');
19.  $window->set_border_width(5);
20.  $text1 = &new GtkEntry();
21.  $label1 = &new GtkLabel("A Text Entry Field");
22.  $button1 = &new GtkButton('Submit Text!');
23.  $button1->connect('clicked', 'submit');
24.  $box = &new GtkHBox();
25.  $window->add($box);
```

SCRIPT 12–4 text_submit.php (Continued)
26. `$box->pack_start($label1, false, false, 0);`
27. `$box->pack_start($text1, false, false, 0);`
28. `$box->pack_start($button1, false, false, 0);`
29. `$window->show_all();`
30. `Gtk::main();`
31. `?>`

Script 12–4 text_submit.php Line-by-Line Explanation

LINE	DESCRIPTION
2	If the GTK class has not been defined, then execute lines 3–7. If the GTK class has been defined, then the script needs to do nothing.
3	Check the first three characters of the PHP_OS environment variable.
4	If it is WIN, then the system is running Windows. Load the PHPGTK library for Windows.
5–7	If the PHP_OS environment variable is not WIN, then assume that PHP is running on a Linux system and load the Linux PHPGTK library.
8–10	Define a function, destroy(), that stops the script when called.
9	Execute the Gtk::main_quit() method to stop the script and close the GTK window.
10	End the function declaration.
11–16	Define a function, submit(), that echoes the user-entered text to STDOUT.
12	Allow the variable $text1 to be accessed by this function.
13	Assign the user-entered text to the $input variable by calling the get_text() method of the $text1 text object.
14	Echo the user-entered text to STDOUT along with a newline character
15	Clear the user-entered text from the text input by calling the set_text() method of the $text1 text object, assigning the new text to be blank ('').
16	End the function declaration.
17	Create a new window object called $window.
18	Connect the 'destroy' method of the window to the destroy() function that you defined earlier. The 'destroy' method is called when the user clicks the "X" on the top right of the window.
19	Set a five-pixel border around the window using the set_border_width method of the window object.

Script 12–4 text_submit.php Line-by-Line Explanation (Continued)

LINE	DESCRIPTION
20	Create a new text-entry object called $text1.
21	Create a new label object called $label1 containing the text "A Text Entry Field".
22	Create a new button object called $button.
23	Connect the 'clicked' method of the button to the hello() function.
24	Create a new horizontal box object called $box.
25	Add the box to the window using the add() method.
26	Pack the label object into the box.
27	Pack the text-entry object into the box.
28	Pack the button object into the box.
29	Issue the show_all() function call to the $window object so that everything within the object is displayed.
30	Call the Gtk::main() method to run the script.

FIGURE 12–6
text_submit.php

Dialog Boxes

Most GUI applications have the ability to display small windows notifying the user that something is wrong or to confirm that the user wants to take the desired action. For example, a dialog box appears asking "Are you sure…" in most word processing applications if you try to close the application without first saving the document on which you are working. PHPGTK also provides an easy way to create simple dialog boxes using the GtkDialog class.

The GtkDialog class is simply a window that contains a vbox, a separator, and an "action area." You place your text in the vbox and place your buttons in the "action area."

This next script shows an example of how to use a GtkDialog box to confirm that a user wishes to quit out of the application. When a user clicks the "Quit" button, or the "X" in the upper right corner of the main window, a dialog box is displayed, asking the users if they are sure they want to quit. If the user clicks "OK" in the dialog box, then the application exits. If the user clicks "Cancel" or the "X" in the upper right corner of the dialog box, then the dialog box closes, but the application remains open. See Figure 12–7 for example output.

SCRIPT 12–5 dialog.php

```php
1.  <?php
2.  if (!class_exists('gtk')) {
3.      if (strtoupper(substr(PHP_OS, 0, 3)) == 'WIN')
4.          dl('php_gtk.dll');
5.      else
6.          dl('php_gtk.so');
7.  }
8.  function destroy() {
9.      Gtk::main_quit();
10. }
11. function close_dialog($button, $dialog){
12.     $dialog->destroy();
13. }
14. function delete_event(){
15.     confirm();
16.     return true;
17. }
18. function confirm(){
19.     global $window;
20.     $dialog = &new GtkDialog;
21.     $dialog->set_title("Are You Sure?");
22.     $dialog->set_default_size('100','100');
23.     $dialog->set_modal(TRUE);
24.     $dialog->set_transient_for($window);
25.     $dialog->set_policy(0,0,0);
26.     $label = &new GtkLabel("Are You Sure You Want To Quit?");
27.     $button_yes = &new GtkButton('OK');
28.     $button_yes->connect('clicked', 'destroy');
29.     $button_no = &new GtkButton('Cancel');
30.     $button_no->connect('clicked', 'close_dialog', $dialog);
31.     $vbox1 = $dialog->vbox;
32.     $vbox2 = $dialog->action_area;
33.     $vbox1->pack_start($label);
34.     $vbox2->pack_start($button_yes);
35.     $vbox2->pack_start($button_no);
36.     $dialog->show_all();
37. }
```

SCRIPT 12–5 dialog.php (Continued)

```
38. $window = &new GtkWindow();
39. $window->connect('delete_event', 'delete_event');
40. $button = &new GtkButton('Quit');
41. $button->connect('clicked', 'confirm');
42. $window->add($button);
43. $window->show_all();
44. Gtk::main();
45. ?>
```

Script 12–5 dialog.php Line-by-Line Explanation

LINE	DESCRIPTION
2	If the GTK class has not been defined, then execute lines 3–7. If the GTK class has been defined, then the script needs to do nothing.
3	Check the first three characters of the PHP_OS environment variable.
4	If it is WIN, then the system is running Windows. Load the PHPGTK library for Windows.
5–7	If the PHP_OS environment variable is not WIN, then assume that PHP is running on a Linux system and load the Linux PHPGTK library.
8–10	Define a function, destroy(), that stops the script when called.
9	Execute the Gtk::main_quit() method to stop the script and close the GTK window.
10	End the function declaration.
11–13	Define a function, close_dialog(), that closes a dialog box. This function takes two arguments: $button and $dialog. See the description for line 30 for a description of the arguments.
12	Call the destroy() method of the $dialog object to close the dialog window.
13	End the function declaration.
14–17	Define a function, delete_event(), that catches when a user clicks on the "X" in the upper-right corner of the main application window and runs the confirm function(). The delete_event() is a special method that is run whenever a user clicks the "X" in the upper-right corner of the application window. "delete_event" is a valid connection point for a window, similar to the destroy connection point. If you do not use a delete_event connection point, then the window is automatically destroyed.
15	Execute the confirm() function to make certain the user wishes to exit the application.

Script 12–5 dialog.php Line-by-Line Explanation (Continued)

LINE	DESCRIPTION
16	Return true. If you return false (which is the default behavior of the delete_event when you don't assign a connection to it), then the window is destroyed.
17	End the function declaration.
18–37	Define a function, confirm(), to confirm that the user wishes to quit the application.
19	Allow the $window object to be used by this function.
20	Create a new dialog object called $dialog.
21	Set the title for the dialog object.
22	Set the default size of the dialog window to be 100 × 100 pixels.
23	Set the dialog window as a modal window. This means that the main application window cannot be accessed while this window exists.
24	Set the dialog window as a transient of the main window. A transient window does not cause an extra taskbar item to be created in the OS for the window. This is currently broken on Windows but works under Linux.
25	Set the resize policy for the window. The resize() method takes three boolean (true or false/0 or 1) arguments: • allow_shrink—Allow the window to be smaller than its children (this should always be set to false). • allow_grow—Allow the window to be made greater than its original size. • auto_shrink—Allows the window to override its default size settings to shrink to the size of any child windows.
26	Create a new label object called $label.
27	Create a new button object called $button_yes. This is used as the "OK" button in the dialog box.
28	Use the connect() method to cause the destroy() function to be called when this button is clicked.
29	Create a new button called $button_no. This is used as the "Cancel" button in the dialog box.
30	Use the connect() method to cause the close_dialog() function to be called. Note that the connect method has an extra argument tagged on at the end. Normally, the connect() method has two arguments: the action (such as clicked) and the function that is called (such as close_dialog). You can add a third argument, which is an additional variable that is sent to the function. In

Script 12–5 dialog.php Line-by-Line Explanation (Continued)

Line	Description
	this case, we are sending the dialog window object $dialog. Since we are sending two arguments, and the connected function usually takes only one by default (which is the object that is making the connection), you must define the default object ($button) and the additional object ($dialog) in the function for which you are creating the connection, in this case, close_dialog().
31	Since the GtkDialog object has built-in "boxes" for content, you need to assign a variable name for that object. Here you assign a variable name to the GtkDialog's vbox.
32	Assign a variable name to the GtkDialog's action_area.
33	Pack the label object into the vbox.
34–35	Pack the OK and Cancel buttons in the GtkDialog's action_area.
36	Show the contents of the dialog box.
37	End the function declaration.
38	Create a new window object called $window.
39	Connect the 'delete_event' method of the window to the delete_event() function that you defined earlier. The 'delete_event' method is called when the user clicks the "X" button in the upper right corner of the application. In the previous examples, we left this method out since we wanted to directly destroy the window.
40	Create a new button object called $button.
41	Connect the 'clicked' method of the button to the confirm function.
42	Add the button to the window using the add() method.
43	Issue the show_all() function call to the $window object so that everything within the object is displayed.
44	Call the Gtk::main() method to run the script.

Figure 12–7 dialog.php—initial window and confirmation dialog box

A Simple PHPGTK Application

This next application uses GTK widgets to create a small application that encodes passwords. You enter a username and password into their respective fields, then click the "Generate..." button to create an encrypted username and password combination that can be used in some of the previous scripts in this book. The username and password are displayed in a text box in the middle of the application. When you have created as many passwords as needed, you can click the "Write To File" button to write the data to a text file. See Figure 12–8 for example output.

SCRIPT 12–6 password_gen.php

```php
1.  <?php
2.    if (!class_exists('gtk')) {
3.    if (strtoupper(substr(PHP_OS, 0, 3)) == 'WIN')
4.      dl('php_gtk.dll');
5.    else
6.      dl('php_gtk.so');
7.  }
8.  function destroy(){
9.    Gtk::main_quit();
10. }
11. function generate(){
12.   global $user_in, $pass_in, $output;
13.   $text = $user_in->get_text() . ":" . encoded($pass_in-
      >get_text()) . "\n";
14.   $output->insert(null, null, null, $text);
15.   $user_in->set_text('');
16.   $pass_in->set_text('');
17. }
18. function encoded($text) {
19.   return md5($text);
20. }
21. function write(){
22.   global $output;
23.   $text = $output->get_chars(0,-1);
24.   $file = fopen("pass.txt", "w") or die("CANNOT OPEN
      FILE");
25.   fwrite($file, $text);
26.   fclose($file);
27.   $output->delete_text(0,-1);
```

```
28.    $complete = "Passwords written to file!\n";
29.    $output->insert(null, null, null, $complete);
30.  }
31.  $window = &new GtkWindow();
32.  $window->set_default_size(300, 300);
33.  $window->connect('destroy', 'destroy');
34.  $user_label = &new GtkLabel("Username: ");
35.  $user_in = &new GtkEntry();
36.  $user_box = &new GtkHBox();
37.  $user_box->pack_start($user_label, false, false, 0);
38.  $user_box->pack_start($user_in, false, false, 0);
39.  $pass_label = &new GtkLabel("Password: ");
40.  $pass_in = &new GtkEntry();
41.  $pass_box = &new GtkHBox();
42.  $pass_box->pack_start($pass_label, false, false, 0);
43.  $pass_box->pack_start($pass_in, false, false, 0);
44.  $button1 = &new GtkButton('Generate Username:Password!');
45.  $button1->connect('clicked', 'generate');
46.  $output = &new GtkText();
47.  $button2 = &new GtkButton('Write To File');
48.  $button2->connect('clicked', 'write');
49.  $vbox = &new GtkVBox();
50.  $vbox->pack_start($user_box);
51.  $vbox->pack_start($pass_box);
52.  $vbox->pack_start($button1);
53.  $vbox->pack_start($output);
54.  $vbox->pack_start($button2);
55.  $window->add($vbox);
56.  $window->show_all();
57.  Gtk::main();
58.  ?>
```

Script 12–6 password_gen.php Line-by-Line Explanation

LINE	DESCRIPTION
2	If the GTK class has not been defined, then execute lines 3–7. If the GTK class has been defined, then the script needs to do nothing.
3	Check the first three characters of the PHP_OS environment variable.
4	If it is WIN, then the system is running Windows. Load the PHPGTK library for Windows.
5–7	If the PHP_OS environment variable is not WIN, then assume that PHP is running on a Linux system and load the Linux PHPGTK library.

Script 12–6 password_gen.php Line-by-Line Explanation (Continued)

LINE	DESCRIPTION
8–10	Define a function, destroy(), that stops the script when called.
9	Execute the Gtk::main_quit() method to stop the script and close the GTK window.
10	End the function declaration.
11–17	Define a function, generate(), that encrypts a username/password combination entered by the user and prints it to a text box inside the application.
12	Assign the $user_in, $pass_in, and $output variables as global so that they can be used inside this function.
13	Assign the user-entered username and password to the $text variable.
14	Insert the username and encoded password into the text box using the insert() method for the text object. insert() takes four arguments: <ul><li>Font—A GDK Font object.</li><li>Color—A GDK color object.</li><li>Size—The number of characters you wish to insert.</li><li>String—The text to be inserted.</li></ul> For simplicity, I set the first three arguments as null so that the default values are used.
15	Clear the user-entered text in the Username field by inserting a blank string into the entry box.
16	Clear the user-entered text in the Password field by inserting a blank string into the entry box.
17	End the function declaration.
18–20	Define a function, $encode, that encodes the entered password.
19	Encode the password using the md5() function and return it to the calling function. You can change the encryption method to suit your needs (for example by using the crypt() function).
20	End the function declaration.
21–30	Define a function, write(), that writes the encoded username/passwords to a file.
22	Assign the $output variable as global so that it can be used inside this function.

Script 12–6 password_gen.php Line-by-Line Explanation (Continued)

LINE	DESCRIPTION
23	Get the entire text from the text object using the get_chars() method and place it into the $text variable. The get_chars() method takes two arguments: • The start position of the text (0 is the first position). • The end position of the text. Using 0 and -1 as arguments causes the entire text in the text object to be collected.
24	Open a file for writing. Note that if you have an existing file with the same name, it will be written over with the new username/password combos. You must also set permissions on the file so that it can be written to by PHP.
25	Write the text to the file.
26	Close the file.
27	Delete the text in the text area.
28	Create a string of text notifying the user that the text has been written.
29	Write the string to the text area. Note that you will need to close and restart the application if you wish to create passwords again.
30	End the function declaration.
31	Create a new window object called $window.
32	Set the size of the window to be 300 × 300 pixels.
33	Connect the 'destroy' method of the window to the destroy() function that you defined earlier. The 'destroy' method is called when the user clicks the "X" on the top right of the window.
34	Create a new label object for the username label.
35	Create a new text-entry object for the username.
36	Create a new hbox in which to place the username label and text-entry objects.
37	Pack the label object into the hbox.
38	Pack the text-entry object into the hbox.
39	Create a new label object for the password label.
40	Create a new text-entry object for the password.
41	Create a new hbox in which to place the password label and text-entry objects.
42	Pack the label object into the hbox.
43	Pack the text-entry object into the hbox.

Script 12–6 password_gen.php Line-by-Line Explanation (Continued)

LINE	DESCRIPTION
44	Create a new button object for the "Generate…" button.
45	Connect the "Generate…" button to the generate() function.
46	Create a new text object to display the output.
47	Create a new button object for the "Write To File" button.
48	Connect the "Write To File" button to the write() function.
49	Create a new vbox to hold the other boxes and buttons.
50	Pack the hbox containing the Username label and entry into the vbox.
51	Pack the hbox containing the Password label and entry into the vbox.
52	Pack the "Generate…" button into the vbox.
53	Pack the text object into the vbox.
54	Pack the "Write To File" button into the vbox.
55	Add the vbox to the window.
56	Show all of the contents of the window.
57	Execute the script.

FIGURE 12–8 password_gen.php

Index

http://www.phptr.com/

Prentice Hall PTR   InformIT   InformIT Online Books   Financial Times Prentice Hall   ft.com   PTG Interactive   Reuters

TOMORROW'S SOLUTIONS FOR TODAY'S PROFESSIONALS

Prentice Hall **Professional Technical Reference**

| Browse | Book Series | What's New | User Groups | Alliances | Special Sales | Contact Us |

Search | Help | Home

Quick Search

PTR Favorites

Find a Bookstore

Book Series

Special Interests

Newsletters

Press Room

International

Best Sellers

Solutions Beyond the Book

Shopping Bag

Keep Up to Date with
PH PTR Online

We strive to stay on the cutting edge of what's happening in professional computer science and engineering. Here's a bit of what you'll find when you stop by **www.phptr.com**:

What's new at PHPTR? We don't just publish books for the professional community, we're a part of it. Check out our convention schedule, keep up with your favorite authors, and get the latest reviews and press releases on topics of interest to you.

Special interest areas offering our latest books, book series, features of the month, related links, and other useful information to help you get the job done.

User Groups Prentice Hall Professional Technical Reference's User Group Program helps volunteer, not-for-profit user groups provide their members with training and information about cutting-edge technology.

Companion Websites Our Companion Websites provide valuable solutions beyond the book. Here you can download the source code, get updates and corrections, chat with other users and the author about the book, or discover links to other websites on this topic.

Need to find a bookstore? Chances are, there's a book-seller near you that carries a broad selection of PTR titles. Locate a Magnet bookstore near you at www.phptr.com.

Subscribe today! Join PHPTR's monthly email newsletter! Want to be kept up-to-date on your area of interest? Choose a targeted category on our website, and we'll keep you informed of the latest PHPTR products, author events, reviews and conferences in your interest area.

Visit our mailroom to subscribe today! **http://www.phptr.com/mail_lists**